Lay Empowerment and the Development of Puritanism

Christianities in the Trans-Atlantic World, 1500–1800

General Editors:

Crawford Gribben, Queen's University Belfast, UK
Scott Spurlock, University of Glasgow, UK

Editorial Board:

John Coffey, Leicester University
Jeff Jue, Westminster Theological Seminary
Susan Hardman Moore, University of Edinburgh
John Morrill, University of Cambridge
David Mullan, Cape Breton University
Richard Muller, Calvin Theological Seminary
Jane Ohlmeyer, Trinity College Dublin
Margo Todd, University of Pennsylvania
Arthur Williamson, University of California, Sacramento

Building upon the recent recovery of interest in religion in the early modern trans-Atlantic world, this series offers fresh, lively and interdisciplinary perspectives on the broad view of its subject. Books in the series will work strategically and systematically to address major but under-studied or overly simplified themes in the religious and cultural history of the early modern trans-Atlantic.

Titles include:

Benjamin Bankhurst
ULSTER PRESBYTERIANS AND THE SCOTS IRISH DIASPORA, 1750–1764

Francis J. Bremer
LAY EMPOWERMENT AND THE DEVELOPMENT OF PURITANISM

Forthcoming titles include:

Crawford Gribben and Scott Spurlock (*editors*)
PURITANISM IN THE TRANS-ATLANTIC WORLD 1600–1800

Mark Sweetnam
MISSION AND EMPIRE IN THE EARLY MODERN PUBLIC SPHERE

Christianities in the Trans-Atlantic World, 1500–1800
Series Standing Order ISBN 978–0–037–31152–8 hardcover
(*outside North America only*)

You can receive future titles in this series as they are published by placing a standing order. Please contact your bookseller or, in case of difficulty, write to us at the address below with your name and address, the title of the series and one of the ISBNs quoted above.

Customer Services Department, Macmillan Distribution Ltd, Houndmills, Basingstoke, Hampshire RG21 6XS, England

---

Lay Empowerment and the Development of Puritanism

Francis J. Bremer
Professor Emeritus, Millersville University, USA

© Francis J. Bremer 2015, First softcover printing 2018

All rights reserved. No reproduction, copy or transmission of this publication may be made without written permission.

No portion of this publication may be reproduced, copied or transmitted save with written permission or in accordance with the provisions of the Copyright, Designs and Patents Act 1988, or under the terms of any licence permitting limited copying issued by the Copyright Licensing Agency, Saffron House, 6–10 Kirby Street, London EC1N 8TS.

Any person who does any unauthorized act in relation to this publication may be liable to criminal prosecution and civil claims for damages.

The author has asserted his right to be identified as the author of this work in accordance with the Copyright, Designs and Patents Act 1988.

First published 2015 by
PALGRAVE MACMILLAN

Palgrave Macmillan in the UK is an imprint of Macmillan Publishers Limited, registered in England, company number 785998, of Houndmills, Basingstoke, Hampshire RG21 6XS.

Palgrave Macmillan in the US is a division of St Martin's Press LLC, 175 Fifth Avenue, New York, NY 10010.

Palgrave Macmillan is the global academic imprint of the above companies and has companies and representatives throughout the world.

Palgrave® and Macmillan® are registered trademarks in the United States, the United Kingdom, Europe and other countries.

ISBN 978–1–137–35288–0 (HB)
ISBN 978–1–349–67497–8 (PB)

This book is printed on paper suitable for recycling and made from fully managed and sustained forest sources. Logging, pulping and manufacturing processes are expected to conform to the environmental regulations of the country of origin.

A catalogue record for this book is available from the British Library.

Library of Congress Cataloging-in-Publication Data
Bremer, Francis J.
  Lay empowerment and the development of Puritanism / Francis J. Bremer, Professor Emeritus, Millersville University, USA.
    pages cm. — (Christianities in the trans-atlantic world, 1500–1800)
  Includes bibliographical references.
  ISBN 978–1–137–35288–0
  1. Puritans. 2. Laity. I. Title.
  BX9323.B26 2015
  285'.909032—dc23   2015001200

*For all my family
and
the memories of
Francis and Marie Bremer
and
Alice Woodlock*

Contents

Acknowledgments	viii
Introduction	1
1 The Experience and Meaning of God's Caress	5
2 Thinking of the Laity in the English Reformation	10
3 Lay Puritans in Stuart England	27
4 Gatherings of the Saints in England and the Netherlands	49
5 Shaping the New England Way	69
6 The Free Grace Controversy and Redefining the Role of Lay Believers	87
7 The Role of the Laity in England's Puritan Revolution	105
8 Varieties of Lay Enthusiasm in New England and England	127
9 Responding to the Challenges of Diversity, 1640–60	144
10 Clergy and Laity in the Later Seventeenth Century	157
Epilogue: Looking Backwards, and Ahead	177
Notes	182
Bibliography	216
Index	233

Acknowledgments

I first began to reflect on the topic of this book while a Long Room Fellow at Trinity College, Dublin in the spring of 2012. I wish to thank Crawford Gribben for encouraging me to apply for that fellowship, and the Long Room staff for making my stay comfortable and productive. I would also like to thank Crawford and his students for valuable conversations during my tenure.

During the course of research and writing I have benefited, as always, from the community of puritan scholars in England and America who are friends as well as scholars and who have shaped my understanding of the field over the years. But in particular I would like to single out L. Baird Tipson, Jr. and Joel Halcomb, both of whom read the entire manuscript and provided numerous helpful suggestions. After the book was essentially finished I benefited from the suggestions of Margo Todd and the students in her graduate seminar at the University of Pennsylvania who were kind enough to read the manuscript and discuss it with me.

This is the first study I have undertaken since my retirement from Millersville University. I thank the university for having granted me emeritus status and the ability to draw upon the library resources in getting access to numerous works cited here. And I would like to thank my family, which has always been the rock on which my life is grounded.

Introduction

Diarmaid MacCulloch has written that religious institutions "create their own silences, by exclusions and by shared assumptions, which...silences are often at the expense of many of the people who could be thought of as actually constituting the Church."[1] My goal in the pages that follow is to examine one such silence—the substantial omission of the role played by countless named and unnamed men and women in the story of the shaping of puritanism. The earliest histories of puritanism were written by clergymen and highlighted the importance of the clergy. William Hubbard, whose *General History of New England* was commissioned by the Massachusetts General Court in the 1670s, stated that "In the beginning of times was occasioned much disadvantage to the government of the church by making it too popular."[2] Clerical authors such as Cotton Mather in New England and Samuel Clarke in England were themselves invested in the importance of the ministry and not unsurprisingly downplayed the role of the laity in the churches and focused on the role of prominent clergy in their accounts.

Later writers, many writing from an institutional perspective, followed their lead, though not all exclusion of the laity was the result of institutional bias. The fact that the vast proportion of surviving puritan writings were composed by ministers reinforced this perspective. I myself titled one of my books *Shaping New Englands: Puritan Clergymen in Seventeenth Century England and New England*.[3] Even those who, like Darrett Rutman, paused to wonder to what extent the message from the pulpit was imbibed by those in the pews took it for granted that the message was shaped by the clergy.[4] The laymen and laywomen who entered the story were typically those described by the clergy of their time and by later historians as radicals—the Anne Hutchinsons and Mary Dyers, the Levellers and the Quakers.[5] Even Christopher Hill, who was more sympathetic than most to the role of ordinary Englishmen and wrote extensively on how some puritans sought to turn the world upside down, devoted his attention to those generally perceived as radical.[6] There were, of course, some exceptions. When I was beginning my professional career Stephen Foster was kind enough to send me a copy of a paper that Patrick Collinson had delivered at a 1966 conference of the Past & Present Society. That paper, "The Godly: Aspects of Popular Protestantism," focused on the role of the laity in early puritanism—even their role in pushing clergy further towards reform than the ministers were prepared to go.[7]

There are of course hints of what was not being written about if one pays sufficient attention to those voices. The fact that arguably the most important sermon in seventeenth-century New England history was preached by a layman—John Winthrop's "Christian Charity"—suggests an important lay role in shaping the thought and practice of that society. The religious life of the Plymouth colony was directed for many years by William Brewster, a lay elder. One of the most vigorous debates over religion as well as governance in Civil War England was conducted by soldiers at Putney and Whitehall. Many of the stories I tell and points I seek to make may be individually familiar to those who have immersed themselves in the scholarship of the puritan movement, though the overall pattern and significance is not.

In revisiting the history of puritanism from its English origins through its development in the Atlantic world of the seventeenth century, I have also been influenced by another essay that I had read long ago. In 1956 James Fulton Maclear wrote of the "mystical element in early Puritan history," focusing on the emotional, Spirit-centered element in puritan experience that existed alongside the rational aspects of puritan theology that had recently been examined by Perry Miller.[8] He explored the tension between the emphasis on individual inspiration and institutional authority. Pursuing this dimension also leads to a focus on lay empowerment. When this book was substantially completed I had the opportunity to read before publication Abram C. Van Engen's *Sympathetic Puritans: Calvinist Fellow Feeling in Early New England*.[9] Van Engen's focus on puritan feeling complements the focus on religious experience depicted by Maclear and the discussion of lay puritanism that is at the heart of my own work in this book.

This study is an attempt to focus on the puritan laity and their role in shaping that religious movement, a story that has been obscured by the silence of those who established what became the structures of the churches. There have been studies that look at various ways in which

Introduction

Diarmaid MacCulloch has written that religious institutions "create their own silences, by exclusions and by shared assumptions, which...silences are often at the expense of many of the people who could be thought of as actually constituting the Church."[1] My goal in the pages that follow is to examine one such silence—the substantial omission of the role played by countless named and unnamed men and women in the story of the shaping of puritanism. The earliest histories of puritanism were written by clergymen and highlighted the importance of the clergy. William Hubbard, whose *General History of New England* was commissioned by the Massachusetts General Court in the 1670s, stated that "In the beginning of times was occasioned much disadvantage to the government of the church by making it too popular."[2] Clerical authors such as Cotton Mather in New England and Samuel Clarke in England were themselves invested in the importance of the ministry and not unsurprisingly downplayed the role of the laity in the churches and focused on the role of prominent clergy in their accounts.

Later writers, many writing from an institutional perspective, followed their lead, though not all exclusion of the laity was the result of institutional bias. The fact that the vast proportion of surviving puritan writings were composed by ministers reinforced this perspective. I myself titled one of my books *Shaping New Englands: Puritan Clergymen in Seventeenth Century England and New England*.[3] Even those who, like Darrett Rutman, paused to wonder to what extent the message from the pulpit was imbibed by those in the pews took it for granted that the message was shaped by the clergy.[4] The laymen and laywomen who entered the story were typically those described by the clergy of their time and by later historians as radicals—the Anne Hutchinsons and Mary Dyers, the Levellers and the Quakers.[5] Even Christopher Hill, who

1

was more sympathetic than most to the role of ordinary Englishmen and wrote extensively on how some puritans sought to turn the world upside down, devoted his attention to those generally perceived as radical.[6] There were, of course, some exceptions. When I was beginning my professional career Stephen Foster was kind enough to send me a copy of a paper that Patrick Collinson had delivered at a 1966 conference of the Past & Present Society. That paper, "The Godly: Aspects of Popular Protestantism," focused on the role of the laity in early puritanism—even their role in pushing clergy further towards reform than the ministers were prepared to go.[7]

There are of course hints of what was not being written about if one pays sufficient attention to those voices. The fact that arguably the most important sermon in seventeenth-century New England history was preached by a layman—John Winthrop's "Christian Charity"—suggests an important lay role in shaping the thought and practice of that society. The religious life of the Plymouth colony was directed for many years by William Brewster, a lay elder. One of the most vigorous debates over religion as well as governance in Civil War England was conducted by soldiers at Putney and Whitehall. Many of the stories I tell and points I seek to make may be individually familiar to those who have immersed themselves in the scholarship of the puritan movement, though the overall pattern and significance is not.

In revisiting the history of puritanism from its English origins through its development in the Atlantic world of the seventeenth century, I have also been influenced by another essay that I had read long ago. In 1956 James Fulton Maclear wrote of the "mystical element in early Puritan history," focusing on the emotional, Spirit-centered element in puritan experience that existed alongside the rational aspects of puritan theology that had recently been examined by Perry Miller.[8] He explored the tension between the emphasis on individual inspiration and institutional authority. Pursuing this dimension also leads to a focus on lay empowerment. When this book was substantially completed I had the opportunity to read before publication Abram C. Van Engen's *Sympathetic Puritans: Calvinist Fellow Feeling in Early New England*.[9] Van Engen's focus on puritan feeling complements the focus on religious experience depicted by Maclear and the discussion of lay puritanism that is at the heart of my own work in this book.

This study is an attempt to focus on the puritan laity and their role in shaping that religious movement, a story that has been obscured by the silence of those who established what became the structures of the churches. There have been studies that look at various ways in which laymen (and some women) played a role in the religious history of the sixteenth and seventeenth centuries. Christopher Hill's *Economic Problems of the Church: From Archbishop Whitgift to the Long Parliament* (1956) examined the important role of powerful men who controlled church property, and I will touch on that subject in the coming chapters. But I am not primarily concerned with the economics of lay involvement in puritanism, seeking instead to focus on how ordinary people influenced faith and practice. Nor will I address the debate conducted by A. G. Dickens, Eamon Duffy, Christopher Haigh, and others over how popular the English Reformation was in England. My focus is on those who embraced reform, no matter how representative they were of the general population. Some of the themes I wish to explore are treated in Claire Cross, *Church and People, 1450–1660: The Triumph of the Laity in the English Church* (1976), but the scope of her book chronologically and in encompassing all religious groups means that at best it provides a broad context for my investigation. And finally, though I have learned much from James F. Cooper's *Tenacious of Their Liberties: The Congregationalists in Colonial Massachusetts* (1999), and draw upon that work in key parts of the following chapters, for the purposes of this book I am less interested than him in the formal exercise of power by the laity in the colonial churches.

So far as the sources permit, we will visit families gathered with their neighbors to pray and debate the meaning of scripture passages. We will accompany bands of believers discussing a sermon they attended as they journey home from a nearby church. We will sit in a church on the New England frontier to listen to a believer instruct his fellow laity through the exercise of the gift of prophesy. We will pause on a London street to listen to a lay preacher, and sit around the campfires of the New Model Army to listen in as soldiers share their religious experiences. Even though we may not have records of exactly what was said, the documentation of the fact that such events were important parts of the puritan movement point to the key role that the laity had in its shaping.

This study is explicitly Atlantic, and draws upon the experiences of puritans in England, in English congregations in the Netherlands, and in New England. I acknowledge that references to Ireland and Scotland are limited. In the case of the former, discussion touches only on some of the congregational churches established in Dublin in the mid-seventeenth century by clergy who came from England or New England. In the case of Scotland I have attempted to draw attention to the role the laity played in the earliest days of the Reformation there and at some key points that followed, such as the protests against Charles I's efforts to change the structure and liturgy of the church there. But the essentially Presbyterian form of the Reformation in Scotland created a framework which resulted in different (though important) roles for the laity than those I have chosen to focus on.

My focus on the lay element in the shaping of the puritan movement may appear at times to unfairly deemphasize the important role played by the clergy, a role that I and many others have written about elsewhere. Such is often the case in revisionist studies. Hopefully, this book will initiate a process whereby we will come to understand the at times supportive and at times antagonistic efforts of laity and clergy. And in writing it I have come to recognize that often those we write of as clergy were acting in a non-professional role as believers. According to Congregational polity, a clergyman was someone who had been selected by a congregation of believers and ordained. Despite their English ordination, which most New Englanders rejected, men such as John Wilson and John Davenport were mere Christian believers until the churches they helped form called them to the ministry. And how are we to classify Roger Williams, the better part of whose life was lived after he rejected the possibility of there being a valid church or ministry?

1
The Experience and Meaning of God's Caress

A constant theme in the history of Christianity has been the struggle between those who rely on divine inspiration to define the faith and those who argue that truth should be established by the institutional church. The chapter of the broader story that this book explores features the tension that shaped the faith and practices of sixteenth- and seventeenth-century puritanism between scripturally aware laymen and laywomen, who believed themselves to be inspired by the Spirit, and university-trained clergy. There was a long prelude to this story. In the earliest days of faith, groups such as the gnostics, who asserted the value of personal, intuitive means to discern truth, were gradually forced to the margins, and their writings excluded from the "canon" of acceptable beliefs.[1] By the start of the third century there was a mainstream Catholic church in the west that asserted itself as the single authority able to "choose sacred texts for canonical status or compare the local creeds in Churches for a uniform direction in teaching."[2] The Nicene Creed was a major step in the process of defining orthodoxy, produced at the general council that the emperor Constantine called to meet in the city of Nicaea in 325, and modified at the First Council of Constantinople (381).

Over the following centuries the institutional Christian church in the west, headed by the papacy, exerted ever-stronger authority in distinguishing acceptable from heretical beliefs and suppressing views deemed heretical. Some of the heresies were rooted in individual divine revelation that produced a different understanding of doctrine. The church asserted that its beliefs were grounded in the canonical scriptures, asserted to be the revealed word of God to men. The interpretation of those scriptures was the responsibility of the institutional church. The fact that until the first Guttenberg Bible was printed in the mid-1540s those sacred books were only available in laboriously copied manuscripts accessible primarily by clergy made it easier to maintain church authority over the meaning of the scriptures. A further safeguard was the fact that the biblical manuscripts were in Hebrew, Latin, and Greek—not in the vernacular tongues of early modern Europe.

As early as the Waldensian movement in the twelfth century and progressing with the Lollard and Hussite movements in the fourteenth and fifteen centuries, some Christians had asserted the equality of all believers.[3] But it took the invention of printing to see such movements achieve significance. The Reformation of the sixteenth century was a critique of Catholic practices and teachings that was rooted in a different reading of the scriptures, but a reading that an ever-increasing number of Christians could test for themselves as a result of the printing revolution that made the texts more accessible. Printing also made available to a wider audience (albeit those who could read Latin) biblical commentaries and theological works by church fathers such as Augustine.[4]

Protestant reformers challenged the need for church authorities to explain what was in the word of God and demanded the publication of the Bible in the vernacular languages of Europe. Leaders such as Luther, Calvin, and Zwingli challenged the authority of the pope with the authority of scripture, but the meaning of scripture was not always clear, leading to variant forms of Protestantism. Luther's doctrine of the priesthood of all believers placed the heart of the believer above the teachings and traditions of the church.[5] Though his assertion of that doctrine was more nuanced than it has often been presented, it was embraced and even enhanced by many who would place the heart of the believer above the teachings and traditions of the institutional church.

As the scriptures became more accessible, believers struggled over how to interpret them. New attention was devoted to the texts themselves. Humanists emphasized the importance of textual accuracy and employed new skills in attempts to perfect the translation of the scriptures, going beyond the standard fourth-century Latin translation of St. Jerome. A key figure was Erasmus, who produced critical editions of a range of Christian texts, including a Greek New Testament.[6]

The humanist approach, adopted by many reformers, emphasized the application of the tools of reason to discern the true meaning of scripture, and thus elevated the role of those who had studied to learn those tools of interpretation. But others, while not denying the value of such learning, believed that human reason itself was corrupted by original sin and that true understanding was achievable only through the grace of God. The inspiration of the Holy Spirit enabled only those chosen by God to make sense of the scriptures. Over time, as we shall see, this emphasis on the inspiration of the Spirit could lead some to go so far as to see such an inner light as making the scriptures unnecessary. But most of the reformers we are dealing with saw the scriptures as God's revealed word and accepted the value of both learning and inspiration as means to understand them, though at times disagreeing on the relative importance of each.

England's puritans did not totally reject the use of reason in the search for truth in the Bible, and valued the scholarship of the church Fathers and other commentators on the scripture, but they placed a greater emphasis on the importance of the inspiration of the Holy Spirit. The Dorchester clergyman John White wrote that "a man when he is regenerate, hath no more faculties in his soul then he had before he was regenerate," but "in the work of regeneration those abilities which the man had before are improved, and receive a farther strength to comprehend and work spiritually."[7] Such an emphasis was not limited to puritans, but it is their views that I wish to discuss briefly here and trace over time in the following chapters.

Puritans believed that those who were saved were transformed by the grace of God in ways that included the ability to read the scriptures with greater understanding than was possible for those who were not of the elect.[8] As expressed by Richard Sibbes, "God, joining with the soul and spirit of a man whom he intends to convert...causeth him to see a divine majesty shining forth in the Scriptures."[9] And Thomas Goodwin wrote that

> If we read the Scriptures, and to get the meaning of them, observe the connection of one thing with another by reason, yet there comes often a light of the Spirit beyond the height of reason, which, by that observation of the connection, seals this up to be the Holy Ghost's meaning.[10]

Like Goodwin, John Davenport believed that while anyone could profit from reading the scriptures, only those whose understanding was illumined by the Spirit could truly understand it.[11] The light received from the "sanctifying spirit of God" was the "new light whereby we are enabled to see other things, or the same truths in a more spiritual and effectual manner."[12]

Scripture was where God's truth was revealed, and the inspiration of the Spirit was necessary for a clear understanding of that truth, and particularly how it applied to the individual believer. If the meaning of the scriptures was revealed by grace provided by the Spirit, and the Spirit bestowed grace on all who were God's elect, then arguably the ordinary believer was as capable of discerning God's truths as the best-educated minister. This was the belief that led to the empowerment of the laity. But, pushed too far, this emphasis on the Spirit could lead to problems.

Puritans believed that the purpose of the Spirit's grace was to enable people to understand the true meaning of scripture. Most rejected the notion that the Spirit might offer insights that contradicted or superseded the message of the scripture. But a critical issue was whether such inspiration was limited to understanding the scriptures, or could reveal truths beyond the scriptures. The claim that she received immediate revelations would ultimately be the key justification for banishing Anne Hutchinson from Massachusetts. The Quaker belief in the breadth of the Spirit's inspiration would lead to the separation of this sect from its puritan roots.

Even limiting the scope of the Spirit's guidance to scriptural interpretation had its problems. Christians did not always agree on what it was that the Spirit revealed. This failure was seen as the result of the remnants of sin, which even those who were elect labored under. The desire to help individuals discern the true nature of their inspiration led many to emphasize the importance of communal discussion as a means of avoiding anarchy and achieving consensus where possible. One of the things that makes puritanism so difficult to define precisely is that many of those who helped shape the movement believed in an evolving understanding of truth, accepting that whatever they believed might be modified by further light. Those who recognized their imperfections were open to the idea that further light might lead to a better understanding of disputed points. John Robinson, the leader of the Leiden Pilgrims who came to the New World in 1620, advised his flock, "The Lord has more truth and light yet to break forth out of his holy word."[13] This was also accepted by John Winthrop who, in his lay sermon on "Christian Charity," offered the hope that if they faithfully sought God, the New England colonists might "see much more of his wisdom, power, goodness and truth than formerly we have been associated with."[14] This openness was viewed less favorably by the Scottish Presbyterian Robert Baillie, who would criticize his Congregational opponents in the 1640s for what he called a "principle of mutability, whereby they profess their readiness to change any of their present tenets."[15]

Empowered by the Spirit, the laity played a large role in seeking that further light and striving for unity if not uniformity. The puritans whom I will focus on urged individuals to read their Bibles, listen to sermons, and discuss the messages they received with friends and family in conferences. Conferences were viewed as a means of counteracting the anarchic tendencies, and reflected the value puritans placed on "sweet consent" and the communion of saints.[16] In many congregations lay members (generally limited to males) were allowed and even encouraged to ask questions and even to present their own views by way of "prophesying." Individuals sought verification of the testimony they received by corroboration from others. The views of educated clergy who were also visibly saints were important, but so too were the lay members of a gathered community of fellow saints.[17] And in cases where a clergyman could not be found to minister to a group of Christians, lay preachers led the congregation in prayer and discussion of the faith.

For puritans the Spirit's guidance in understanding the scriptures and thus God's will was offered only to those who had been saved. The inspiration of the Spirit was not produced by a clergyman's ordination or a layman's education. While puritans believed strongly in the value of education, no amount of education could make one regenerate. God alone bestowed upon an individual the grace to see more clearly and understand more profoundly. The act of regeneration was an act of God whereby a new understanding and a new will was instilled in the elect. It was "wrought irresistibly, not issuing from the liberty of our choice."[18]

The major part of the story that will be followed in this work is the ways in which the belief in the Spirit's guidance of individuals led to various ways in which laymen, and even laywomen, were encouraged not only to take responsibility for their own faith, but to reach out in various ways to edify other members of the fellowship of saints. Another part of the story is the attempts to curb the democratic and individualistic elements of these beliefs. For some this would mean emphasizing the leadership role of the clergy within the congregation. Others would seek to curtail lay authority by requiring congregations to defer to the authority or advice of synods or assemblies.[19]

It is a mistake to read too much of later denominational forms into the evolution of puritanism in the sixteenth and early seventeenth centuries, though for the most part those who sought greater lay empowerment favored congregational forms. Numerous individuals, some lay and some clerical, were searching for a better understanding of God's way. Inspired by the Spirit and shaped by circumstances, they struggled to reform England. The communities they created were expressions of their sense of being elect and their experience of communion. What follows is their story.

2
Thinking of the Laity in the English Reformation

The English Reformation was begun by a layman who happened to be king.[1] Henry VIII, of course, saw himself as a special layman, divinely anointed as king. But the fact remains that the impetus against the right of the papacy to define doctrine and practice in the Catholic Church came from a layman who placed his own interpretation of a key text in Leviticus above that of the pope and then sought learned opinion to support his position. Equally important in our story is that when the split with Rome became inevitable, it was the English Parliament, comprised mostly of laymen (abetted by churchmen in the House of Lords) that invested the king with the title of Supreme Head of the Church in England. Some would later claim that since the monarch's authority derived from Parliament, that body actually had the right to determine the affairs of the church, a position strongly rejected by future monarchs, but supported by those who saw Parliament as means of pushing for further reform. And while Archbishop Thomas Cranmer arguably played the critical role in shaping the Protestant Church of England, an important role was also played by the layman Thomas Cromwell, whom Henry VIII appointed vicar general and vice-regent of the king in "Spirituals."[2]

There was, of course, a long history of clashes between powerful laymen and the Catholic Church. One thinks of the Investiture Controversy of the eleventh century, with Pope Gregory VII excommunicating the future Emperor Henry IV over the latter's claim to present bishops with symbols of sacred authority. In England one of the most famous clashes was between King Henry II and the Archbishop of Canterbury, Thomas Beckett, which led to the Archbishop's murder in his own cathedral in 1170.[3] These and similar controversies centered on issues of power and wealth debated between secular and religious princes.

There were also clashes resulting from the efforts of ordinary believers to shape religious understanding and practice. Looking at Europe as a whole these would include the Waldensian movement started by the wealthy Lyon merchant Peter Valdes, or Waldo, around 1170, and the fifteenth-century preaching by the German shepherd and street entertainer Hans Bohm, or Behem.[4] Focusing on England, the Lollards of the fourteenth century relied more on "the secret motions in private men" than they did on priests for defining the faith, with laymen engaged in reading and discussing scripture as well as preaching.[5] Lollards met together in groups that ranged from a handful to over a hundred, where, according to one scholar, "they read and discussed the scriptures, heard sermons, and distributed books. These sessions, often called 'conventicles and schools,' could on occasion last through the night."[6] John Skilly, a miller in Norfolk, was but one of many who, when confronted by the authorities, expressed views that challenged the authority of priests and asserted lay authority.[7] An Oxford scholar who was a Lollard claimed that "every man, holy and predestined to eternal life, even if he is a layman, is a true minister and priest ordained by God to administer the sacraments necessary for the salvation of man, although no bishop shall ever lay hands on him."[8] Women as well as men were encouraged to read the scriptures at Lollard sessions. There is evidence of female preaching, and some Lollards went so far as to suggest that some women might be qualified for the priesthood.[9]

Other evidence of lay empowerment is the fact that the initial growth of Lollardy was made possible by the support of prosperous and powerful laymen with important court connections.[10] Despite the best efforts of the authorities to root out the movement, there is evidence of its survival through the fifteenth century and up to the time of the broader Protestant Reformation. The Chilterens and the Thames Valley in particular were areas where laymen distributed Lollard manuscript books and instructed their fellow believers. Coventry was another center of strength where 74 people were examined for heresy in 1511. Seven men and two women were executed in that city between 1512 and 1522. In London, the Coleman Street ward was a center of Lollard activity. It would also be a particular center of lay religious activity in the sixteenth and seventeenth centuries.[11]

A similar emphasis on lay empowerment would cross from the Continent during the early Reformation. Though he would later backtrack because of concerns about the disruptive consequences of the doctrine, as late as 1523 Martin Luther asserted that the laity needed no papal or other ecclesiastical authorization to preach in their own parishes.[12] This influenced William Tyndale, who undertook the task of translating the scriptures into English. Tyndale's goal was to enable "the boy who drives the plow to know more of the scriptures" than the clergy, arguing that "there are many found among the laymen which are as wise as their officers." Gradually the distinction between the clergyman who could read the scripture and the layman who could not was eliminated, allowing ordinary believers to engage in discussions of their faith. He also pointed out that for husbands to follow the scriptural command to instruct their wives they needed to be able to read and understand the Bible.[13] Tyndale himself was involved with a group that met in merchants' houses to read and expound on scripture.[14] In regard to the church, Tyndale translated the key scriptural term *ekklesia* as "congregation."[15]

Though Archbishop Thomas Cranmer was skeptical of trusting laymen too far, he did encourage the settlement in England of Continental reformers such as Peter Martyr Vermigli and Martin Bucer who were open to the laity playing a greater role in the church.[16] And Cranmer allowed the establishment of "Stranger Churches" in London. These were congregations of immigrants who were allowed to practice their own forms of reformed faith, some of which emphasized the role of the laity in making decisions.[17]

There were other signs of a growing lay involvement in religion during the reigns of Henry VIII and Edward VI. The dissolution of monasteries and religious houses led to the advowson for many churches passing into lay hands, which meant that the choice of parish clergy was increasingly exercised by lay landowners, and sometimes by the parishioners themselves, albeit with episcopal approval of the choice required.[18] In some cases this simply became a means whereby a powerful layman was able to acquire for himself the wealth of a church living while employing a poorly paid clergyman to serve or, more typically, fail to serve, the spiritual needs of the people. But when the owner of the living was a godly patron, this was a means for such a layman to nourish a reformed vision.

Another part of the new legal order also provided zealous laymen a chance to promote reform. A 1535 statute required all inductees to clerical livings worth more than eight marks to pay a tax known as "First Fruits" in installments. Because some of those appointed to such livings did not have the ability to pay the tax, lay supporters stood surety to do so. Godly clergymen relied on like-minded laymen to support them in this regard.[19] William Winthrop, the uncle of the future Massachusetts governor John Winthrop, stood surety for a number of clergymen both in London and in his home county of Suffolk.[20]

While the patronage of prosperous laymen was a means of furthering reform, there is also evidence of a striving for godliness emanating from ordinary believers. The Suffolk parishes of Stratford St. Mary and Hadleigh were among the first parishes to use an English liturgy, ten years before it was made legal in 1548.[21] Early instances of iconoclasm—the destruction of rood screens and religious images—were generally an expression of the outrage of ordinary believers who were persuaded that such church furnishing was idolatrous.[22] During the reign of Edward VI authorities began to complain about parishioners exercising their own judgment about religious matters by "gadding" off to neighboring parishes where the worship and preaching was more to their liking.[23]

Perhaps the strongest impetus for lay involvement in the shaping of English Protestantism came from the Marian persecutions. During her reign (1553–58), Mary Tudor's determination to restore Roman Catholicism led to the execution of over 300 men and women and to the decision of many Protestants to flee to hospitable refuges on the Continent. Those who fled settled in centers of continental reform such as Geneva, Strasburg, and Frankfurt. There, lay exiles along with clerical friends worked to craft their own congregations. In some of these cases, as in Frankfurt and Geneva, those forming the church drew up an agreement that members subscribed to, anticipating the formal covenants that would be utilized by later reformers.[24] Their discussions and their observations of the reformed churches in the cities where they settled would shape the positions these exiles brought back to England at the end of Mary's reign.

Many of those who chose to remain in England paid the ultimate price for upholding their faith. The stories of the Marian Martyrs told by John Foxe in his monumental *Actes and Monuments of these latter and Perillous Days, Touching Matters of the Church* (1563) included numerous stories of lay believers who "had refused to bow their knees to Baal."[25] Along the Stour River, in Stoke-by-Nayland, three years into Mary's reign all but two of the parishioners refused to receive communion in the prescribed Catholic form.[26] When the clergyman in Hadleigh was arrested by the Marian authorities, the layman John Alcock stepped in. A woad setter, he used the Edwardian Prayer Book in the parish church, offered up prayers in English, and instructed the parishioners on scripture.[27] He preached till he too was put in prison, where he died. Ralph Allerton of Much Bentley, Essex was burned following his arrest for leading fellow laymen in scripture reading and discussion. Edmund Allen, a miller in Kent, was burned for having conducted his own religious services and claimed that he could do better than the Marian priests. He asserted that all Christians should be "lively stones to give light to others," and that "out of Christians should spring beams of the gospel, which should inflame all the world."[28] These and numerous other examples testify to the religious commitment of ordinary laymen during the time of persecution.

As narrated by Foxe in the *Actes and Monuments* (popularly known as the *Book of Martyrs*) such stories provided inspiration for laymen during the reign of Queen Elizabeth and beyond. In 1652 a treatise that had been written in Mary's reign by the martyr John Bradford was published with the hope that it would "stir up men of parts and experience to impart their experiences ... as little knowing how many drooping and desponding souls their surviving works might help."[29] Much of the material gathered by Foxe was in the form of letters that had been sent by those awaiting martyrdom in prison. Typically addressed to "faithful friends," "sisters," "brethren dispersed abroad in sundry prisons," "brethren which constantly cleave unto Christ," and the like were read aloud in secret gatherings of believers, helping to strengthen their faith.[30]

There were other Englishmen who decided against emigration and were also able to evade the attention of the authorities. Many of these formed underground congregations that worshipped in secret locations, often without clergymen. John Hooper, the Edwardian bishop of Gloucester and Worcester who was himself burned by the Marian authorities, had been an advocate of further reforms in the church. Concerned about the quality of the clergy he had ordered ministers in his diocese to attend quarterly training sessions that likely anticipated the prophesying exercises of the early Elizabethan church.[31] And he had justified lay religious gatherings as well. Early in Mary's reign he urged Protestant laymen to "have assemblies together ... and there to talk and renew among yourselves the truth of your religion. Comfort one another, make prayers together, confer with one another." Hooper recommended that such underground groups have someone "out of the scriptures speak unto you of faith and true honoring of God."[32]

The very fact that these groups met secretly makes it difficult to quantify how many there were, and how many laymen and laywomen were members. But there is evidence that the authorities suspected that such communities were widespread and involved strong lay participation. We know something about a few of them, particularly the London underground churches. William Winthrop was a member of one such church, which met in private homes and occasionally on ships in port.[33] Another London group of young merchants, French and Dutch as well as English, met in a tavern in Stepney to read and discuss the Bible and to share information on their fellow Protestants abroad.[34] The Protestant layman, Edward Underhill, recorded that "there was no such [better] place to shift in in this realm as London, notwithstanding the great spying and search." Underhill had a bricklayer seal his Protestant books in a wall near his chimney, where they remained until Elizabeth came to the throne.[35]

Outside of London, the layman Geoffrey Hurst of Shakerley, Lancashire, was forced to leave his home but returned secretly to gather together over 20 fellow believers to pray and worship. He kept hidden a Tyndale New Testament and an Edwardian Prayer Book. Thomas Watts of Billericay, Essex was accused of holding conventicles. Edmund Allen of Frittenden, Kent was a miller who was accused of preaching to followers.[36]

With the death of Mary Tudor and the accession of Queen Elizabeth in 1558 the sun rose again on the Protestant cause in England.[37] Clergy and laity emerged from underground while others returned from abroad. But the Elizabethan settlement did not go far enough in reforming the church to satisfy those who increasingly came to be labeled "puritans," precipitating decades of local and national debates over the proper nature of the church. Laymen played a large role in the struggle. Faced with the need to fill the many parish vacancies caused by the departure of Catholic priests, Archbishop Matthew Parker lowered the standards for ordination, allowing many men with no university training to enter the ministry, but also licensing laymen to read the church services.[38]

Thomas Upcher, a weaver who had been arrested in 1553 for hosting a conventicle of fellow laymen who read and discussed the scriptures, was ordained deacon by Bishop Edmund Grindal.[39] Grindal granted Upcher permission to preside over worship without wearing the hated surplice which advanced reformers saw as a remnant of Catholic practice. Grindal also ordained others who had no formal ministerial training, including William Betts and Walter Richardson, the former a weaver and the latter likely to have been a weaver.[40]

Despite the efforts of Grindal and other returning exiles to take up the reformed momentum from where it had been when Edward VI died, Queen Elizabeth imposed a more moderate church settlement and blocked efforts for further reform. During her reign the most successful efforts to purify the church were local and regional initiatives promoted by godly laymen in conjunction with puritan clergy. Their agenda included a strong commitment to Calvinist orthodoxy, the settlement of preaching ministers in the nation's pulpits, the stripping of the church of the remnants of Catholic belief and practice, and a greater exercise of discipline to keep notorious sinners from the table of the Lord's Supper. These positions were not limited to puritans, but an especially zealous pursuit of them did come to be identified as puritanism, particularly by the enemies of change.

The advance of this agenda varied from region to region. The efforts of godly laymen of substance were largely responsible for the growth of puritanism in those areas where it began to flourish, and are easier to document than those of ordinary men and women. Patrons who supported further change in the church named reformed clergy to livings for which they held the advowson. Between them Sir Robert Jermyn and Sir John Higham had the rights to present clergy to 14 Suffolk benefices, and, calling upon the advice of clergy such as John Knewstub, they appointed godly preachers to those livings and then protected them from episcopal interference.[41] This was complemented by the efforts of other laymen to pay the "First Fruits," a payment required of all inductees to clerical livings worth a certain amount. As previously noted, the merchant William Winthrop, the former member of the London underground church in Mary's time, paid the assessment for clergy in a variety of livings in London and in Suffolk, where his family had its roots.[42] Prosperous puritans financed lectureships in select parishes and in market towns to enable the reform message to reach a larger audience.[43] Because the various parish ministerial posts in Ipswich, Suffolk were poorly compensated, it was difficult to find university graduates who could successfully guide believers, Samuel Bird of St. Peter's being an exception. As a result the magistrates of the corporation worked to obtain a town preacher who would serve the purpose, in 1605 settling on Samuel Ward, who became one of the region's most influential puritan clergy.[44]

In the absence of government efforts to reform the church, ordinary Christians embraced the responsibility of advancing their faith through religious interaction with family and neighbors. They were encouraged to pray in their homes and invite friends to join with them. They read and discussed the scriptures in such domestic settings.[45] Committed to such efforts, Henry Hastings, the puritan Earl of Huntingdon, stated that

> my days are not given to me to be spent securely and carelessly... but religiously and soberly, which must give assurance to myself and yield testimony to others that I am one of the number of those who are chosen to be children of so holy a Father.[46]

John Bruen led family devotions in rural Cheshire and later in Chester; in both settings neighbors and friends joined him. In Cheshire neighbors slipped through the garden behind his home to attend sessions, with, according to a contemporary account, "many converted, and many confirmed, and many convinced."[47]

Laymen clearly were responsible for household exercises such as these, but often took a prominent role in broader neighborhood gatherings as well. According to Alexander Topp one did not have to be a clergyman to expound on scripture, since the "Holy Ghost is a divers gift unto the chosen," clergy or lay.[48] As early as the 1520s some London evangelicals were sharing Protestant books and meeting to discuss them. In the 1570s William Carnsew recorded the practice of sharing London reformed publications with friends and neighbors in Cornwall.[49] Many clergy encouraged such practices. The noted divine William Whitaker wrote that it was the Spirit and not reason that enabled one to understand the scriptures. "Scripture," he asserted, "cannot be proved by scripture." Rather, "all Christ's sheep know his voice and are internally persuaded of the truth of Scripture."[50]

Other clergy, however, worried that such practices might lead laymen to encroach on the prerogatives of the ministerial office, and that without the benefit of university training ordinary believers might stumble into error.[51] As the Church of England became more effectively established, some clergy—particularly those who supported the settlement of 1559—began to advance a self-definition of themselves as members of a profession with special expertise that distinguished them from ordinary Christians. They believed that knowledge of ancient languages and of the writings of Church Fathers and contemporary theologians, as well as training in logic made them especially qualified to interpret the Bible. This placed them at odds with laymen who relied on the Spirit to guide their reading of scripture and with those reformed clergy who relied on lay support.[52] The tension involved in trying to balance lay empowerment with clerical authority was to remain a significant element in the evolution of puritanism.

In the early years of Elizabeth's reign some church leaders who had witnessed large degrees of lay empowerment during their time of exile on the continent sought to involve ordinary Christians in the process of reforming England. Bishop John Jewel encouraged Bible reading by laymen. He believed that in the early days of Christianity lay believers had participated in church councils and that the apostles had recognized that ordinary people often judged things better than more prominent Christians.[53] Thomas Lever, William Fulke and other Elizabethan reformers expressed similar positions regarding lay authority.[54] Early in the 1570s Thomas Cartwright "claimed that the first Christian missionaries had sanctioned local autonomy, broad lay participation, and lay leadership."[55]

The stranger churches in London employed practices whereby believers could engage with the clergy in order to find answers to questions they might have about doctrines or church order. This was in large measure a way of dealing with issues that if unaddressed might lead some church members to heretical positions. The clergy of the French Church primarily focused on discussion of the Bible to achieve this end, while the leaders of the Dutch Church allowed public time for questions on recently preached sermons.[56] These practices were known to English reformers, some of whom were engaged in the affairs of the stranger churches. William Winthrop, for example, was elected one of the elders of the Italian Church in London in 1570, and on more than one occasion came to the assistance of the French Church.[57]

Laymen were also involved, to some degree, in the similar practice known as "the godly exercise of prophesying," which was employed for a time by numerous English bishops as a way of enhancing the quality of the clergy. This typically featured the gathering of clergy in an area who would listen to and discuss sermons preached by ministers of distinction as a process of collective edification, referred to by Patrick Collinson as "an open university, as it were."[58] Frequently laymen attended the sermons, many of them with the Bibles open in front of them as they followed the preacher's scriptural references.[59] In such cases it is likely that the laity were able to engage the clergy with questions and perhaps to offer their own insights into the scripture texts. Certainly those who complained of the exercises highlighted such involvement and its subversive implications, and even the chronicler William Harrison, sympathetic to the reformers, acknowledged that some laymen "intruded themselves with offense" at the exercises.[60] There were also reports that preachers who had been suspended for their controversial views were continuing to participate in some of the exercises.[61] Though the majority of the bishops in those dioceses where the practice was most prevalent stressed their value, Queen Elizabeth ordered the exercises ended in 1576. Her order complained that "in sundry parts of our realm there are no small number of persons presuming to be teachers and preachers of the church" who gathered "unlawful assemblies of a great number of our people out of their ordinary parishes and from places far distant...to be hearers of their disputations and new developed opinions upon points of divinity."[62] When Archbishop Edmund Grindal questioned the queen's directive and defended the prophesyings he was suspended from his duties.[63]

The concern about lay participation in prophecy was likely heightened by the fact that some authors were explicitly arguing that laymen could possess the gift of prophecy. Thomas Paynell argued that "if any man have the gift of prophecy, let him have it, that it be agreeing with the faith," and that those who were thus filled with knowledge were "able to exhort one another."[64] The prophesying may have come to an end but the same objectives were often achieved through the unregulated preaching of suspended or deprived preachers as well as some who remained in good standing through the protection of patrons but were every bit as energetic in promoting further reforms.

The image of a layman following a preacher's scriptural references in a Bible he had brought to a prophesying or sermon is indicative of an important dimension of the ongoing English reformation. Between 1525 and 1640 there were over a half-dozen separate English translations of the Bible published, most of which went through multiple editions. In that same period there were a total of 280 editions of the complete Bible in English published, with an additional 175 editions of the New Testament.[65] From the start, making the Bible available in English was not designed merely for clergy and university students. In the "Prologue" to the Great Bible published in 1540, Archbishop Thomas Cranmer wrote that "all manner of persons" could, through the guidance of the Holy Spirit, profit from the Bible—"men, women, young, old, learned, unlearned, rich, poor, priests, laymen, lords, ladies, officers, tenants, and mean men, virgins, wives, widows, lawyers, merchants, artificers, husbandmen, and all manner of persons of what estate or condition they may be."[66]

To aid the reader various editions provided prefaces explaining how the scriptures should be read, and some had marginal commentary offering explanations of unfamiliar terms and occasional paraphrases to clarify difficult passages. Other editions provided doctrinal glosses. In the case of the Geneva Bible, some glosses contradicted the official positions of the English church. Such commentary was fodder for discussions among lay and clerical puritans in prophesying and conferences.[67]

During the Elizabethan period a number of puritan writers published works in which a layperson served as spokesman for true doctrines, something that would have been inconceivable had not the authors believed that it was actually possible for laymen to play such a role.

Of course, depicting laymen who could address matters of faith was a formula that harkened back to William Langland's fourteenth-century *Vision of Piers Plowman*, which asserted lay anticlericalism in its expression of a believer's search for Christian truth. Robert Crowley, a mid-sixteenth-century printer, published a popular edition of *Piers Plowman* as well as the works of some of the Edwardian reformers.[68] At the time of the English Reformation this tradition came to include published dialogues in which two or more individuals exchanged views that were intended to edify readers about matters of faith. Thomas Becon was one of the early reformed pioneers of the genre.[69] He was a follower of Hugh Latimer, a theologian, and the author of four dialogues, beginning with *A Christmas Bankette* (1542) in which he assumed the persona of Philemon in setting forth the importance of scripture as the sole guide to truth.[70]

Anthony Gilby, one of the Marian exiles, wrote *A Pleasant Dialogue between a Soldier of Berwick and an English Chaplain* shortly after returning from exile, though it was not published until the 1570s. In it, Gilby's lay soldier, Miles Monopodios, is critical of the uneducated, multi-beneficed clergyman who was the epitome of all that puritans found wrong with the English ministry. Not only did the layman have the best of the argument, not surprisingly, the fictitious chaplain complained about the efforts of those who "would make all men as wise as themselves" in spiritual matters.[71]

In 1581 George Gifford, lecturer in the Essex town of Malden, published *A brief discourse of certain points of religion which is among the common sort of Christians, which may be termed the country divinity, with a manifest confutation of the same*, generally abbreviated as the *Country Divinity*. In it Zelotes, a godly layman, engages an uneducated country person named Atheos in a discussion of the religious issues of the day, including the need for an educated ministry, the importance of preaching, the value of scripture reading by the laity, and the relationship between faith and works. As in Gilby's work, the layman is depicted as one assuming the responsibility of evangelizing the ignorant.[72]

This genre continued to be popular. In 1589 an anonymous author published *Sophronistes: A dialogue persuading people to reverence and attend the ordinance of God in the ministry of their pastors*. This was actually a work that countered the argument for sermon gadding, urging instead the duty to attend to the parish ministry, though making some allowance for attendance at other sermons. But it is significant that here too the published arguments were in the form of dialogue between two laymen.

William Perkins was one of the foremost theologians of the Elizabethan church and a fellow of Christ's College, Cambridge. In 1590 he published *A Treatise tending unto a Declaration whether a man be in the Estate of Damnation or in the Estate of Grace*, a major portion of which consisted of "A Dialogue of the State of Christian Man, between Eusebius, a perfect Christian, and Timotheus, a wise Christian." Like Monopodios in Gilby's dialogue and Zealotes in Gifford's, Eusebius was a layman who had mastered the reformed message and was able to articulate it persuasively to others. For Perkins, grace transformed a lay person's consciousness, which enabled him or her to properly understand the scriptures.[73] Grace was, he wrote, "like the sun, shining upon all to who it is proclaimed, but with no effect among the blind." All men were by nature blind, so that they could not understand the scripture "unless the Spirit, as the inner teacher, through his illumination makes entry for it."[74] Elsewhere, Perkins wrote that "anyone who would encourage godly affections and desires in others must first have godly affections himself," a position that could be read to mean that a layman blessed with grace was a better guide to the faith than an educated clergyman who was not so gifted.[75]

Yet another example of this genre was Arthur Dent's *A Plain Man's Pathway to Heaven*, which appeared in 1601. Dent's approach differed from that of the previous authors in that he expanded the dialogue into a conversation between four participants: Theologius, a minister; Asunetus, an unlearned layman; Philagathus, an "honest" man; and Antilegon, a scoffer with no interest in exploring religious ideas.[76] Such works not only demonstrated what the authors saw as the ability—and responsibility—of ordinary believers to defend their faith, but likely gave believers who read them confidence in their own power to do so.

Without demonstrating the point through imagined dialogues, other authors also sought to promote lay power. Thomas Cartwright was, like Perkins, another Cambridge stalwart of the Elizabethan puritan movement. In the 1570s he argued that the earliest missionaries to England had encouraged lay participation and even leadership of the church.

As Elizabeth's reign progressed without any sign that the queen would change the structure of the national church, some puritans began to offer their own suggestions as to what a reformed church might look like. While the suggestions came primarily from clergy, many of them included an important role for laymen, in which ordinary believers (from whom those clergy drew their own support) not only were empowered to address religious matters, but also to govern. In their desire to purify the church, various reformers advanced the ideal of a visible church in which all would be doctrinally orthodox and contain the sacraments that would be denied to anyone who was guilty of profane and sinful acts. Walter Travers argued that those who were "brutish and ignorant" and "given to all sin and wickedness are to be cast out and banished from the church." Ralph Udall likewise argued that "drunkards, papists, etc." were not truly part of the church. William Perkins likewise envisioned Christian communities in which all would have knowledge of God's will and a commitment to godly obedience.[77]

In such a reformed church a godly laity could be entrusted with considerable power. William Fulke, a leader of a puritan faction at St. John's College, Cambridge in the 1560s and eventually master of Pembroke College, argued that "whatever matters to all ought to be decided by all."[78] He was the author of *A Briefe and Plaine Declaration concerning the Desires of all the Faithful* which circulated in 1584 and made the case for a broad and comprehensive participation by lay parishioners, who would form a kind of interpretive community.[79] Fulke envisioned learned, godly, and moderate men meeting in debates in which

> there be much searching of the truth by sufficient reasoning... when the spirit of every prophet shall be subject unto the spirits of the other prophets, & the judgment of all shall be sufficiently heard, without stopping of free & sufficient answer, without Lordly carrying away of the matter.[80]

Dudley Fenner likewise argued that the people should be involved in decision-making in "every matter of great weight and importance." Thomas Cartwright was convinced that no weighty or light matter could be decided without the consent of the laity.[81] And Lawrence Chaderton, the master of Emmanuel College, Cambridge, wrote that believers were to be actively engaged with each other, that each "must be one another's member," "serving to the benefit of all... by diligence and love," which included laymen reading the Word in public and preaching in private gatherings.[82]

Of course, this would have called for enormous transformations in the national church. But part of the significance of such writings was that they stimulated many laymen to express themselves on the need for reform. In 1575 Richard Fletcher, the Bishop of London but rector of the parish of Cranbrook, complained that "it is a common thing now for every pragmatical prentice to have in his head and mouth the government and reformation of the church." During a sermon that Fletcher preached on the necessity of conformity, some of the lay members of the parish openly challenged him while he was in the pulpit. He noted that many of those listening were taking notes and later arguing and advancing their own views.[83]

The puritan agenda called for rejecting various ceremonies associated with Roman Catholicism. Among these were the wearing of clerical vestments and kneeling to receive the Lord's Supper. Many clergy stretched the limits of how far they could avoid conforming to prescribed practices seen as popish—such as wearing vestments and requiring that recipients kneel to receive the Lord's Supper—because they were pushed by their lay supporters. The Brownist Robert Harrison pointed out that often the spiritual "children" were "forwarder than their father."[84] Explaining to Norfolk pastor Edward Fenton why his parishioners were moving beyond him, Harrison pointed to their "fruitful edifying of gracious speech and godly conference."[85] Clergy who became figures of consequence in the movement stood out because they responded to such pressure from their parishioners. As a result godly men and women frequently flocked from outside the parish to hear their sermons.[86]

It is hard to unravel the extent to which the positions taken by puritan clergy in adopting certain practices and rejecting prescribed procedures were the result of their own initiative, consultation with other clergy, or popular pressure by the hotter advocates of reform in their parishes. But Patrick Collinson argued that as early as the Elizabethan period "the conduct of a puritan minister, including his own nonconformity, was partly a response" to pressure from those in the pews. While ministers would clearly be loath to acknowledge that they were bowing to popular pressure, Collinson found evidence that "the strongest prejudices against the most concrete and symbolic of popish survivals in the Church of England, the surplice, resided not in the puritan clergy but among 'simple gospellers'." Thus, for instance, when some Suffolk puritans crossed the Stour River to attend services at Boxted, Essex, the vicar there decided not to wear the vestment, since "some that came out of Suffolk side would have liked him the worse if he had worn it."[87] Similarly, in Bury St. Edmunds, Suffolk, George Withers refused to wear the clerical four-corned cap because of the views of his congregation about it.[88]

Those who travelled to hear the word preached effectively were "gadding," a practice of travelling to attend the word. This had begun in the early stages of the Reformation and continued as an important way of both building enthusiasm for the cause and connecting puritans throughout a region. As explained by an Essex layman cited for the practice in 1585, "he goeth to other places, viz., sometimes to Maldon, sometimes to Langford, where the word is more purely preached."[89] Frequently laymen and laywomen travelled together to listen to such a preacher, talking of religious matters en route and discussing the sermon they had heard as they returned home.

Not all reformers were comfortable with unfettered lay participation in church affairs and the types of pressure just described would have heightened such concerns. While most were critical of the hierarchical episcopal national church, there were differences over how it should be modified. There were two connected issues—how power should be distributed within a local church, and the relationship of the individual congregation to a superior authority. At one extreme were those who advocated a system of classes and synods that exercised authority over local congregations and chose and ordained the local ministers. This system also envisioned the officers of the congregation, including lay elders, exercising the governing power of the local church. On the other side of the reform polity debate were those who argued for a system similar to what was being put into practice by the Separatists in England and the Netherlands—lay control of the affairs of the local church (including electing ministers and determining membership) and the absolute autonomy of the local congregation, though a loose system of consultation between churches was allowed and even encouraged.[90]

There were numerous other ideas spread on the spectrum between these extremes, and space does not allow an examination of the multiple proposals for church government and the particular roles of lay elders and members set forth in various clerical treatises. But it is necessary to examine some of the ideas advanced regarding the relationship between the clergy and the lay members of a church as a whole. Thus, for instance, the proposed Presbyterian *Directory of Church Government* prepared by Walter Travers in the 1580s, asserted that a minister "was so bound to [the church that chose him]...that he may not after be of any other, or depart from it without the consent thereof," and that he could not exercise his ministry elsewhere, even on a temporary basis, without the approval of his own church.[91] And positions sometimes shifted. The reform agenda presented as *An Admonition to Parliament* in 1572 stated that a minister was to be elected by the "consent of the whole church," but later editions modified this to "by the elders with the consent of the whole church."[92]

The Presbyterian movement that surged late in Elizabeth's reign sought to reorganize the national church into a system of classes and synods. In the late 1580s these reformers did set up what approximated an underground Presbyterian Church within the Church of England, with separate regional classes, procedures for classical meetings, and measures for connecting the various classes. In point of fact, however, in the absence of any ability to enforce the system, the classes had only that authority which was willingly granted to them by those they intended to supervise. It is important to distinguish the aspirations of those spearheading this effort from the reality on the ground. The most famous and well documented of the regional classes, that which met in Dedham, Essex, resisted the centralizing tendencies of the effort and was, in the words of its most famous historian, "at the risk of anachronism one might say more Congregational than Presbyterian."[93] When the church authorities became aware of the movement they took steps to suppress it.

While Elizabethan puritan reformers could not agree on the precise role of the laity in the governance of the church, many continued to encourage practices that in fact did empower the laity. Glimpses of local prayer meetings can be found in the records of the period. In Aythorp Roding, Essex, in the 1580s a dozen or so laity met in a private home after the Sunday service to dine and discuss doctrine they had heard, concluding with a reading from the *Book of Martyrs*.[94] One such involved the town of Mildenhall in Suffolk, where the curate Thomas Settle conducted meetings of the godly in a chamber at the local inn. There they "used certain prayers whence the noise might be heard to the further side of the street, so as the other guests of the house complained of the disquiet they received thereby." Patrick Collinson has suggested that the behavior of such groups "was extended and verging on behavior that might nowadays be associated with Pentacostalism and other spirit-filled versions of Christianity."[95] And that of course is the point. For many puritans theirs was a spirit-filled version of Christianity—the Spirit empowered them to see God's truth and compelled them to spread the word.

The authorities were often critical of these practices, branding such meetings conventicles and seeking to suppress them. But puritans evaded such attempts for the most part, and occasionally challenged the official position. John Wilson, a godly clergyman in northern Yorkshire, when challenged by Edwin Sandys, the Archbishop of York, of urging the laity to hold such meetings, denied the fact but responded, "My lord, you now put me in mind of a duty I have not yet done, but by the grace of God I will remember it hereafter, and will exhort the people of God to meet together, to comfort and edify one another in these things which they have been taught and learned."[96]

Another practice that also engaged the laity was fasts. Puritan fasts were not part of the regular calendar, as was the case with Roman Catholics, but were called for special purposes. They could be private periods of meditation and abstinence from food. Most commonly they were public events. Locally, friends and neighbors might gather in one home to fast, read scripture, and join in prayers with or without a clergyman present. Those on a parish or town level often involved a full day of preaching capped by reception of the Lord's Supper and a shared meal. Some were more regional and could stretch to more than a single day, resembling the so-called "holy fairs" that flourished in Scotland in the seventeenth century and then spread to North America. A famous description of one of these was written by the Jesuit William Weston, who described an open-air gathering outside of Wisbech Castle, where he was being held captive.[97] A fast held in Warwickshire in 1596 was attended by hundreds of believers and featured sermons by three ministers. Another, in Bedfordshire in 1603, lasted from nine in the morning till five in the evening and included sermons by four ministers.[98]

During the reign of Queen Elizabeth Protestantism became firmly established in England, but the nature of that faith remained contested. While many Englishmen were content to allow the leaders of church and state to make decisions about belief and practice, a strong and growing minority felt compelled to use the graces God had bestowed upon them to reach their own conclusions about what the scripture set forth. Encouraged by some clergy, laymen and laywomen met in family groups and larger gatherings to debate uncertain matters of faith and practice. They gadded to sermons, participated in fasts, and through these and other means sought to exercise their influence on the nation's religious course.

3
Lay Puritans in Stuart England

Following the death of Elizabeth in 1603, her Scottish kinsman James Stuart, James VI of Scotland, came to the throne of England as James I. Because Presbyterian reform had accomplished in Scotland many of the changes long sought by English puritans, English reformers hoped that the new monarch would be receptive to modifications of the Church of England. Few realized that the Scottish monarch's apparent sympathy to English reform was calculated to insure that he would succeed Elizabeth, and that it cloaked a distaste for the puritan-like Presbyterian system of his native land. A petition to the king supposedly signed by over a thousand Englishmen sought his approval for a variety of reforms. But at the Hampton Court Conference King James rejected most of the puritan program, though he did agree to a new, authorized translation of the scriptures (what has become known as the King James Bible).

As had been the case under Elizabeth, puritans were again forced to build support for reform from the bottom up. Continuing and expanding the tactics they had employed to effect change in the previous decades. Modest reforms in church practice occurred in those parishes where godly patrons or puritan congregations had influence over the appointment of a rector, curate, or lecturer and where the implicit support or inattention of the diocesan authorities made changes possible. Thus, for instance, the parishioners of the two churches in Bury St. Edmund's, Suffolk claimed the right to elect their own clergy despite the objections that had been lodged in Elizabeth's time by Bishop Edmund Freake.[1] Many parishes clearly had the legal right to choose their ministers, subject to a bishop's approval. When John Wilson was invited to become lecturer at All Saints Sudbury in 1617, he demurred until the parishioners as a whole confirmed the call by their vote.[2] In 1624 the vestry of St. Stephen's Coleman Street chose John Davenport to be their vicar.³ John Burgess, in debating with John Robinson regarding whether the Church of England was a true church, pointed to the fact that in parishes like St. Andrew's in Norwich the congregation voted to choose their minister.⁴

During the early decades of the new century puritan merchants in numerous towns sponsored Sunday afternoon and weekday lectureships—the latter often on market days. These offered lay people in the surrounding area an opportunity to attend godly preaching if it was not available closer to home, or to supplement the preaching of the local ministry if it was. Some of these were so-called combination lectures, where a group of clergymen took turns filling the pulpit. Because lecturers did not have to officiate in religious services they were able to avoid the use of vestments and ceremonies viewed as papist, and this made such positions attractive to reformers.⁵

In addition to the efforts of local merchants to sponsor such lectureships, laymen and laywomen were engaged in other plans to significantly alter the ministry of the church by purchasing the rights to install godly ministers to parish livings. Thus, for instance, Mary Lady Weld left £2000 to a London livery company with instructions that they use the funds to buy up church livings.⁶ More ambitious was the organization of the Feoffees for Impropriations in 1625. This was a London-based group that initially included four clergymen, four lawyers, and four prominent merchants. The orders they drew up stated their objective to be "the purchasing of impropriations for the maintenance of the preaching of the word of God." Between 1625 and the time when the government put an end to the enterprise in 1632, they claimed to have succeeded in placing over 40 godly preachers around the land.⁷

The practice of gadding to sermons by parish clergy or lecturers continued in the new century. Godly laity travelled up to 20 miles to hear the puritan divine Samuel Fairclough preach at Ketton, Suffolk so that "the churchyard [was]...barricaded with horses, tied to the outward rails."⁸ In Derbyshire laymen and laywomen carried lunches with them as they traveled to hear Julines Herring, and discussed his sermons as they returned home together.⁹ Many men and women from various parts of Lincolnshire—likely including the Hutchinson family of Alford—traveled to Boston to hear John Cotton preach.

The popularity of a preacher such as Cotton or Dedham's John Rogers was largely established by the number of such individuals who voted with their feet by traveling to hear him.¹⁰ Rogers was noted for his powerful preaching style and, in the words of a contemporary, "multitudes of people flocked from the parts adjacent and his plain preaching was blessed with a large harvest."[11] Margaret Winthrop wrote to her husband John in May 1629 of "the going of the young folk to Dedham, where many thanks were given to God."[12] One such believer urged a friend to "go to Dedham to get a little fire."[13] Sermons could draw so many lay listeners from outside a parish that the church fabric might have to be expanded to accommodate them. In 1629, for instance, the parish of St. Stephen's on Coleman Street in London built a new gallery along the south side of the church to fit the many coming to attend the sermons of John Davenport.[14]

While attendance on the preached word was a major part of a godly life, believers also gathered in private meetings. Clerical and lay conferences were important as occasions for fasting and prayer, but also settings in which various views of where the Spirit seemed to be inclining believers might be discussed and hopefully be reconciled. Conferencing was a term puritans used for godly interaction between saints, whether it be a casual meeting between two friends or more formal groups that gathered for spiritual sustenance. It could be a means for mobilizing support for a particular clergyman or the reform of disputed practices, but it was also a critical means whereby laymen and laywomen strengthened their own faith and supported that of others.

Nicholas Bownd, who presided for a time over the combination lecture at Bury St. Edmunds, was a strong advocate of clerical and lay conferencing. He wrote that "though every one give but a little yet the sum amounteth to a great deal," and that "though every man hath some grace of God's spirit in himself, yet it is greatly increased by conference."[15] It was like "a great many firebrands laid together."[16] John Cotton used similar imagery. If an individual believer meets with "two or three like himself," he preached,

> they presently begin to kindle one another, and the breath of such Christians is like bellows, to blow up sparks one in another, and so in the end they breathe forth many savory and sweet expressions in their hearts, and edify themselves by their mutual fellowship with one another.[17]

The noted polymath Samuel Hartlib recorded in his notebook in 1634 that "The benefits of conference are very many and great." For ministers it was a way to test the knowledge of those to whom they preached. It helped those who participated to focus their discussions and enabled some to edify others. A person could experience "the greatest meditations, upon which happily we should never have lighted all our lifetime in our retired and private meditations." And, Hartlib stated, it was more quickening to the spirit than just listening to one person.[18] Those who heard John Rogers roar from the Dedham pulpit were encouraged by that clergyman to have "society and conference with our fellow-brethren... who may confirm us by their counsels and consolations." "He that walks with the wise," he stated, "shall be the wiser. Much good may we learn, and comfort may we get, by conversing with them that be truly godly."[19] According to Thomas Hooker, a man whom God had bestowed saving grace upon might not be aware of it until he "haply drop into the congregation or falls into a house where there is conference."[20]

At the heart of the practice was a humility in recognizing that one could profit from the further light shared from others. Richard Bernard talked about how conferencing involved asking advice from clergy, "reasoning with equals, and teaching inferiors, all in reverence and humility to understand that [which] I know not, to be resolved in all that I doubt of, and to call to memory what I have forgotten."[21] While Thomas Hooker warned of the type of man who "in conference... would have it known that he is learned, full of knowledge," such use of the practice for self-aggrandizement appears to have been rare.[22] Christians should, wrote Thomas Watson, "when you meet give another's soul a visit, drop your knowledge, impart your experiences each to other... Christians should take all occasions of good discourse when they walk together, and sit at table together... What makes it a communion of saints but good conference?"[23] Richard Sibbes saw such gatherings as providing "better encouragement in these sad times, and to help our trust... It were a course much tending to the quickening of faith of Christians if they would communicate one to another their mutual experiences."[24] When Lady Joan Barrington was feeling anxiety over her spiritual condition, her former chaplain Ezekiel Rogers encouraged her to seek "the society of God's saints," and particularly those "such as could help... by telling what God had done for their souls."[25]

Often called conventicles by the church authorities who sought to suppress them, conferences could include clergy along with laymen or be for the laity only.[26] In 1593 the government passed an act prohibiting "any such assemblies, conventicles, or meetings under color or pretense of any such exercise of religion."[27] The Canons of 1604 prohibited conventicles but the wording was directed to ministers who would preach, administer the sacraments, pray, or conduct fasts in a private house.[28] Nevertheless, the authorities broadly interpreted these canons to include any such activities, whether a minister was present or not, leading John Winthrop to include "many unjustly traduced for conventicles" in a list of "Common Grievances Groaning for Reformation," which he prepared for puritan MPs to present to Parliament in 1624.[29]

Begun in Elizabeth's reign, conferencing became more prevalent and more controversial under the rule of the early Stuarts. One form, in which believers formally bound themselves together, became particularly contentious. Thwarted by the authorities from effectively fencing off notorious sinners from the table of the Lord, some clergy gathered parishioners self-identified as godly to participate in informal religious exercises. In 1588 nine laymen in Dedham, Essex, joined in a covenant to live godly lives and thus be examples for their neighbors.[30] Years later, John Cotton recalled how "some scores of persons in Boston in Lincolnshire...entered into a covenant with the Lord, and one with another" to share spiritual gifts.[31] In Chelmsford, Essex Thomas Hooker presided over a "community within a community."[32] This may have been what John Eliot was referring to when, in a 1657 letter to Richard Baxter, he recalled how "I have known before I came to New England in the Bishops' times, a company of Christians who held frequent communion together."[33] There were other, less-documented examples of such efforts as well.

Aside from their other objections, church authorities viewed such gatherings as a potential half-way house toward separatism. An indication of the prevalence of the practice in the early decades of the seventeenth century and the concern they prompted can be found in the Visitation Articles prepared by bishops to root out dissent and nonconformity in their dioceses. Some of the articles also identify what was believed to be the setting for such meetings and what transpired in them. The 1601 articles prepared by Richard Bancroft for the diocese of London asked parish authorities "whether any within your parish do resort to barns, fields, woods, private houses, or to any extraordinary expositions of Scripture, or conferences together."[34] When Bancroft became Archbishop of Canterbury he incorporated a similar question into the 1605 articles for the ten dioceses that he supervised. Bishop Richard Vaughan asked about conventicles in the 1605 articles for London.[35] His successor in the London diocese, John King, asked in 1612

> whether your minister, or any other that hath taken holy orders now silenced or suspended, or other person or persons, either of the ministry or laity, within or near your parish...hath been at or used to

meet in any barns, fields, woods, private house or houses, and held private conventicles or meetings: whether at any such meeting do any of them preach, confer, or agree upon nay private orders for divine service, prayers, preaching or expounding the scriptures.[36]

To the north, Archbishop of York Tobie Matthew included like questions in his archdiocesan articles in 1607. Other examples can be found in the 1612 articles for Gloucester, and the 1617 articles of Peterborough.[37] John Overall's 1619 articles for Norwich inquired if anyone had "been present at any unlawful assemblies, conventicles, or meetings, under color or pretense of any exercise of religion."[38] Richard Montagu's articles for the Chichester diocese in 1628 specifically listed "repeating of sermons, [and] expounding of scripture in private houses" as activities to be investigated.[39] Countless other examples testified to official concerns about such private religious meetings.[40]

Many conferences involved the discussion of sermons. Laymen were encouraged to take notes of the sermons they heard and review them with their family. But there was also value in friends coming together for the same purpose.[41] Various puritan writers identified Sunday evenings as a particularly appropriate time for believers to gather for the discussion of that day's sermon. The puritan clergyman John Udall wrote that "after the sermon we ought at our coming home to meet together and say to one another, 'Come, we have all been where we have heard God's word taught. Let us confer about it.'"[42] Typically ten or more gathered for supper and then "conferred together of such profitable lessons as they had learned that day at a public catechizing," after which they read from the Book of Martyrs, sang psalms, and "so departed about ten o'clock at night." In one Essex town godly laity met "sometimes... at one neighbor's house, sometimes at another's."[43] Many of those who attended Julines Herring's sermons in Shrewsbury in the 1620s and 1630s gathered to discuss what they had heard, rotating their meetings through different houses to avoid suspicion. Also to avoid discovery, in Bristol such meetings were held at various times in the homes of a grocer, a writing master, a farrier, a victualizer, and a butcher.[44]

Prayer was a key element in such gatherings, but not the use of formal petitions such as the prescribed prayers of the English liturgy. Reformers stressed the importance of extemporaneous, free-form prayers in which believers drew on the inspiration of the spirit to reach out to God for favor or in praise. While some clergy became noted for their extemporaneous prayers, a critical point is that puritan teachings not only allowed but encouraged individual Christians to form their own prayers in public and private.⁴⁵

There are numerous examples of laymen sustaining their faith and that of others by these means. In 1603 Richard Rogers published one of the key puritan guides to leading a godly life. In this *Seven Treatises* he urged believers to join together with fellow saints to achieve the benefits of sharing their experiences and their ideas. He provided an "example of a covenant made by certain godly brethren" in his parish of Wethersfield, Essex for "the continuance of love and for the edifying one of another." "They were," he emphasized, "no Brownists; for they were diligent and ordinary frequenters of public assemblies with the people of God. Neither were their meetings conventicles for the disturbing of the state of the Church and the peace thereof." They prayed together, shared experiences, counseled one another, and discussed matters of faith. Their interaction "did knit them in that love, the bond whereof could not be broken." Rogers expressed the hope that what had worked in Wethersfield would be attempted elsewhere, so "that godly conference may be had in more account among Christians."⁴⁶

The covenant drawn up by the Wethersfield believers included activities to be engaged in by the whole group, but also ways in which individual members might interact with one or more brethren, lay saints coming to the assistance of other laymen without the presence of a clergyman. The signatories pledged

> weekly, and by days... to communicate our estate with some faithful brother, with whom we may freely and faithfully open and impart our whole course: what means, and how far we use them; what we see cause to complain of; and what is more required of us than that which we do.

"It doth not a little help," they attested, "to have this communion with some... that we ourselves should be helpers of others."⁴⁷

One of those influenced by Richard Rogers was John Winthrop. Winthrop had been raised in the Stour Valley, where clergymen such as John Knewstub and Henry Sandes were frequent guests at his father's table. He had considered the ministry himself, but left Cambridge when he married Mary Forth. The future governor of Massachusetts settled with her in Great Stambridge, Essex where he thrived under the spiritual guidance of Ezekiel Culverwell, a close friend of Rogers. Culverwell had spoken of how, "when as by some good measure (as some sweet conference), my affection is enlarged to any of God's saints" he had a "taste of the happiness to come" in heaven.[48] And he had written that "there are no stronger means to make man and wife, or two brethren or sisters living together, in peace and love, than to join together often in prayer and Christian conference."[49] Inspired by Culverwell's teachings, Winthrop reached out to fellow Christians in the region, comforting an elderly man and offering spiritual counsel to fellow believers who respected his judgment. Later, having moved back to Suffolk, he continued to engage with fellow saints. He joined with John Knewstub, Henry Sandes, and fellow laymen in their own form of "godly conference," pledging themselves to aid one another and be "knit in that love, the bond of which could not be broken." They agreed to recall their covenant and communion every Friday, even if distant from one another.[50]

The puritan clergyman Oliver Heywood recalled secret fasts held in his father's house in the 1630s, when he was but a boy. When he was in his early teens he was himself initiated into "the society of some godly Christians" who held "conference every fortnight and prayed."[51] In 1640 the layman Roger Quartermayne, called before the High Commission for participating in what was branded a conventicle, argued that there was nothing illegal in what he and his fellow saints were doing. "We pray," he stated, "and we read the scriptures, and as well as we are able find out the meaning of the Holy Ghost therein, and what we understand of the word we impart to our company." "It is nothing but godly conference," he argued, "which every Christian man is bound to do and perform; for it is our duty to edify and build up one another in our moist holy faith."[52]

One of the important features of conferencing was describing one's personal experiences of grace. Sharing stories with others who could understand them reinforced a sense of saintly communion and could be a means of leading others to a closer relationship with God. Thomas Goodwin pointed to "the success which our examples, or gifts, or graces have upon others" as one of the fruits of saving grace.[53] The London puritan clergyman Thomas Taylor referred to godly conference as "a whet-stone of grace."[54] It was, he wrote on another occasion, a means of drawing "thy friends along to heaven with thee."[55] Richard Rogers used a similar image in describing godly conference as "whetting on one the other."[56] It was a means for "the continuance of love and edifying of one another."[57] The preaching of godly clergy and the reading of scripture were both important, but according to Vavasor Powel, "amongst the various ways of God's teaching, experience is one of the chiefest."[58]

In sharing their experiences laymen and laywomen assumed what was in essence a pastoral role in helping others to understand their own spiritual progress. Samuel Petto believed that "the declaring of experiences is one means which we may expect the Lord will make successful unto the conversion of sinners."[59] Petto set forth a variety of ways in which the sharing of experiences with fellow believers could help. Richard Sibbes complained that many Christians were "too backward that way to treasure up the benefit of experience," which when reflected on helped to strengthen faith.[60] In explaining how "by their experiences, you will learn how various God is in his ways and workings," Dublin's John Rogers wrote that "By these experiences of saints you will learn that God hath divers ways, and divers times, and divers means to work with; and some that seem very contemptible too, so that if he does not work on thee or thine in one way, he may another."[61]

Richard Gilpin, who became the puritan rector of Greystoke, Cumberland, during the Protectorate, went so far as to argue that "so great and many are the blessed helps arising from the society and communion of such as fear the Lord (as counsel, comfort, encouragement from their graces, experiences, and prayers, &c.) that the woe pronounced to him that is alone is not groundless." Gilpin went on to argue that "Christians in an holy combination can do more work, and so have a good reward for their labor. They can mutually help one another when they fall, they can mutually heat and warm one another; they can also strengthen one another's hands to prevail against an adversary."[62] Robert Bolton talked of how "comfortable communion in prayer, godly conference, mutual communication of their spiritual state and how they stand to God-ward, [and] days of humiliation" were ways of "helping one another towards heaven, and that joyful forethought of most certain meeting together in the ever lasting mansions of glory, joy and bliss above." "Such divine fellowship would...make that state a very earthly paradise to those...that love so sweetly and graciously together."[63]

In the aftermath of the Restoration of 1660, Richard Vines recalled how, in the 1630s, "time was (and indeed the worst of times) when Christians, the professors of Christian religion in England, were practical, and exceedingly addicted to practical holiness, keeping a sweet inward communion with God, and among themselves." "Their conferences were savory," he wrote, "and their inward experiences communicated were excellent, edifying and building up."[64]

Scottish Presbyterians agreed with their English brethren on the spiritual value of conferencing. Indeed, as Alec Ryrie has shown, such practices had deep roots in Scotland. Early in the process of reform in that kingdom the embers of faith were nourished in small gatherings of Christians. This was in keeping with the thrust of reform throughout Europe. As Ryrie points out, "For early modern Protestants, the core religious activity was getting together with other Protestants, and reading and talking about being Protestants."[65] In the seventeenth century leading Scots endorsed conferencing. Samuel Rutherford saw value in it, "providing none invade the Pastor's office."[66] He wrote that "Christians meeting for prayer and conference want not God, who rains down impressions of grace upon them as his people, especially when they warm one another; as many coals in one heap make a great fire." "Let the saints meet," he urged, "and by conference and prayer draw down new influences of the spirit."[67] Robert Rollock also advocated conferencing, but emphasized that "when the saints are exercised in godly conference and in spiritual and heavenly exercises... then they should be separated from the world, and from the society of profane men."[68]

Christians learned from other Christians—even the humblest. The lay role is clear. Some authors suggested that the role of a fellow Christian in stimulating godly communion could exceed that of the clergy. Thomas Gouge urged his readers to "communicate thy counsels, comforts and experiences to the poorest and meanest Christians, and to partake of their counsels, comforts, and experiences; not disdaining to learn any good thing of those who in several respects are much thine inferiors."[69] Agreeing that one could learn from lay believers, John Owen recognized that "men not solemnly called and set apart to the office of public teaching may yet be endued with useful gifts for edification."[70] Richard Sibbes went further, arguing that "a carnal man can never be a good divine" and that "an illiterate man of another calling may be a better divine than a scholar" because mere "notional" or "discursive knowledge" is knowledge without a taste of the Spirit.[71] When puritans extolled the importance of prayer they were referring not to set forms but to the spontaneous outpourings of fervent believers. In 1635 the lecturer Samuel Ward of Ipswich asserted that "there was not that life to quicken either hearer or speaker in the reading of an homily or prayer, though penned never so elegantly, as there was by prayer and preaching by the Spirit, and that a parrot might be taught to repeat forms without affection."[72]

At a time when many godly men and women did not have access to puritan clerical guides, the ability of fellow laymen to minister to one another, in essence adopting a pastoral role, was particularly important. James Janeway wrote that one of the "season[s] wherein God meets the soul, and the soul is visited by God, is when Christians are met together to communicate experiences, or to discourse together about the great things of God." Simonds D'Ewes found that in conferring with a godly friend in 1624 he "learned more touching the nature of signs, causes, and effects of faith...than ever I had done before."[73] Even when such meetings were "prohibited by the public magistrate" and "but few dare meet together, "though there be but two or three of them, he [God] will make the number one the more, he will be in the midst of them."[74]

Sharing one's religious experiences not only celebrated the salvation of the individual but shaped communities of saints.[75] As the laity came together in such groups the very act of doing so was a means of detecting fellow Christians who had been touched by God's grace.[76] John Saltmarsh wrote of a "manifestation of Spirit...in which spiritual men are known and revealed to each other, and have as full assurance of each other in spirit and truth as men know by the voice, features, complexions, statures of the outward man." Those who had "the Spirit of God in them" could detect "the workings and manifestations of the same Spirit in others, as in prayer, preaching, prophesying, conference, conformity to Christ [and] spiritual conversation."[77] Walter Craddock made a similar point, that "A man that hath the spirit may know the spirit in another by the spirit."[78] John Goodwin wrote of the "connaturality of spirit in the saints" that brought them together.[79] For Nathaniel Byfield, "Nothing bringeth more feeling joy, comfort, and delight (next the communion with God in Christ) than the actual communion of saints, and the love of the brethren."[80] This ability to recognize fellow saints was important when puritans wished to come together in conferencing or to gather their own churches, as they would in the Netherlands and in New England, and then in England itself in the 1640s and 1650s.

It should be noted that personal narratives such as were shared in conferences were not assertions or celebrations of having reached a final goal. Typically, those who shared a conviction that they had received God's caress subsequently would experience challenges to their assurance, and would continue to share the story of their ongoing struggles with their fellow believers. Telling and discussing those events with other godly men and women was a source of continuing comfort and a further means of binding together the community of saints.[81] Saints who shared their experiences served as lights, candles, tapers to guide others, to mention some of the common images used at the time.[82] A friend of James Janeway wrote that by sharing their experiences with others the godly, such as Janeway, "may be such proficient in Christianity as shining like lights yourselves to hold forth the word of life for convincing the incredulous."[83] Those who neglected to share their experience, wrote Richard Rogers, "had been dim lights."[84]

While most lay advice on religious matters was shared in conferences and other informal settings, some laymen were able to publish their views despite the censorship of the times. Others celebrated in sermons and print the stories of exemplary Christians. Over 40 laymen, including some women, published works of scriptural devotion before 1640.[85] In 1625 the lawyer and judge Sir John Bennet published a meditation on Psalm 51 which he dedicated to the puritan clergyman John Downane. When Sir Richard Baker was criticized for publishing meditations on scripture he responded with *An Apology for Laymen Writing in Divinity*.[86] In 1611 an author writing under the pseudonym Miles Micke-bound published *Mr. Henry Barrowes Platform* in Amsterdam. Following in the tradition of earlier works by Thomas Becon, Anthony Gilby and George Gifford, the author discussed religious reformation in the form of a dialogue between two laymen.[87] William Hinde extolled the life of John Bruen, a layman whom he identified as "a nursing father to the children of God."[88] Such lay writings were criticized by many, eventually prompting responses such as Sir Richard Baker's *An Apology for Lay-mens Writing in Divinity* (1641).

In recent years scholars have pointed to the importance of what have been referred to as "scribal publications," manuscript works that were circulated among family, friends, and other believers. Though many of these works were by clergymen, laymen and laywomen also authored such works. Most students of the period are familiar with the over 50 notebooks of scriptural reflection, self-examination, and life incidents recorded by the London artisan Nehemiah Wallington and the devotional meditations and autobiographical reflections of Lady Grace Mildmay, but these are only two of many such collections composed by lay puritans and shared with other members of the godly community.[89]

If indeed it was possible for even an illiterate man with the gift of the Spirit to be a better guide than a scholar untouched by God's grace, it is not surprising that occasionally laymen preached in secret gatherings. Patrick Collinson found that "at Ramsey there was a preaching place in the woods, with straw and moss for seating, 'and the ground trodden bare with much treading' " where dozens of individuals, most of them women, "gathered in this clearing to eat roast beef and goose while listening to one William Collett, who expounded St. John's gospel from a ladder." Elsewhere in Essex a schoolmaster names John Leach was the leader of what authorities labeled a conventicle.[90] According to a tract published in 1651 there had been a sect of "an united people" led by the layman Christopher Cob worshipping in Ely for the previous 20 years.[91] At Scrooby, in Nottinghamshire, the layman William Brewster was cited in 1598 for preaching to a group of local believers, initially by reviewing and commenting on sermons preached in local churches.[92] There is evidence that in the late 1630s Oliver Cromwell, living in St. Ives, "regularly preached in other men's houses as well as his own."[93]

Defining the limits on such practices would be a challenge for puritans, and the anxiety felt by some about the dangers of lay preaching grew as the prevalence of the practice grew. The Water Poet John Taylor, no puritan, mocked the practice, referring to "this new talking trade, which many ignorant coxcombs call preaching."[94] Though Nehemiah Wallington decided that the idea came from the Devil, it is significant, as Kate Narveson has observed, that at one point Wallington recorded that "it came to my mind what need I go to the walls of church for thou mayest read as good and sweet matter at home."[95] It is not surprising that many clergy felt that lay empowerment threatened their pastoral office. Even Richard Rogers, the Wethersfield puritan clergyman who urged lay engagement with one another, advised that when laymen encountered difficult passages in the scripture they should consult the opinion of a learned pastor whenever that was possible.[96] Yet in the absence of a godly clergyman, lay believers would continue to look for a guide from among themselves.

A critical point in understanding the eventual fragmentation of the reform movement was that while most of those who trusted in the guidance of the Spirit did so in order to find the true meaning of scripture, others would come to place the inspiration they received as supplanting the scripture. The former trusted that they would come to agree on the true meaning of the Word, and all, even those who trusted the Spirit independent of the Bible, believed that there was but one truth to be discovered. Some would be willing to await further light when consensus was not achieved, but others were less tolerant of differing views, rejecting the possibility that they could be in error.

Though it appears to have been less common, some women as well as men were known to share their religious insights, and I have previously noted women compiling and sharing spiritual reflections. Stephen Geree believed that "grace makes men and women excel," so that women might achieve the "sharpness of apprehension and soundness of judgment" not normally associated with their sex.[97] The ministers of the Dedham conference debated whether it was "convenient" for a woman to lead family prayers if she had a greater gift than her husband, and reached no conclusion.[98] Richard Rogers believed that a wife could lead family prayers if her husband was not available, but went further to argue that she should do so if he had insufficient knowledge or was sinful. And even in cases where the husband was suited to do so, he might "allow her... or request her to undertake it."[99] Margaret Hoby discussed sermons with the gentlewomen who waited upon her, specifically referring in her diary to conferences with "a religious gentlewoman" and "some that came to see me." On one occasion she noted that she "had some conference with John Browne, unto whom I gave the best advice I could."[100] In Scotland, Elizabeth Melville led gatherings of prayer in her chambers in 1630.[101] Elizabeth Juxson sought to spend her Sundays in fellowship with God and fellow saints.[102] Jane Radcliffe's godly discourse was able to "inkindle the same holy fire (in their heart who heard her) which burned in her own bosom."[103] Interestingly, the "society of some godly Christians" that the young Oliver Heywood was a member of had been "joined together by the instigation of an ancient godly widow woman."[104]

The society Heywood recalled may not have been that unusual. The conventions of the day made it unlikely that gatherings of believers led by women were readily acknowledged. Yet there are some that we do know about. Brigit Cooke was a married woman of modest means living in the town of Kersey, not too far from John Winthrop's Groton. Occasionally she would walk to Dedham to hear John Rogers preach, or to other local communities, though she appears not to have been as devoted to gadding as many other puritans in the region. She became known as someone of particular piety and became the leader of a conventicle in that Suffolk town in the 1640s, and perhaps earlier. Gathered in her home local saints read the scripture, prayed, and discussed sermons and their religious experiences. Brigit was reported to be particularly powerful in prayer. Weaker Christians came to rely on her for advice.[105]

In the 1620s Anne Hutchinson is generally believed to have frequently traveled to Boston, Lincolnshire from her Alford home in order to hear John Cotton preach, and it is likely that she was a member of the covenanted group that he assembled in the church. But she also sought to discern God's will by reading the scriptures with the guidance of the Holy Spirit, reflecting the puritan belief that a layperson could, with grace, discern God's will. While there is no evidence that she participated in the type of conventicle that she would organize in the Boston, Massachusetts church, it is highly likely that she would have shared her religious illumination with her family and friends. Her ease and success in doing so in New England, and the speed with which members of the church there came to respect her insights, suggest experience.[106]

In the 1620s Mistress Anne Fenwick of Northumberland came to the attention of the authorities. As David Como has documented, Fenwick, the details of whose life are unknown, was a godly prophetess and religious writer who was highly critical of some of the practices of the national church. She was held in high esteem by men and women in the area for, according to the godly lecturer Robert Jenison, the "extraordinary faculty she had in praying."[107] Her insights were initially offered in informal gatherings of saints, where, as Como points out, "effusive, powerful, and emotive outpourings of the spirit were not merely tolerated but in fact highly prized."[108] Brought before the Durham High Commission, she challenged Bishop Richard Neile, stating, "I acknowledge no reverence belonging to you, you are the bastard brood of Antichrist, literally descended from the whore of Rome."[109]

Mary Simpson was eulogized by the Essex clergyman John Collings as an "elect vessel" who "did more good to poor souls in the three years of her sickness by telling them of her experiences, directing, quickening, exhorting, strengthening, satisfying them than God hath honored any of us who have been preachers." She counseled those who came to her and inspired them by her example. Indeed, Collings referred to her as "an eminent preacher."[110] A tract published in 1641 identified women who preached in Lincolnshire, Ely, Hertfordshire, Yorkshire, and Somerset.[111]

It is clear that women actively participated in conferences of the faithful and, as in the above cases, actually could exert leadership. It also became acceptable in the seventeenth century for women to share their religious insights in writing. Anne Fenwick shared her prophetic views in manuscripts that eventually saw print as *A Collection of Certain Promises Out of the Word of God*.[112] Anna Trapnell would publish *Several Experiences of the Dealings of God with Anna Trapnel* in the hope that "these mourning experiences may be of great use to the sorrowful and troubled spirit that lieth languishing for want of the light of assurance."[113] Later Katherine Sutton would write of her prophetical experiences and offer "these crumbs which I have gathered from my bountiful Lord's table" in the hope that they would be "savory to... hungry, brokenhearted Christians."[114]

The banding together of laymen and laywomen into godly communities could be found throughout the nation. In areas where there was no settled puritan clergyman to hear, lay meetings could evolve into a gathered congregation. During the Elizabethan reign Walter Travers had conceded that while a well-established church should have a minister, a true church could stand without one if a godly clergyman could not be found.[115] Patrick Collinson identified the Broadmead Baptist Church in Bristol as one which, according to tradition, "grew by degrees out of the practice of repetition, the godly 'repeating their notes to one another, whetting it on their hearts.' After twenty years of this activity a few, and especially the women in the circle, 'had strength to begin to go farther.'"[116]

While some puritans were willing to recognize the value of lay preachers in circumstances where there was no clergyman to serve their needs, some went beyond this to question the value of a formal ministry. John Morrill has pointed out that "the claims of many Protestant clergy to be (by ordination in the Established or Dissenting churches) the sole authorized preachers of the Word of God, to have a superior and ultimately decisive authority to interpret Scripture, generated an especially powerful reaction amongst many highly educated laymen."[117] That was certainly the case, but it was not only educated laymen who believed that the grace of the Spirit was as important, if not more important, than education in discerning the will of God.

The records of laymen and laywomen advancing reform can be found for most parts of the nation, but are most abundant for London. That city had traditionally been a center of the puritan effort to reform the church, in part because its size, its fluid population, and the large number of parishes made regulating affairs there more difficult than in many parts of the country. It was in London that in the 1520s groups of laymen exchanged and discussed Protestant writings smuggled from the continent. During the Marian persecutions the city was the location for underground congregations with strong lay leadership. The Stranger Churches in the city provided a constant inspiration for many English reformers. A number of parishes had obtained the right to choose their own clergy, giving to some laymen an opportunity to put reformers in office. It was a city with countless bookshops, legal and underground presses, the extensive circulation of manuscripts advocating various religious doctrines and practices, and lay gatherings in which the ideas circulating could be debated. It was in London that the challenge of how lay-centered religion could succeed in separating error from truth was most dramatically posed.

The diversity of puritanism revealed in the scholarship of the past decades was most evident in the city of London. The richness of the movement can be gathered by looking at how many of the lay activities we have been examining manifested themselves there. There were numerous examples of London churches where the parishioners played a significant role in governance. Some examples can be found in the career of John Davenport, eventually to become one of the leading architects of puritan New England. Davenport's first position in London was as curate and lecturer of the poor parish of St. Michael in Wood Street, to which he was chosen by lay trustees who had acquired that right during the reign of Queen Elizabeth. He then went on to be chosen to lectureships by the lay vestries of St. Botolph's Bishopsgate and St. Lawrence Jewry. In all of these posts he attracted sermon listeners from throughout the city. In 1624 he was elected vicar of St. Stephen's Coleman Street, one of the largest and wealthiest parishes in the city. The story of that appointment speaks to the influence of prominent laymen in directing the affairs of some parishes. The advowson, the right to appoint the vicar subject to the approval of the Bishop of London, had been sold to the parishioners in 1590. The choice, as well as other parish business, was determined by a general vestry of about a hundred householders. In the early 1620s the parishioners had used their power to force the departure of Samuel German, the parish vicar who was deemed unsound "both in life and doctrine," following which they chose Davenport.[118] When there were doubts about whether his choice would be ratified by the Bishop of London, powerful lay patrons at court intervened to have the appointment confirmed. Over the years Davenport relied on lay support and opinion, even giving the parishioners a deciding voice on whether he should resign his living when faced with episcopal discipline.

In addition to the fact that many vicars were chosen by lay supporters of reform, the proximity of parishes and the abundance of lectureships provided laymen the opportunity to vote with their feet for preachers who reflected their own views. The London craftsman Nehemiah Wallington recorded in his diaries having attended 19 sermons in one week! While this was clearly exceptional, there is ample evidence of others who travelled through the city to feed their spiritual appetites. Robert Keayne, a London merchant who would later settle in Boston, Massachusetts, attended at least two and sometimes three sermons on any given Sunday. Lady Mary Vere, whose husband was the commander of English forces in the Netherlands, was a strong supporter of puritan clergy. When in England, she listened to sermons at a variety of London churches, and befriended John Davenport and other clergy.[119] Edward Montagu, Viscount Mandeville, kept a sermon notebook in which he recorded the preaching of Davenport, Sidrach Simpson, Richard Sibbes, and William Greenhill among others.[120]

William Kiffin was another such sermon gadder. When he was only nine years old, Kiffin's parents had died from the 1625 outbreak of the plague. As a young apprentice in 1631 he followed a crowd of Londoners into St. Antholin's church in London, where he heard and was moved by the puritan preacher Thomas Foxley. He began to visit other churches, including St. Stephen's Coleman Street, where a sermon by John Davenport "was of great use to my soul. I thought I found my heart greatly to close with the riches and freeness of grace which God held forth to poor sinners."[121]

Moderate clergy such as Davenport encouraged gadding, conferencing, and other activities designed to strengthen the communion of saints. This was a concept that had meaning on two levels. On the one hand these ministers sought to build the national and international reform causes. During his years at St. Stephen's, Davenport emerged as one of the leading proponents of religious reform at home and the Protestant cause abroad. Together with clergy such as Richard Sibbes, Thomas Taylor, and others he organized the Feoffees for Impropriation, raising funds to purchase the rights to install puritan clergy in positions in London and throughout the realm. Sibbes and Taylor also joined him in a fundraising effort to raise funds for the relief of Protestant refugees from the fighting in the Thirty Years War.[122] Contributing to such causes allowed lay donors to help advance God's plans.

On the other hand, these larger movements were rooted in the small gatherings of saints whose faith was strengthened by face-to-face contact and shared religious practices. Davenport was a friend of the clergyman Henry Scudder. Davenport wrote the preface to Scudder's *The Christian's Daily Walk with God*, which became one of the more popular puritan guides to the godly life. In that work Scudder laid stress on the importance of lay fellowship. He urged his readers to "be much in good company, especially in theirs who are full of joy and peace in believing." Nothing, he wrote, "giveth a more sensible evidence of your conversion" than "Christian society in brotherly love." Indeed, though clerical guidance was of value, "though there be never such an excellent ministry in any place, you shall see little thriving in grace amongst the people until many of them become of one heart, showing it by comforting together in brotherly fellowship, in the communion of saints."[123] These were lessons embraced by Davenport and passed on to his parishioners in London, later in the Netherlands, and then in New England.

We can also find in Davenport's story examples of discussions about church polity that suggest a willingness of mainstream puritan clergy to interact with those reformers on the fringe. Alexander Leighton was a physician who had been a member of the semi-separatist London church of Henry Jacob. Around 1625 he wrote to Davenport to challenge him on the clergyman's acceptance of the practice of kneeling to receive the Lord's Supper. Davenport responded in a letter in which he argued that it was more important for reformers to unite on fundamentals than divide over ceremonials. But he evidently found it appropriate to discuss such matters with a layman, knowing that the manuscript exchange would circulate widely.[124] About a half dozen years later he was prompted to reconsider his own conformity in part as a result of communications with imprisoned lay members of the London congregation formed by Henry Jacobs but at the time headed by John Lathrop.[125]

Thomas Taylor and Richard Sibbes were also strong proponents of lay conferencing. In a work published in 1612 Taylor bemoaned the fact that such conferencing seemed on the decline, asking, "Where is the communion of saints become? When do professors meet together to edify themselves by godly Conference?" Calling for greater efforts, he asserted that "such a fellowship as this [is] likest unto the purest primitive church in the days of the Apostles."[126] Sibbes likewise urged believers to "remembrance of former experiences, [which] serve to excite endeavor, so to stir up hope."[127]

The consequences of such encouragement can be found in the life of William Kiffin. Having been stirred by the preaching of puritan divines, Kiffin later recalled that

> About this time I began to be acquainted with several young men who diligently attended on the means of grace. It pleased God to make known, much of himself and his grace unto them. And, being apprentices as well as myself, they had no opportunity of converse, but on the Lord's days. It was our constant practice to attend the morning lecture... We also appointed to meet together an hour before service, to spend it in prayer, and in communicating to each other what experience we had received from the Lord; or else to repeat some sermon which we had heard before. After a little time, we also read some portion of Scripture, and spake from it what it pleased God to enable us; wherein I found very great advantage, and by degrees did arrive to some small measure of knowledge.[128]

Kiffin eventually emerged as a leader of the Particular Baptist movement in London.

Gatherings of similar groups were held throughout the city, and in each of them laymen and laywomen sought to identify the answers to questions about faith and practice. Peter Lake has done the most to help us understand the various currents in the London puritan underground of the period and has concluded that "We can now envisage a series of debates and altercations between a variety of different schools of thought, or styles of divinity or doctrinal assertion, all advanced by persons accepted as in some sense members of the godly community."[129] Some gatherings involved prominent political leaders. Sir Robert Harley, who we know attended some of John Davenport's sermons, joined with other laymen in private homes to pray for the success of the Protestant cause in the Thirty Years War as well as other godly causes, and to offer thanks to God for the blessings he had bestowed on them.[130]

By the end of the 1630s there were numerous such gatherings in London that would have been seen as more radical. Some featured believers gathering to listen to lay preachers such as the cobbler Samuel How and the tailor Richard Lee.[131] How was noted for a sermon he preached at the Nag's Head Tavern on Coleman Street in January 1639 that was subsequently published as *The Sufficiency of the Spirit's Teaching*. Addressing a gathering of over a hundred, including the then rector of St. Stephen's, John Goodwin, How challenged the monopoly on preaching claimed by university-trained clergy.[132]

Radical ideas such as those How espoused were debated in some conferences. The London clergyman Thomas Gataker wrote to his friend Samuel Ward that in the search for truth "private discussions, for ought I see, do best for the discovery of it, wherein men are most free either to take or given leave mutually of retracting and drawing back ought again."[133] The hope was that with a free exchange of ideas truth would emerge. For the most part, the godly were resigned to living with disagreement until the Spirit provided further light. But a number of disputes tested how willing puritans were to allow certain views to circulate. A few controversies bubbled to the surface in this period that highlighted the process of striving for conformity and its limits. These disputes also exposed the issues of governance that would occupy many puritans in the coming decades—What were the proper roles of the laity and the clergy within a congregation, and how could a movement consisting of many individual congregations maintain unity?

Early in 1611 a godly lecturer named Anthony Wotton prepared a series of manuscript position papers in which he challenged the traditional Calvinist view that men were justified by imputation of Christ's righteousness. He was soon attacked by George Walker, a young clergyman on the make, who first triggered a debate on the issue in godly circles and then violated the norms of procedure by taking his attacks public. Walker was staking his reputation in the court of godly opinion, seeking the support not only of fellow ministers but also of the lay puritan community in the city. In 1626 the clergyman Stephen Dennison publicly attacked John Etherington, a boxmaker who had set himself up as a lay preacher for heretical views. Defending himself, Etherington argued he was exercising his rights as an ordinary Christian to test the assertions made in the pulpit against his own understanding of scripture.[134] In 1629, when the authorities were determined to reduce puritan influence, Peter Shaw was brought before the ecclesiastical court of High Commission and charged with various heterodox opinions, including antinomianism. The testimony revealed further tensions and disagreements within the godly community.[135]

While these three incidents have left a record of discussion and dispute among London puritans, there were undoubtedly more. One of the consequences of valuing the insight of each individual—layman or clergyman—as potentially Spirit-guided was that each conference of fellow saints would be a forum in which rival claims would be presented in the hope that through discussion a greater understanding of the truth would arise. The larger community of similar gatherings might be consulted through correspondence, circulated manuscripts, and personal conference as the movement as a whole strained for agreement. Because there was no authoritative godly body to decide on such issues, unity required humility to accept what could not be agreed on while awaiting further light. When an individual or group was so convinced that one belief was the truth, the result might be splintering within a conference or in the wider movement. As Peter Lake and David Como have suggested, what might be called the "puritan public sphere" was a "social and discursive space in which a number of different ideological and emotional currents might mingle and miscegenate, react, and repel."[136] Of particular danger were disputes over the meaning and consequences of true godliness that on more than one occasion became acrimonious and gave rise to antinomianism.[137] Thomas Taylor published an attack on antinomian errors in 1631 in which he identified a variety of lay preachers who had promulgated the error, including one "who taught a number of silly women who gathered into his house on the Sabbath day."[138]

Foreshadowing what would become common in the following decades, the larger puritan community in London was disrupted in the late 1630s by the preaching of a variety of laymen, some of whom questioned the value of an educated ministry. Samuel How, who attracted large crowds in the Coleman Street Ward, argued for *The Sufficiency of the Spirits Teaching without Humane Learning* in a tract of that name published in 1640. In it he described a debate he had some years before with John Goodwin, the rector of St. Stephen's.[139] Displaying an impressive ability to cite and interpret scripture, the cobbler-preacher claimed that it was "such as are taught by the Spirit, without Humane-Learning, [who] are such persons as rightly understand the Word." Indeed, he went so far as to argue that if faced with a choice between "two men, both alike imbued with grace from God, and alike gifted by his Spirit," it was the unlearned man who "should be chosen to the ministry of Christ in his church." This was because a learned man would expect more respect than an ordinary Christian, and because since the gospel message was one of simplicity it was better for it to be presented by a simple man. University learning was of great use for "Statesmen, Physicians, Lawyers, and Gentlemen," and the ability to translate the scripture was vital lest those "that are unlearned could not come to have the letter of the word," yet not requisite for the ministry. He pointed out that "a lantern you know is of good use to contain the candle, but let one carry it on a dark night and it will do him no pleasure without a candle lighted in it." Likewise, the letter of the word is like a lantern without light; it is the Spirit that provides the light. Such "as are destitute of the Spirit's teaching, though furnished with human-learning, are the perverters and wrestlers of these and all other scriptures to their own destruction."[140] How was arrested for his activities and died in prison in September 1640.[141] But the authorities would soon lose all ability to control lay preachers in London and elsewhere.

The London scene was replicated on a smaller scale elsewhere. Through the reign of James I and into that of Charles I, lay puritans came together to discuss sermons they heard and passages of scripture they had read. They traveled to near or far parishes to listen to the sermon of a well-regarded preacher and talked about the message as they returned home. They recorded their spiritual experiences in writings that they shared with family and friends. Puritans were not alone in undertaking such efforts in their desire to serve God and lead exemplary lives, but it was puritans who were more likely to have the commitment required to devote the time and effort required to do so, a commitment they attributed to the blessing of God's grace. Bound together by such shared experiences into a communion of saints, such men and women would be uncompromising in their dedication to reform.

4
Gatherings of the Saints in England and the Netherlands

Most of those discussed in the previous chapter retained the ideal of a national church while seeking to transform it. John Cotton's "inner congregation" was located in St. Botolph's, Lincolnshire. John Davenport and John Wilson sought approval of parishioners to take up livings in established parishes. But the slow pace of reform led some of the godly to question their adherence to the Church of England. The more fervent their commitment to the task of leading godly lives, the more reluctant they were to compromise. Increasingly, many puritans found in their communion with fellow saints a community they valued above that of the national church. This chapter examines those who separated themselves from the Church of England either formally or by relocating in the Netherlands, where they found a greater freedom to reform, even if some still claimed kinship with the English church.

Shortly after Elizabeth came to the throne, some Londoners, frustrated by the queen's refusal to embrace a full reform agenda, began meeting secretly in London in a way reminiscent of the activities of the London underground church of Queen Mary's reign. Using the prayer book developed by the Scottish reformer John Knox, they conducted their own services in churches such as Holy Trinity Minories and in private houses. When over a hundred were discovered at a meeting in Plumbers' Hall in 1567 they were brought before the authorities.[1] But it was impossible for the bishops to totally suppress such efforts. And it is impossible for us to correctly gauge how common such practices were since for the most part we can only learn about those meetings that were eventually discovered by the authorities.

In the early 1580s Robert Browne had decided to join together in communion with fellow saints, "the worthiest, be they never so few." He was arrested for holding conventicles in private homes. On his release he joined in forming a separate congregation, the members of which chose him as pastor and Robert Harrison as teacher. Forced to leave England, the group settled in Middleburg, in the Netherlands. There Browne published his *A Treatise of Reformation without Tarrying for Any* (1582), in which there was an emphasis on the responsibilities of ordinary Christians. He accepted that while the chosen officers of a church had "the grace and office of teaching and guiding... every one of the church is made a King, a Priest, a Prophet under Christ to uphold and further the kingdom of God."[2] In forming his congregation he acted on the belief that Christians could find holiness only in a church where "any might protest, appeal, complain, exhort, dispute, reprove."[3] In *A Booke which Sheweth the Life and Manners of All True Christians*, Browne wrote of "prophecy, or meetings for the use of every man's gift, in talking or reasoning, or exhortation and doctrine."[4] Returning to England, he was arrested and persuaded to submit to the authority of the Church of England. But his ideas continued to circulate in reformed circles.[5]

Debates over separation as opposed to compromise continued to trouble puritan clergy following the accession of James I to the throne. Frustrated by the failure of the Hampton Court Conference to usher in a thorough reform of the church, some reformers were pushed towards separatist solutions, while others continued to seek reform incrementally on the local level.[6] The clergyman William Bradshaw published a series of works arguing that the episcopal structure of the national church was unscriptural and that the individual congregation held the power to reform itself and govern its own affairs. He asserted that "every Company, Congregation or Assembly of men, ordinarily joining together in the true worship of God, is a true *visible church* of Christ... equal and of the same power and authority."[7] His emphasis on congregational authority implied a strong lay role in the church. While his position was similar to the arguments of many who decided to separate from the national church, Bradshaw himself rejected the separatist choice.[8]

In 1606 the puritan laywoman Lady Isabel Bowes hosted a meeting in Coventry of a group of clergy including Arthur Hildersham, John Dod, Richard Bernard, John Smyth, Thomas Helwys, and possibly Thomas Cooper, Humphrey Fenn, and Robert Cawdrey. The subject of their deliberations was whether the failure of the church to purify itself meant that godly Christians were obliged to leave the church and establish their own congregations. The majority determined that doing so would only encourage Catholic critics of reform.[9] Bernard would, however, dabble with separatism before returning to the fold of the national church, while Smyth and Helwys would organize separatist churches.

Frustration with the pace of reform had led to the decision of men like Robert Browne and Robert Harrison to seek change without tarrying for the approval of the magistrates and bishops. Challenged about how they could justify rejecting the parish clergy if their own faith came from the preaching of those ministers, these reformers emphasized the ability of laymen to apprehend God's will through their own reading of the scripture as facilitated by the Holy Spirit. Lay saints could both find faith on their own and assist others to find it by sharing their insights with family and neighbors. Ultimately this type of thinking would lead to the conclusion that a true church rested on the faith of individual Christians and was formed through their coming together in covenant.[10] Michael Winship has observed that it is likely that such gathered congregations, "given that they were underground and voluntary, had a larger role for the laity in practice than Presbyterian clerical theorists would have been pleased with."[11]

Given the belief that any Christian, with the assistance of the Spirit, could discern God's truth, it is not surprising that one of the most prominent Elizabethan proponents of lay empowerment was a layman, Henry Barrow, the son of a Norfolk gentleman who had studied at Cambridge and then read law at Grey's Inn, though he never practiced. Something of a rake and man about town, Barrow was, according to his own account, transformed by hearing a fiery London puritan preacher. Devoting himself to a study of the religious issues of the day, he became a proponent of reform and developed an association with the separatist minister John Greenwood, the two organizing a congregation in London in the late 1580s. Greenwood, was seized by the authorities along with other separatists meeting in the home of Henry Martin in the London parish of St. Andrew by the Wardrobe in 1587. Barrow was shortly thereafter also arrested and imprisoned. Over the following years Barrow defended his positions against the ecclesiastical High Commission and other spokesman for authority while still being able to counsel members of the London separatist community and to smuggle out works which were published in the Netherlands. In 1593 he and Greenwood were executed for writing and publishing seditious literature.[12]

In his writings Barrow justified his activities by strongly asserting the importance of the lay role in the church. He was critical of what he saw as the clericalism of many fellow reformers. Indeed, he argued that the decay of the church of Apostolic times had come about because "the people...first neglected their duty, and gave up their Christian liberty, power, and interest in all the church affairs, the choice, insuring, and deposing of their officers, etc. into the hands of their presbytery." If church elders failed in their duty,

> then may any of the congregation, or any Christian whatsoever...ought to reprove such transgression and error, unless he will be guilty of betraying the faith of Christ, [and] of the destruction of the whole congregation, knowing...the suddenness of the wrath of God for such things.[13]

Barrow denied that the ministry was a necessary part of the true church. Members should take part in all of the action of the church. They could not only elect ministers but dismiss them.[14]

While puritans such as Barrow were struggling with how to perfect reform in the face of a hostile establishment in England, others found refuge in the Netherlands. The experience of English puritans there forced them to consider and implement new understandings of the nature of the church and the role of the laity in church affairs. They had to define what a church was, how it was to be organized, how its membership was determined, and how it was to be governed.

Francis Johnson, educated at Christ's College, Cambridge, initially accepted Thomas Cartwright's advocacy of polity that vested power in the hands of church elders. That position was anathema to the authorities and led to Johnson's brief imprisonment and expulsion from his university fellowship. Johnson traveled to the Netherlands, where he became pastor of an English merchant congregation in Middleburg. He soon sought to reform the congregation on the basis of a covenant whereby the members pledged themselves "to live as the church of Christ, watching one over another, and submitting our selves unto them, to whom the Lord Jesus committeth the oversight of his church, guiding and censuring us according to the rule of the Worde of God." Shortly thereafter Johnson returned to England. In September 1592 he was elected pastor of a newly formed separatist congregation in London. This led to his arrest and over four years in prison, during which he was able to continue to write and smuggle works out of prison to be published in the Netherlands. Upon his release, Johnson was involved in an abortive attempt to establish a colony in the gulf of the St. Lawrence River in North America, and then settled in Amsterdam in 1597, where he rejoined the exiled members of his London congregation, forming what became known as the "Ancient Church," which they hoped would serve as a "light upon a hill" for the people of England.[15]

Johnson's *A True Confession of the Faith* (1596) included attacks on the Church of England and directions for organizing a gathered, covenanted separatist congregation in which church officers were elected by the laity and final authority resided in the congregation. He called for covenanted congregations with membership determined by a statement of belief and a pattern of godly living. The applicant's life had to testify to the beliefs espoused. A "verbal profession," he declared, "helps little when men in practice and particulars deny that which in word in general they seem to hold."[16]

John Smyth was another Cambridge graduate who ran afoul of the authorities late in Elizabeth's reign for opposing various prescribed ceremonies. In 1605 he took part in the conference at Coventry where the question of separating from the national church was discussed. Dissuaded from separatism at that time, by early 1607 Smyth had organized a group of followers and left the church. He journeyed to the Netherlands and settled in Amsterdam. He did not join the Ancient Church because of his increasingly radical ideas on the use of set prayers, the role of church elders, and the practice of infant baptism.[17] But Smyth did share with other reformers the belief that church membership should be limited to those who possessed knowledge of doctrine and Christian obedience.[18] He believed that it was the laity and not the clergy who were the essence of the church. "Ordination doth give nothing at all to the minister," he wrote. As for the laity, "the chief care of every member must be to watch over his brother in bearing each others burden, admonishing the unruly, comforting the feeble minded, admonishing the excommunicate, [and] restoring them that are fallen." He also went so far as to argue that women and children of sufficient age should be asked to consent in the selection of church officers.[19]

While most separatists followed the lead of Johnson and Smyth and rejected participation in any religious activities with those who considered themselves part of the national church, John Robinson took a more moderate view. Robinson was a 1596 graduate of Corpus Christi College, Cambridge, who first came to the attention of the authorities when he attacked abuses in the Church of England in a sermon he preached at St. Andrew's in Norwich in 1603. Refusing to subscribe to the church canons he was ejected from his living in 1604 and moved back to near where he had been raised in Nottingham. By 1606 he had rejected his holy orders and embraced separatism. He soon joined Richard Clifton as leader of a group of godly believers that met in Scrooby, and ordained Robinson as their pastor. Faced with persecution from the authorities, the congregation began an emigration to the Netherlands in 1607. They first settled in Amsterdam but, disturbed by the contention they found in the Ancient Church and among other separatist groups, in 1609 they successfully petitioned the magistrates in Leiden for permission to settle there. Ultimately, it was a portion of this congregation, whom we know as the Pilgrims, that would settle the Plymouth Colony in 1620.[20] In his writings on church government Robinson argued for the formation of congregations of visible saints. The criteria to be used in admitting individuals to membership was sound knowledge and holy practice.

The Netherlands was also a refuge for some clergy who were forced from their livings in the Church of England but refused to take the step of separating themselves from it. The Netherlands was a Protestant country, just over 200 miles from London, and was relatively tolerant of religious differences. Early in the seventeenth century the number of English residents in the Netherlands numbered in the tens of thousands, most of them in good standing with the national church. This included merchants, soldiers assisting the Dutch in their fight to maintain their independence, and students. There were over 20 churches in which Englishmen worshipped in addition to the congregations of separatists. Some of these were affiliated with Dutch classes; others would become members of an English classis organized in 1621.[21] Removed from the close oversight of England's bishops, reformers in virtually all of these churches sought to institute new practices and articulate new visions of reformed churches. Among the puritan clergy who spent time in the Netherlands in the late sixteenth and early seventeenth centuries would be many who wrote about the role of the laity and who contributed to the development of congregational practices. Among the non-separating puritans were Robert Parker and William Ames.

Robert Parker originally came to the attention of the English authorities in the 1580s when he was at Magdalen College, Oxford. He refused to wear the prescribed vestments and tried to avoid subscribing to the church canons. He did finally subscribe in 1591 but his nonconformity became evident once again in 1607 when he published a work against the practice of signing with the cross in baptism, a practice puritans saw as a popish remnant in church ceremonies. Shortly thereafter he journeyed to the Netherlands, perhaps with William Ames. He spent some time with the separatist English congregation in Leiden led by John Robinson, but in 1611 he moved on to Amsterdam, where he was elected an elder of the English congregation there headed by John Paget. This was one of many churches established in the Netherlands by English merchants resident there. Parker's supporters in that church sought to elect him to be co-pastor but opposition from the English authorities led the local magistrates to block the appointment. Parker then found employment as a chaplain to English troops in the east of the country, but he died in 1614 after only eight months in the post.[22]

In various printed and unprinted works Parker argued for limiting church membership to those believed to be numbered among God's elect. He supported the practices of "other reformed churches" whereby candidates were to provide a statement of faith, evidence of a godly life, and a commitment to continue in the path of Christian obedience. He distinguished what was expected in the statement of faith from a mere catalogue of doctrines—what many called historical or general faith. As would others whom we will encounter, he believed that a truly effectual confession of faith was one that reflected the changes that the Spirit had wrought in the believer.[23]

William Ames would be one of the most referenced reformers among the settlers of New England. Born in Ipswich, England, Ames was raised from an early age by kin in Boxford, the town next to the Winthrop family's Groton manor. He was sent to Cambridge where he studied and then became a fellow at Christ's College. His nonconformity on ceremonial matters and his outspoken criticism of pastimes such as celebrating Christmas and playing cards eventually cost him his college post. After a brief stint as a lecturer in Colchester, Essex Ames moved to the Netherlands. He spent some time with John Robinson's congregation in Leiden before finding a post in 1611 as chaplain to Sir Horace Vere, the commander of English troops in the Netherlands. He had emerged through his publications as a skilled defender of Calvinist orthodoxy, which led to an appointment as a paid adviser to the president of the Synod of Dort, called to reject Arminian views on salvation. From 1622 to 1633 Ames served as Professor of Theology at Franeker University. His views on theology, church governance, and morality became very influential through his publications and drew many students to study under him. In 1633 he moved to Rotterdam to accept a ministerial post in an English church there, but died before taking office.[24] Like Parker, Ames believed that church membership should be limited to the godly, to those effectually called by God. They were to demonstrate an actual faith, meaning one that was manifested in the activities of a godly life.[25]

Henry Jacob was a reformer who spent time in the Netherlands but returned to England. He doesn't fit neatly into either the separatist or non-separatist categories. Jacob graduated from Oxford in 1583. His activities for the next two decades are obscure. When King James came to the throne in 1603 Jacob was living in London. He campaigned to influence the king in favor of church reform, helping to draft and garner support for the millenary petition. His efforts led to a brief imprisonment, after which he evidently traveled to Middleburg in the Netherlands. There he published *Reasons Taken Out of God's Word* (1604). Though it was a modest and reasonable statement of reform principles it led to his arrest upon his return to England. Released after agreeing not to speak publicly against the Church of England for six months, he and his family traveled again to the Netherlands. There he met with John Robinson, William Ames, and Robert Parker among other exiled reformers. He remained in the Netherlands till 1616, when he returned to London and joined with others in forming a covenanted gathered church in Southwark, on the south side of the Thames. Having prayed and fasted with one another, the group of men and women

> joined both hands each with other Brother and stood in a ringwise: their intent being declared, H. Jacob and each of the rest made some confession or profession of their faith and repentance... Then they covenanted together to walk in all Gods ways as he had revealed or should make known to them.

This was not a separatist church as its members were allowed to also attend services and receive communion in parish churches. Jacobs had petitioned the king for the toleration of congregations such as this within the structure of the Church of England. While the request had been denied there was no effort at the time to suppress the congregation. Jacobs himself likely emigrated to the Virginia colony in about 1623, dying there a year later.[26]

In setting forth his understanding of what should be expected of church members, Jacobs asserted that a congregation should "consist only of such people as are not ignorant in religion, nor scandalous in their life." In essence, he demanded faith and Christian practice.[27] The church thus formed was to exercise the power of Christ in governing its affairs "substantially, essentially, and fundamentally." United in a communion of saints, the congregation became in essence the body of Christ.[28]

All these reformers—separatists as well as non-separatists—found themselves wrestling with a number of issues involving the nature of the church. They had to decide what was meant by the very term "the church." They had to decide what the relationship was between individual congregations. And they had to decide how authority and power were distributed within a congregation. Their conclusions were relevant not only in the specific circumstances they found themselves in, but in shaping the course of puritanism over the remainder of the seventeenth century, and particularly the puritan understanding of the role and power of the laity.

Critical to all these discussions was the interpretation of two particular scriptural passages. One involved the proper definition of what was the church and involved the meaning of Matthew 18: 17: "And if he shall neglect to hear them, tell it unto the church: but if he neglect to hear the church, let him be unto thee as a heathen and a publican." The puritans—separatists and non-separatists alike—who would be defined as Congregationalists, agreed that the individual congregation was the "church" to which Christ had referred. William Bradshaw, whose *English Puritanism* was translated into Latin by William Ames, asserted that ecclesiastical power was held "within the limits of one particular congregation." The *True Confession* (1596 and 1602) of the Ancient Church of Amsterdam asserted that "Congregations be thus distinct and several bodies, every one as a compact City in itself."[29] While conceding some utility for synods, Bradshaw, like later Congregationalists on both sides of the Atlantic, maintained that they could only offer advice and had no coercive powers.[30]

Also at issue was who Christ addressed in Matthew 16:19: "And I shall give unto thee the keys of the kingdom of heaven: and whatsoever thou shalt bind on earth shall be bound in heaven: and whatsoever thou shalt loose on earth shall be loosed in heaven." It was generally agreed that Peter, to whom Christ was speaking in this passage, here represented the church. But, as John Cotton would express it, "it hath proved a busy question, how Peter is to be considered in receiving this power of the Keys, whether as an apostle, or as an elder (for an elder also he was, 1 Peter 5:1), or as a believer professing his faith before the Lord Jesus, and his fellow brethren."[31] The answer would determine who was to exercise the power of the keys. Some asserted that the laity were the ultimate authority within the church. Others believed that the authority of the keys was to be wielded by the officers of the church. William Bradshaw took the position that while the ministers were to be chosen by the laity, their authority derived from God.[32] Others countered this somewhat aristocratic view with a more democratic position. William Ames believed that the power of Christ was communicated to the members of the gathered congregation. Robert Parker, citing Thomas Cartwright, argued that Matthew 16:19 was to be read as Christ giving "the keys to the whole church." Parker did believe that the ministers were to administer the keys, but only as the agents of the laity. The people were the rulers; the ministers their servants.[33]

The meaning of these passages would continue to be debated within the puritan movement. To some extent how individuals interpreted them would distinguish Presbyterians from Congregationalists. But while true to a degree, that distinction is overly simple. Few "Presbyterians" would push ministerial authority to the point where it denied the importance of the laity, and authors who argued for lay authority often trimmed their positions to avoid discounting the importance of the ministry. Though explicitly asserting that a congregation held governing power "immediately under Christ" as a right, Jacob saw the officers of the church as the congregation's instruments in exercising authority.[34] This question, which had been largely of theoretical importance during Elizabeth's reign, became a matter of practical concern as puritans began to organize actual congregations in England and the Netherlands. And, as we will see, consensus was difficult to achieve, so that in the 1640s the Scottish Presbyterian Robert Baillie would observe about the Congregationalists that "so far as we can learn, there is yet no full agreement among them, either in New or Old England, in setting the march-stones of power betwixt the eldership and the brotherhood...They cannot come to accord."[35] But it was not only Congregationalists who wrestled with these issues. When they were debated in the Westminster Assembly, Lord Saye and Sele would point out that the Presbyterians did not agree on these matters either.[36]

The emphasis placed by some reformers on believer covenants as the foundation of the church offered the potential for an expanded lay role, including fostering the faith of other believers. A commitment to lay involvement in the teaching mission of the church was a distinguishing characteristic of the London congregation organized by Henry Jacob. " 'Any understanding member of the church (but women)' might with the church's permission undertake 'the sober, discreet, orderly, and well governed exercise of expounding and applying the Scripture in the congregation.' "[37] The records do not reveal how commonly laymen engaged in the practice, but it was significant enough for Richard Mansell, one of the original supporters of the church, to leave the congregation because of the right extended to the laity to preach by way of prophecy.[38]

A commitment to lay prophesying was central to congregations being formed in the Netherlands. The 1596 *Confession* of the Ancient Church in Amsterdam had asserted the legitimacy of the practice, particularly when a congregation had not yet found a minister. It is not clear how widely that particular church anticipated that power was to be exercised once a minister was in place.[39] Francis Johnson, who believed that governing authority was to be exercised only by the elders, upheld lay participation in the exercise of prophesying, including asking and answering questions, discussing disputed points of religion, and interpreting the scriptures.[40] Henry Ainsworth emphasized the responsibility of laymen in

> the mutual exhorting and building up one of another in the faith, laboring together unto the truth, admonishing the unruly, comforting the feeble minded, bearing with the weak, considering one another to provoke unto love and good works, rebuking for sin and trespass, confessing of faults one to another, and praying for another, bearing one another's burden, etc.[41]

Prophesying was an essential part of the congregation established by John Smyth after he had rebaptized himself. According to a description written by one of the members of his church in 1609, the normal service consisted of reading and expounding of scripture, prophesy, and prayer. In the morning, an initial speaker, perhaps Smyth, would speak for about 45 minutes, following which other members of the church would speak for varying amounts of time.[42]

John Robinson was another proponent of lay participation in the teaching mission of the church, though he believed that the authority of a minister rested on the possession of special gifts.[43] There was a tradition of prophesying in Norwich and elsewhere in England that Robinson would have been familiar with, and when he wrote *The Peoples Plea for the Exercise of Prophesie* he dedicated it to his "Christian friends in Norwich." Defending the practice against critics, Robinson urged that "a man (out of office) having received a gift of God, whether extraordinary or ordinary, by which he is able to prophesy, that is to speak to edification, exhortation, and comfort of the Church should so use the same good gift of God in his time and order." When multiple believers joined in such an exercise the result was "a joint feast of that heavenly repast, the word of God."[44] Robinson's principal target in his tract was John Yates, himself the puritan incumbent of the civic church of St. Andrew the Apostle in Norwich, who had been critical of lay prophesying. Robinson cited scripture as well as the authority of "the public Professor in the University of Leiden" who had supported the practice, "expressly proving it lawful for others than ministers to preach publicly." Robinson further pointed out that "they who prophesy at one time may learn at another; it is the disease of the exalted clergy to scorn to learn anything of others than themselves, and almost of one another."[45] In the Leiden Pilgrim church prophesying was normally conducted after the sermon by laymen approved by the congregation to do so, and with their contributions moderated and commented on by the elders.[46]

In justifying the practice, Robinson also pointed to the position of the Reformed Synod that met at Emden in 1571 where the Dutch Reformed Church was organized. Among the conclusions advanced was that "into the fellowship of that work are to be admitted not only the ministers, but the teachers too, as also of the Elders and Deacons, yea even of the multitude, which are willing to confer their gift received of God, to the common unity of the Church," though only "as they first be allowed by the judgment of the ministers, and others."[47] Furthermore, the synod had decreed "that in all the churches...the order of prophecy should be observed...and that into this fellowship, to wit of prophets, should be admitted not only the ministers, but also...of the very common people."[48]

Jeremy Bangs, whose study of Robinson's church is the most thorough, has concluded that lay prophesying was one of the elements that made the religious life of the Leiden congregation exciting: "Robinson emphasized that interpreting the Bible was not a skill restricted to the clergy, and that among the laymen of any proper congregation it should be expected that some could be found whose words should be heard."[49] "It may so come to pass," he wrote, "that some in the church, though no ministers, may excel the very pastors themselves."[50] William Brewster and Robert Cushman were among the lay members of the Leiden congregation whose views were highly regarded. Robinson even went so far as to "find a general rule that at times women should legitimately speak to the church in contrast to the particular contradictory instance when the apostle Paul wanted women to be silent," and he cited scriptural precedents that included Miriam, Deborah, Huldah, and Anna.[51] Citing 1 Corinthians 13:34, Robinson wrote that

> It seems most plain that he [Paul] hath no eye, nor respect at all, to these extraordinary gifts and endowments of prophecy, authorizing even women furnished with them to speak publicly, and in men's presence, as appears in Miriam, Deborah, Huldah, Anna, as also even Jezebel herself in regard of order, and others.[52]

While most separatist congregations were led by individuals who had been ordained as clergymen, ran afoul of the authorities, and finally split with the national church, some were headed by men with no formal ministerial qualifications. Henry Ainsworth had studied at Cambridge but left without receiving a degree. Soon thereafter he repudiated the Church of England and was arrested in London for separatist activities. He journeyed briefly to Ireland, but by the 1590s was settled in Amsterdam, where he became teacher of the Ancient English Separatist Church in that city. He soon became a prominent defender of lay-empowered congregations. Ainsworth identified the origins of a church in the coming together of believers determined to "walk forward in the ways of Christ for their mutual edification" through prophesy. "People fit and men furnished with meet and necessary gifts" were to "continue the exercise of prophesy... but also upon due trial proceed unto choice and ordination of officers for the ministry and service of the Church."[53] Describing the practices of his Amsterdam church, he wrote that "reading the book of the law and expounding it was their ordinary service every Sabbath." The participation of the congregation went along with the preaching of the minister, so that "when we pray, prophesy, or sing, we utter matter out of the heart unto the ear of the church."[54]

Soon after his arrival in Amsterdam Ainsworth experienced the centrifugal forces that lay empowerment could generate. Some members questioned Ainsworth's right to serve as a church officer based on the fact that at one time he had conformed to the Church of England. Though this was resolved in his favor, other disputes divided the church. A quarrel between the pastor Francis Johnson and his brother George led to the latter's excommunication. A further rift in the congregation was caused by John Smyth, who was critical of the use of English translations of the scripture in worship, arguing for extemporaneous translation of the original Hebrew and Greek texts, and also urging, according to Ainsworth, that men "lay aside the scriptures and hear what men should prophesy out of their hearts."[55] Ainsworth rejected the idea of prophesying concerning what was not tied to scripture, and published a defense of the church practices against Smyth, who left the congregation. Smyth had argued that "Christ intendeth the power of binding and loosing to be given to every brother," and that placing the elders above the members was Antichristian.[56] Reacting to Smyth's contention that the officers of the church must be subject to the wishes of the congregation, Francis Johnson had triggered another conflict in the church. Johnson asserted that the ultimate authority in the church rested with the elders in theory and in practice and that assertions of lay authority were an error. When Christ said "tell the church" he meant "tell the elders," according to Johnson.[57] This caused yet another split in the Amsterdam church, with Ainsworth defending lay authority and eventually becoming pastor of a dissident congregation that seceded.

Another layman to achieve prominence as a religious leader was Thomas Helwys, who had been at the 1606 Coventry conference that discussed conformity along with his friends Richard Bernard and John Smyth. In 1607 he followed Smyth to Amsterdam. Having joined Smyth in leaving the Ancient Church and been rebaptized, Helwys later split with Smyth. During the winter of 1612–13 he returned to England, where he became the founder and leader of the first Baptist church. By that time he had drifted far from the Calvinist orthodoxy which characterized most puritans, but his story does reinforce the willingness of laymen to put their understanding of scripture against university-trained clergy.[58] He expressed his belief that "the most simplest soul that seeks the truth in sincerity may attain unto the knowledge of salvation contained in the Word of God," and that "any disciple of Christ in what part of the world soever coming to the Lord's way, he by the word and spirit of God preaching that way unto others, and converting he may and ought also to baptize them."[59]

Though uncommon, there were other examples of laymen assuming pastoral responsibilities. The Ancient Church in Amsterdam had no minister for a long time in the 1620s, and was led by the lay elders, in particular Jean de L'Ecluse, who preached frequently.[60] The Pilgrim congregation in Leiden functioned for a time without a minister following John Robinson's death in 1625.[61] Following Jacob's departure to America in 1622, the members of his London congregation were relegated to "edifying one another in the best manner they could according to their gifts received from above" until they chose John Lathrop as their new pastor in 1624.[62] The so-called "Duppa church," formed by a small group that seceded in the 1630s from the congregation organized by Jacob, was led by John Duppa, a layman characterized in one report as a "cow-keeper." Katherine Chidley, who would later emerge as an important religious figure in her own right, was a member of this church.[63] There were other London congregations led by laymen in the 1630s. A congregation initially organized by a Mr. Hubbard flourished under the cobbler Samuel How in the Coleman Street area. How had earlier been a member of Henry Jacob's church and had learned his Bible by reading while mending shoes.[64] Another such church was led by a London clothier named Edmund Rosier. Richard Rogers was a glover in the city who was a preacher to a group meeting in Goat Alley.[65]

While many reformers were willing to accept the right of the laity (at least men) to preach by way of prophesy, the issue of administering the sacraments was a separate issue. During the sixteenth and early seventeenth centuries very few puritans were willing to concede any administration of the sacraments—baptism and the Lord's Supper being the only two sacraments they recognized—by laymen. While Henry Jacob did accept that "when a church is destitute of guides... then the people themselves have full power to accomplish any ecclesiastical action in the best order they can," he was presumably referring in that statement to matters such as admissions and censures, although he appeared to be open to lay baptism if the church was without officers. The Lord's Supper, however, could never be administered by a lay person.[66] John Robinson took a similar position, emphasizing in the 1620s that the Lord's Supper was not to be administered by William Brewster in the Pilgrim congregation in America.[67]

During the 1620s and 1630s the non-separatist English churches in the Netherlands became the stage for further debates over lay involvement in the church that would shape the formation of New England puritanism and the debates over church reform in England in the 1640s and 1650s. Some of these originated in the English church in Amsterdam. This was a church constituted in 1607 to provide worship for those Englishmen in the city who did not wish to worship in the Dutch churches, nor to join the separatist Ancient Church. It was organized as an English congregation that would nevertheless administratively be a part of the Dutch Reformed Church. The Amsterdam civic authorities provided a place for worship—a chapel and buildings called the Beguinage, which had formerly belonged to a female Catholic religious group—and agreed to pay the salaries of the congregation's ministers.[68] John Paget, an English clergyman who had migrated to the Netherlands after being ejected for nonconformity in 1605, was chosen pastor. Thomas Potts was installed as his associate in 1617.[69]

During the first decades of the congregation's existence Paget was heavily committed to the task of opposing the Ancient Church in the city. He engaged in a pamphlet war with Henry Ainsworth, defending his congregation against Ainsworth's attacks on the ceremonies of the English Church, the fact that it joined the Dutch in observing various holy days, conducted worship in a former Catholic chapel, and other matters. But Paget also was concerned with the activities of the growing number of former separatists who had left the Ancient Church to join his own congregation. Some of these were prosperous men who gradually rose to positions of leadership in the congregation. The result was a faction in the English Church that espoused a strong belief in congregational authority. In opposing the views of both the separatists and the Congregationalists in his own church, Paget moved toward a greater commitment to Presbyterian authority—that of the minister within the church and the higher authority of the classis.[70]

When Thomas Potts became seriously ill in 1628, those advocating a greater role for the laity sought to bring in a new clergyman who would share their views. They proposed a series of candidates, including a number of clergy who, forced from their livings in England, would eventually go on to play a large part in the shaping of New England's religious life. A dispute over who would pay his salary blocked the call of Hugh Peter. Thomas Hooker did preach to the congregation for a time but Paget succeeded in engaging the Dutch Classis to block his call, overriding the wishes of the congregation.[71] Paget's invoking the threat of the disapproval of that classis was enough to stop consideration of Thomas Welde. In 1633, with Potts dead and Paget himself very infirm, John Davenport was invited to assist the church in its needs. Davenport had left St. Stephen's Coleman Street under intense scrutiny from Bishop William Laud. He was very successful in Amsterdam, a success which in itself worried Paget, who utilized the Dutch classis to block the call, despite the strong support Davenport enjoyed in the congregation. With his path to the ministry of the church blocked, Davenport preached for a time in the private home of one of its members before moving on to a position in the Rotterdam church.

Anger at Paget's actions led one of the lay leaders of the church, William Best, to publish *A Just Complaint Against an Unjust Doer, wherein is declared the miserable slavery and bondage that the English Church of Amsterdam is now in by reason of the tyrannical government and corrupt doctrine of Mr. John Paget* (1634). This triggered a tract war over the issues in question, including the distribution of authority in the church. Paget published his *An Answer to the Unjust Complaints of William Best...Also, An Answer to Mr. John Davenport* in the summer of 1635. William Best was first to respond to Paget, publishing *The Churches Plea for her Right, or, A Reply to an Answer made of Mr. John Paget against William Best and Others* (Amsterdam, 1635). In it he explained that he had chosen to "not follow him [Paget] step by step throughout his book, but have principally insisted upon two points, viz., promiscuous Baptism and the due power of the church, because on these depend all our differences."[72] Dragged into what had become a public fray, Davenport sought to refute Paget point by point in his own *An Apologetical Reply to a Book Called An Answer to the Unjust Complaint* (1636), and his answer marked the first time that he publicly questioned the authority of classes and synods over individual churches and asserted his belief in congregational principles.

Davenport did not reject the idea of synods or assemblies entirely. "The combination of particular churches in classes and synods is either such a combination of them as is between equals, or such subordination of them as between unequals," he wrote.

> The first is by way of counsel, or brotherly direction. The second is by way of command, or masterly subjection. This we condemn as being the first step whereby the Pope ascended into the chair of pestilence, and a mere inlet for tyranny to invade and usurp the church's right. The other is approved by the practice of the most ancient churches and by good reason.[73]

In his defense of his positions here and elsewhere, he drew on the writings of, among others, Dudley Fenner, Thomas Cartwright, William Perkins, William Ames, and Robert Parker. According to Samuel Eaton, who had briefly ministered to the dissidents in the English Church in Amsterdam after Davenport's departure, at this time Davenport asserted that "a Classic Presbytery sets up many Bishops instead of one."[74]

Davenport's response to Paget was written when he was in Rotterdam, where he had joined Hugh Peter in an English congregation that encouraged strong lay involvement. Peter had arrived in Rotterdam in 1629 and began a process of reforming the church. Early in 1633, disdaining (in the words of a critic, Stephen Goffe) to "be called by the vulgar English of Rotterdam," he insisted on his call to the congregation's ministry by "the Godly, and so he framed a new covenant in paper to which all must put their hands, and none but those which were of that covenant should have any vote to call him."[75] There were 15 articles to the covenant, many of which reflected the importance of lay participation and conferencing. The first agreed that all who sought membership in the church should undergo a "meet trial for our fitness to be members." In other articles the members pledged to "labor for growth of knowledge and to that end to confer, pray, hear, and meditate"; to "submit to brotherly admonition and conference without envy or anger"; and to "be thoroughly reconciled one to another even in judgment before we begin this work."[76]

The Rotterdam congregation having been re-formed by those who took the covenant, John Forbes, representing the English Classis, called upon the members to approve Peter as their pastor. Looking out at the congregation Forbes (again, according to Goffe's account) said, "'I see the men choose him, but what do the women do?'...Hereupon the women lift up their hands too."[77] This is one of the few descriptions of congregational formation in England, the Netherlands, or New England which explicitly documents the vote of women in choosing their pastor. How common this might have been in the absence of explicit evidence one way or the other is an open question.

The obligation of conferring with and hearing one another in the Rotterdam church included the practice of sharing religious experiences. Daniel Bradford and his wife, who had come to Rotterdam from Norwich early in 1636, reported how they "did each give an account of the work of God's grace in our souls. Then Mr. Davenport asked if we were willing to join with them in the covenant. We said we were. They did then vote to receive us members of the church. Afterwards we turned to prayer."[78] Later that same year, perhaps after Davenport had left, Sidrach Simpson desired admission to the Rotterdam church following the afternoon Sunday service. Simpson was a graduate of Emmanuel College, Cambridge, who had been deprived of his church living by Archbishop Laud. According to a contemporary account,

> two things were required of him, a profession of his faith, and a confession of his experience of the grace of God wrought in him. Both of which he did so excellently perform, that the hearts of all there present were much affected, professing that this had been the fruit of prayers and tears, and many were upon the wing for heaven, saying, "Now, Lord, lettest thou thy servants depart in peace, the glory of church-communion being so brightly discovered, and the state of godly souls so graciously anatomized." ... For a whole hour he poured out his soul into our bosoms, and we as heartily embraced him in the beauty of the church.[79]

Following the departure of Peter and then Davenport to New England, the Rotterdam church was led by a number of clergy who would emerge as strong advocates of Congregationalism in England during the 1640s and 1650s. William Bridge and John Ward were ministers who renounced their English orders and joined the church as private men, after which they were chosen to the ministry in 1636. Also joining the church as private individuals were Sidrach Simpson (as noted above), Joseph Symonds, and Jeremiah Burroughes. Shortly after this a dispute developed in the church over the practice of lay prophesying. Tradition in the church allowed lay members to ask questions of the ministers and offer opinions following the sermon on the Sabbath. Bridge evidently wished to put an end to the practice or at least modify it. Simpson, who had spoken so movingly to the members at the time of his admission, opposed Bridge and the congregation became deeply divided. Ward was caught in the middle and was deposed by a vote of the congregation, which in January 1639 chose Jeremiah Burroughes as his replacement in the ministry. Those who had favored the maintenance of prophesying withdrew and formed a new church under the ministry of Simpson and Joseph Symonds. The new congregation had no support from the Dutch authorities. The bitterness that divided the two groups led to an intervention by Thomas Goodwin and Philip Nye, who were at the time ministering to the English church in Arnhem, where prophesying was the practice.[80] Eventually, in 1643, the two Rotterdam congregations reunited, but lay prophesying was only permitted in private homes.[81]

It is difficult to fully discern the role of women in the puritan movement at any point in the sixteenth or seventeenth centuries. Women were clearly expected to play a large role in the religious formation of their children. Glimpses of female involvement in conferences and as supporters of godly clergy have been noted in earlier chapters. Critics noted (and likely exaggerated) examples of female preachers. But puritans tended to accept the contemporary wisdom that viewed women as subordinate, which means that they would have been unlikely to advocate a strong role for women in the church and unlikely to publicize any inclination to do so. Yet there are clues in the story of Dutch puritanism that suggest more female empowerment than we might suspect.

Separatists had long emphasized the spiritual equality of both sexes, and while access to the ministry was denied to women, some separatists believed that women should have a role in church government. Henry Ainsworth believed that women should be included in all congregational deliberations but not allowed to vote. John Smyth accepted that women might vote in elections to membership and other church business, but not preach in any form. As noted above, John Robinson found scriptural justification for some role for women in the congregation. In arguing for lay empowerment, he wrote that "one faithful man, yea, or woman either, may as truly and effectually loose and bind, both in heaven and earth, as all the ministers in the world."[82] Robinson rejected female prophesying in normal circumstances but that "in a case extraordinary, namely when no man will, I see not but a woman may reprove the church, rather than suffer it to go on in apparent wickedness."[83]

The history of the Rotterdam church offers further examples of female empowerment. John Forbes's specifically asking the women in the congregation to express their vote in the election of Hugh Peter as the pastor is the only documented example of women voting for a minister, though it suggests that the practice may not have been unheard of. Furthermore, women in that church "met for their own weekly communion, prayer, and fasting meeting."[84]

As hopes for the reform of England's national church dimmed in the early seventeenth century, more and more laymen were unwilling to tarry longer in accommodating themselves to ceremonies they believed smacked of popish error. They put into practice the idea that churches rested upon the gathering together of godly men and women in covenanted union. Such groups—many but not all explicitly declaring themselves separate from the national church—acted on the belief that godly laymen could organize a church and control its affairs. Most sought clerical leaders chosen and ordained by the congregation, but also recognized that God's gifts could also enable laymen to instruct their fellow believers, even more effectively than some pastors could do so.

5
Shaping the New England Way

While separatist and non-separatist puritans were wrestling with issues of church formation and governance in England and the Netherlands, beginning in 1620 other reformers were dealing with the same issues on the other side of the Atlantic. In that year members of John Robinson's Leiden congregation settled at Plymouth, along Cape Cod in New England, and organized their own congregation. Later in that decade members of that Plymouth church traveled up the coast to Salem to offer material and spiritual assistance to the first settlers of the Massachusetts Bay Colony. Freed from the close supervision of English bishops and Dutch authorities, New England puritans crafted a religious culture that offered lay believers considerable power. Indeed, the decades of the 1620s and 1630s in New England can be judged to have witnessed the fullest expression of lay empowerment in the history of puritanism. By the early 1630s one colonist claimed that "the order of the churches and of the Commonwealth was so settled, by common consent, that it brought to his mind the new Heaven and the New Earth, wherein dwells righteousness."[1]

When the *Speedwell* carried members of the Leiden congregation to England on the first leg of the journey that would end up bringing them to the New World on the *Mayflower*, the expectation was that the remainder of the congregation and their pastor John Robinson would follow them in the coming few years. Other members of the Leiden congregation did come over in the years that followed, but John Robinson did not, though hopes for his joining the emigrants continued until the clergyman died in 1625. During most of the 1620s religious services in Plymouth were led by the lay elder William Brewster, and the church flourished. William Hilton, who arrived in November 1621, was able to report that the colonists were "for the most part very religious honest people; the word of God sincerely taught us every Sabbath: so that I know not anything a contented mind can here want."[2]

William Brewster had studied at Cambridge but left before receiving a degree. Settling in Scrooby he became a supporter of religious reform and of ministers such as Richard Clifton and John Robinson. The separatist congregation that ended up in Plymouth by way of Leiden met for a time in his manor house. In Leiden he was chosen a lay elder of the church and he became the leader of the congregation in the New World. The colony's governor William Bradford commended Brewster for having "labored diligently in dispensing the word of God unto us." Bradford assessed his friend to be the equal of many ordained clergy "in gifts or learning."[3] Brewster was able to draw upon an extensive library of over 400 books which he brought with him to America.

In Bradford's account of his friend we have a detailed account of a lay leader of a puritan congregation. According to the governor, Brewster "taught twice every Sabbath, and that both powerfully and profitably, to the great contentment of the hearers, and their comfortable edification; yea, many were brought to God by his ministry." In his sermons "he was very moving and stirring of affections, also very plain and distinct in what he taught, by which means he became the more profitable to the hearers." In addition to his preaching, "he had a singular good gift in prayer, both public and private, in ripping up the heart and conscience before God... He always thought it were better for ministers to pray oftener and divide their prayers than be long and tedious in the same." He supervised the government of the congregation, "careful to preserve good order in the same, both in the doctrine and communion of the same, and to suppress any error or contention."[4] Brewster consulted Robinson on whether he could administer the sacraments and when the Leiden pastor indicated that it would not be appropriate, members of the Plymouth congregation proposed ordaining Brewster, but he declined, for reasons which are not clear.

William Hubbard, writing his *General History of New England* later in the century, noted that in addition to Brewster's preaching, "several of his people were well gifted, and did spend part of the Lord's day in their wonted prophesying, to which they had been accustomed by Mr. Robinson."[5] We know that Robert Cushman, who had been one of the laymen who prophesied in Leiden, preached a sermon in Plymouth in December 1621 before returning to England.[6] It is likely that Samuel Fuller also preached, and Edward Winslow and Governor Bradford may have done so as well. When Samuel Hicks, a member of the congregation, challenged the practices of the church in the 1630s, it was several lay leaders who were deputed to answer the charges.[7]

In June of 1628 John Endecott, with about 50 other planters, was dispatched by the newly formed New England Company to take charge of a number of small fishing villages along the coast of New England that fell under their jurisdiction. Endecott established his base in Naumkeag, which he renamed Salem. In exploring the region he came upon and dispersed a small settlement on the south side of Boston harbor where there was a trading post that had been run by Thomas Morton, who had been accused of selling guns and alcohol to the natives. Based on these charges the Plymouth authorities had previously seized Morton and shipped him back to England. They would have been pleased to hear that Endecott had completed the task. This might explain the fact that when asked for help by Endecott, the Pilgrims willingly agreed to send their physician, Samuel Fuller, who was also an elder of their congregation, to help treat the new colonists who had contracted scurvy on their voyage to America.[8] At this time there was no minister in Salem and so it is likely that religious guidance was being provided by Endecott himself, who may have read scripture or even preached by way of prophesying. Certainly he would have been eager to discuss with Fuller how the believers in Plymouth were coping without an ordained clergyman.

On May 11 a grateful Endecott wrote to Plymouth's governor Bradford thanking him for sending Fuller as a physician. But he also discussed religious matters in a way that demonstrates a good deal of affinity for the faith of the Pilgrims. There was an intuitive element to the test of sanctity that determined how puritans viewed others. As historians Raymond Phineas Stearns and David Brawner explained regarding the admission of members to the semi-separatist London congregation formed by Henry Jacob,

> To recognize a saint was, at once, a difficult and easy task: difficult because one could never be sure; easy because the criteria for determining the probability of sanctification were both abundant and clearly established. To put the matter crudely, we can be reasonably sure that Henry Jacob could tell a saint when he met one.[9]

Various puritan authors made the same point. Thomas Hooker was confident that God's saints could "tell how to judge" those who were also sanctified.[10] Walter Craddock wrote, "A man that hath the spirit may know the spirit in another by the spirit."[11] John Saltmarsh stated that the "manifestation of the Spirit is that in which Spiritual men are known and revealed to each other, and have full assurance of each other in Spirit and Truth as men know men by voice, features, complexions, statures of outward men."[12] However God had implanted his grace on one of the elect, godly puritans believed that they could, with a high probability of success, discern a fellow saint. Similarly, during England's Civil Wars, Oliver Cromwell would characteristically dismiss doctrinal niceties and believed he could discern those who had "the root of the matter in them."[13]

We find this same tendency in Endecott, and it speaks to his role in helping to shape the religious culture of early New England. Writing to Bradford, Endecott referred to the Pilgrims and his own group of puritans as "servants of one master and of the same household." "God's people," he explained, "are all marked with one and the same mark, and sealed with one and the same seal, and have for the main one and the same heart, guided by one and the same spirit of truth, and where this is there can be no discord, nay, here must be sweet harmony." Not concerned with how the non-separating leadership of the company that had sent him to America might look on a close relationship with the Plymouth separatists, he requested of Bradford that "we may, as Christian brethren, be united by a heavenly and unfeigned love, bending all our hearts and forces in furthering a work beyond our strength, with reverence and fear, fastening our eyes always on him that only is to direct and prosper all our ways."[14] Samuel Fuller was a deacon of the Pilgrim congregation with a library that included numerous works of theology and piety.[15] He was one of the lay leaders who had likely preached to the congregation in the absence of an ordained minister. His discussions with Endecott left the Salem leader "satisfied touching your judgments of the outward form of God's worship." That pattern was, "as far as I can yet gather, no other than is warranted by the evidence of truth." Interestingly, Endecott confessed that the Plymouth way was "the same which I have professed and maintained ever since the Lord revealed himself to me."[16] What exactly that pattern was is not made clear, but presumably it would have included the idea of a church gathered by saints and framed by a congregational covenant, with the laity empowered to make decisions and to share their own spiritual insights.

Fuller's visit was not the only contact between the Salem settlement and the Plymouth church. There is evidence of correspondence between Bradford and Endecott prior to this, and Endecott expressed his hope of meeting with Bradford. And in a letter that the Salem settler Charles Gott sent to Bradford in July 1629, he thanked Bradford for his hospitality during a visit Gott had made to Plymouth.[17]

While these events were occurring in America the New England Company evolved into the Massachusetts Bay Company, which in the Spring of 1629 dispatched three clergymen to the colony. The clergy arrived in Salem on June 29. Samuel Skelton and Francis Higginson settled at Salem. Francis Bright, who had been a curate for John Davenport in St. Stephen's Coleman Street, moved south to the town of Charlestown, but returned to England in the following year. The Massachusetts Bay Company had not determined what the religious institutions of the new colony were to be, which left the decisions to Endecott, Skelton, and Higginson.

It is possible that a church had been formed by Endecott and other lay leaders in Salem even before the arrival of Skelton and Higginson, though their presence would have contributed to the further shaping of the congregation.[18] Endecott appointed July 20 as "a solemn day of humiliation for the choice of a pastor and teacher." The detailed description of the events of that day written by a member of the church a few weeks later is very clear that the proceedings involved "members" and this would imply that a church had been formed earlier.[19] Endecott could well have undertaken this together with other leaders of the community following his discussion with Samuel Fuller, and the similarity of what is thought to be the earliest covenant of the Salem church to that of the Scrooby–Leiden congregation points in that direction. A few years later potential members were also asked to assent to a Confession of Faith, but it is not clear that this was the one prepared at the time of the original formation of the church.[20]

Neither Higginson nor Skelton assumed that their ordination in England authorized them to minister to the members of the community, though they likely preached in their private capacity.[21] After time spent in prayer and teaching (by way of lay prophesying), the members proceeded to the election. Higginson and Skelton acknowledged that they each had a

> twofold calling, the one an inward calling, when the Lord moved the heart of a man to take that calling upon him, and fitted him with gifts for the same; the second was an outward calling, which was from the people, when a company of believers joined together in covenant to walk together in the ways of God, and every member (being men) are to have a free voice in the choice of these officers.

With each "fit member" writing down the name of the individual the Lord led them to believe was qualified for each post, the members chose Skelton to be their pastor, and Higginson their teacher. Endecott and other leaders of the church then ordained the two by an imposition of hands.[22] On August 6 the church gathered again for the purpose of choosing lay elders and deacons.[23] Governor William Bradford and other members of the Plymouth church traveled to Salem on that day and acknowledged the new congregation as a valid church by offering it the "right hand of fellowship."[24]

There has been a long debate among historians concerning the degree to which the church polity and practice of the puritan colonies in New England were influenced by Plymouth. Perry Miller, the scholar who did so much to revitalize an interest in American puritanism in the twentieth century, argued in *Orthodoxy in Massachusetts* (1933) that the formation of the Salem church and the subsequent evolution of the New England Way would have been no different had Plymouth not even existed. He connected the development of the New England Way to a tradition of puritan non-separating congregationalism, pointing to the influence of the writings of clergy such as Paul Baynes and William Ames. That view became a scholarly paradigm for a long time among those who studied colonial New England.[25] There is much to say for Stephen Foster's assertion that "Quite simply, the earliest New England ecclesiastical foundations were the only way according to both theory and practice (at about 1630) that professing Christians could have been organized in a church way."[26] The puritans who came to America would have had sufficient knowledge of the theories and examples documented in the previous chapters and some of them had already experimented with covenanted communities of various sorts. Recently, however, Michael Winship has effectively challenged these positions in *Godly Republicanism: Puritans, Pilgrims, and a City on a Hill* (2012). As Winship points out, there were a number of opportunities for Endecott and his fellow colonists in Salem to discuss the practicalities of congregational formation and governance with representatives who were lay leaders of the Plymouth church, and the organization of the Salem church was in some respects at least modeled after and endorsed by the Pilgrims.[27]

What is striking is the degree to which the events leading to the formation of the Salem church were driven by lay believers, and particularly by John Endecott. Following conversations with lay leaders of the Plymouth church, a self-selected group of laymen who recognized themselves as godly formed a congregation that they believed to be an independent and self-governing church as identified in scripture. They then chose as officers two individuals who had put aside any claim to authority that they may have had as a result of ordination by English bishops. Lay members of the new church then ordained and thus empowered Skelton and Higginson.[28]

The influence of the older colony is further demonstrated by the Salem church seeking advice from Plymouth on some of the issues they subsequently faced. Francis Higginson exchanged letters with Plymouth's elder Brewster regarding the implications of baptism for the children of members. Based on Brewster's response it was determined that those baptized as children had to seek membership and accept the covenant in their own right when they reached adulthood. Implementing this, Higginson's own son answered questions about his faith and accepted the covenant in order to be accounted a member of the congregation and receive the Lord's Supper. Since Higginson died in August 1630, the letters had to have been exchanged during the first year of the new church's existence.[29] If indeed this narrative is accurate, then John Endecott might be identified as the colony's first "separatist congregationalist," which would shed new light on the relationship between Endecott and the Salem church with Roger Williams over the following years.[30]

Not all of the colonists were supporters of these developments. The New England Company had acquired small fishing outposts in America that had been established earlier by the Dorchester Company. Endecott had assumed the governance of these settlements and worked to smooth relations between those "Old Planters" and the new arrivals who had come with him. The "Old Planters," led by Roger Conant, had clashed with Plymouth's Pilgrims during the previous years and were opposed to the religious separatism of the latter.[31] Also opposed to the practices of the new Salem church were the brothers John and Samuel Browne. A prosperous merchant, John Browne was one of the Massachusetts Bay Company's assistants and a member of Endecott's council. He and his brother, supported by some of the Old Planters, protested the limited membership of the new church, as well as the fact that Higginson and Skelton had abandoned the use of the ceremonies and prayers specified in the Book of Common Prayer. They accused the members of the new church of separatism and of Anabaptism and gathered on their own to conduct readings from the Prayer Book. Endecott responded by shipping the Brownes back to England.[32] At the time when the Brownes arrived there, the new Massachusetts Bay Company had elected John Winthrop governor of the company and had approved a proposal to remove the charter, and with it its governing headquarters, to the colony. To avoid drawing the attention of the bishops and the king to the complaints emanating from the colony, the papers that the Brownes had sent over were seized and their case referred to arbiters.[33]

Late in March of 1630 additional settlers preparing to emigrate to Massachusetts gathered in the Church of the Holy Rood in Southampton. There the Reverend John Cotton addressed them in a sermon that would be published as *God's Promise to His Plantation*. Following this, John Winthrop ascended the pulpit to address the audience.[34] His sermon on "Christian Charity" sought to define the goals of the colony and the obligations that those who were preparing to sail owed to God and to one another. This was the first recorded lay sermon preached by Winthrop, but it would not be the last. In it he drew on scripture to explain that members of the new society would be bound to one another as members of the body of Christ, connected by sinews of Christian love. In the New England they would be expected to adhere to God's will as they had done in Old England, but even more so. Winthrop offered no single pattern as representing God's plan. Rather, he told them that if they served God as he wished he would provide them with a greater understanding of their faith than they currently professed. And if they thus came together to "delight in each other, make others' conditions our own; rejoice together, mourn together, labor and suffer together," then God would make them as a City upon a Hill, an inspiration to other Christians everywhere.[35]

Winthrop knew of the decisions that Endecott and the Salem ministers had made in organizing their church, and he had heard the Brownes' complaints, but he was likely not prepared for what occurred when his ship, the *Arbella*, docked at Salem on June 30. Evidently when Winthrop, Deputy Governor Thomas Dudley, and other new arrivals wished to receive the Lord's Supper with the Salem congregation, they were denied permission to do so. The reason given was that the newcomers were not members of a particular reformed church. Underlining that point, the Salem church did allow a new arrival who had been a member of the Jacobs–Lathrop church in London to receive communion, and they baptized that individual's son, while the son of William Coddington, a member of John Cotton's St. Botolph's church, was not baptized.[36]

When John Cotton heard about the decision to exclude members of his own church, as well as others, from the sacraments, he wrote a strong letter to Samuel Skelton. Cotton knew Skelton and expressed his surprise at the proceedings, assuming that Skelton, who "went hence of another judgment," had been influenced by the "new-Plymouth men, whom though I much esteem as godly & loving Christians, yet their grounds which they received for this tenant from Mr. Robinson, do not satisfy me."[37] Yet Cotton went on to acknowledge that the nature and definition of a church lieth in this: that it is a flock (1) of saints (2) called by God into the fellowship of Christ, (3) meeting together in one place, (4) to call upon the name of the Lord (5) to edify themselves in communicating spiritual gifts (6) & partaking of the ordinances of the Lord.

Further, he granted that "a covenant [such as that adopted by the Salem congregation] is very requisite for the wellbeing & continuance of a church," while arguing that there was an implicit covenant of the godly in the churches of England, and that some of those refused the sacraments by Skelton had been members of the covenanted group within St. Botolph's.[38] While critical of the exclusion of his former parishioners from the sacrament, Cotton's points emphasized the role of godly laymen in shaping what was a true church.

The fact that John Winthrop made no mention of the exclusion of the new arrivals from the sacraments in his journal (which was not prepared for publication) or in his correspondence suggests that he found the explanation that was offered satisfactory. Indeed, Winthrop had made the point in his "Christian Charity" that by doing God's will the colonists could expect to "see much more of his wisdom, power, goodness and truth than formerly we have been acquainted with."[39] Presumably the practices of the Salem church qualified as such a further truth.[40]

Over the following months Winthrop engaged with members of the Plymouth church as he sought to shape the institutions of his own colony. In late June, deacon Samuel Fuller was back in Massachusetts and partook in discussions over church matters as well as ministering to the settlers as a physician. He spent time in Dorchester, where, he said, he "held conference with them till I was weary," trying to dissuade the Rev. John Warham from the belief that "the visible church may consist of a mixed people, godly and openly ungodly." He was pleased to find that George Phillips, previously the rector at Boxted, Suffolk would leave if the congregation he was forming in Watertown "will have him stand minister by that calling he received from the prelates in England." Watertown also chose as a ruling elder the wherryman Richard Browne, who had been a member of a London Separatist congregation.[41] Fuller found Winthrop "a godly, wise, and humble gentleman." The two of them "had conference... both in private and before sundry others." He found that "opposers there is not wanting, and Satan is busy," but Fuller believed that "if the Lord be on our side who can be against us," and noted that Winthrop hoped that Plymouth would continue to help the newcomers. Interestingly, Fuller related that William Coddington, whose exclusion from the sacraments at Plymouth troubled John Cotton, had told him that "Mr. Cotton's charge... was that they should take advice of them at Plymouth, and should do nothing to offend them." John Endecott continued to be a strong supporter of the congregational principles being implemented, and Fuller referred to him as "my dear friend, and a friend to us all," and as "a second Burro," referring to the noted separatist lay leader Henry Barrow.[42]

Weakened by the long voyage and suffering from lack of adequate food and shelter, many of the colonists who had arrived in the Winthrop fleet sickened and died. It was necessary for the surviving newcomers to organize churches, and Plymouth again was willing to assist. Fuller, Isaac Allerton, and Edward Winslow of that colony advised the settlers of Charlestown, Watertown, and Dorchester. A day of fast and prayer was observed in each of those towns so that, according to Winslow,

> they may humble themselves before God, and seek him in his ordinances; and that then also such godly *persons* that are amongst them and known each to other, publicly make known their godly desire, and practice the same, viz. solemnly to enter into covenant with the Lord to walk in his ways.

They had asked the church at Plymouth to set apart the same day for prayer and fasting, and to beseech God to "direct them in his ways."[43]

In Charlestown on the set fast day, July 30, four individuals—John Winthrop, Thomas Dudley, Isaac Johnson, and John Wilson (formerly minister in Sudbury, Suffolk)—entered into a church covenant whereby the church was formed. A few days later the four admitted five more men into the membership. Samuel Fuller, who had observed the events, planned to return to Plymouth accompanied by Johnson and John Endecott. Winthrop expressed a wish to do so but his responsibilities did not allow him to leave the Bay at that time.[44] At the same time churches were established by covenant in Watertown and Dorchester. On August 30 the Charlestown church met for another fast day and chose its officers, including John Wilson as teacher. By the Fall the majority of the members of that congregation had crossed to Boston, where the supply of water was better.[45] While there were men who had served as ministers in England (Wilson, Phillips, and Warham) who participated in the process of church formation in their towns, the driving force behind the organization of these churches, as had been the case in

Salem, were laymen such as Winthrop. And as in the cases of Plymouth and Salem, the new churches were formed as autonomous congregations with authority to admit members and select church officers in the hands of the lay members.

The same pattern would be followed as further arrivals came to Massachusetts and new churches were formed. In virtually all of these communities the process began with sessions where residents came together for what Stephen Foster has called "a friendly look into each other's souls" as a basis for choosing the pillars of the church and entering into covenant.[46] The most detailed description of the process comes from the formation of the Dedham church in 1637. The 30 families who settled the town agreed to "meet every 5th day of the week at several houses in order, lovingly to discourse and consult together such questions as might further tend to establish a peaceable and comfortable civil society, and prepare for spiritual communion in a church society." The meetings were the epitome of the types of lay conferencing we have previously examined, as the members strived towards unity. In them the household head who was hosting the gathering

> began and concluded with prayer, and he first speaking as God assisted to the question [that had been posed], others that pleased spoke after him as they saw cause to add, enlarge or approve what was spoken by any... or else to propound any questions pertinent to the case or any objections or doubts remaining in any conscience about the same.

The results were "peaceable, loving and tender, much to edification." The first question posed for the gathering of a church society was whether, since a church had yet to be organized, "such as in the judgment of charity look upon one another as Christians, may assemble together, speak and hear the word, pray and fast, or confer together," which was agreed affirmatively. They agreed that the church should be created by a covenant of those deemed saints, who were to demonstrate their suitability by "a confession and profession of their faith, and that this be publicly testified," and, that their "profession of an inward work of faith and grace [be] declared by an holy life." They discussed and endorsed the practice of prophesying, and gradually identified the pillars of the church through a process whereby those being considered spent time "in fasting and prayer, exercising the gifts of prayer in every one at their sessions."[47] The whole process was driven by lay believers and reflected the conviction that godly laity were empowered by the

Spirit with the ability to instruct one another and come together as a community of saints.

The churches thus formed were congregations of visible saints. As was the case with the Separatists and with some congregations in the Netherlands such as the Rotterdam church presided over by Hugh Peter and John Davenport, membership required a charitable judgment by fellow laity that an individual was one of those selected by God for salvation and blessed with the special graces associated with that gift. While some New England congregations came to require a statement of personal transformation as criteria for membership, initially the judgment was based upon a profession of faith, evidence of godly behavior, and a willingness to swear to the church covenant. Puritans believed that they could distinguish between a rote recitation of doctrine and a sincere and feeling profession of faith animated by the grace of the spirit. And they similarly were confident that they could generally distinguish behavior shaped by the transformative power of grace from counterfeit actions. And these were decisions that would be made by the laity.[48]

John Cotton had questioned the Salem church's refusal of sacraments to members of the Winthrop fleet, expressing concern that the new church might be asserting a complete separation from the Church of England. This was a position that might stir actions from the English authorities. Anticipating that their colony might be labeled separatist, on the eve of their departure Winthrop and other leaders of the Great Migration had signed the *Humble Request*, a letter denying any attempt to separate from the Church of England, making the point that "such hope and part as we have obtained in the common salvation we have received in her bosom and sucked it from her breasts."[49] While borrowing heavily from Plymouth in organizing their congregations, the Massachusetts leadership asserted a non-separatist position, which distinguished them from the Pilgrims to their south. Not all who came to Massachusetts agreed with this balancing act. Roger Williams, whom Winthrop described as "a godly minister," arrived in Boston in January 1631.[50] He was invited to join the Boston church but "refused to join with the congregation at Boston because they would not make a declaration of their repentance for having communion with the churches of England while they lived there."

Williams also had declared his opinion that the magistrate might not punish the breach of the Sabbath nor any other offense as it was a breach of the first table" of the Commandments.[51] Williams settled briefly in Salem, where his strong separatist beliefs might not have been as controversial. In fact, that church took steps to elect him to the ministry to replace Francis Higginson, who had died the previous August. The colony magistrates wrote to John Endecott and the Salem church leaders expressing opposition to the plan, and Williams soon moved on to Plymouth.[52]

Samuel Fuller's letters imply conferences with numerous settlers as they planned the details of their new religious institutions and practices. Many of those who were thus engaged would have been familiar with such conferences from their days in England. Thomas Dudley and others from the Lincolnshire area had been members of the covenanted inner church in John Cotton's parish. John Winthrop frequently engaged in conference with other Christians. While the forms of the churches they organized may have been new to them, the habit of meeting with fellow Christians to pray and discuss matters of faith and practice were not, and such conferencing would continue to play an important role in the religion of New England. John Eliot, who had engaged in such gatherings in England, continued such "private meetings, wherein we pray, and sing, and repeat sermons, and confer together about the things of God," after his arrival in New England.[53]

An example of such conferencing came when some members of the Boston church journeyed to Plymouth in October 1632. Following morning services,

> in the afternoon, Mr. Roger Williams [who was settled in Plymouth at the time], (according to their custom) propounded a question, [presumably whether a church officer could also hold civil office], to which the pastor, Mr. [Ralph] Smith spoke briefly. Then Mr. Williams prophesied, and after, the Governor of Plymouth spoke to the question; after him the Elder, then some two or three more of the congregation. Then the Elder desired the governor of Massachusetts [Winthrop] and Mr. Wilson speak to it, which they did.[54]

The discussion at Plymouth was one example of both conferencing and the practice of prophesying, which had a long tradition among the reformers, particularly in the Netherlands. Prophesying could also take other forms, including lay preaching before a congregation. Early in 1631 John Wilson was planning to return to England to fetch his wife and settle various business affairs. In the end he would be absent from the Boston church for 13 months. Addressing the church, he prayed and exhorted "the congregation to love, etc., and commended to them the exercise of prophesy in his absence, and designed those he thought most fit for it, viz. the Governor [Winthrop], Mr. [Thomas] Dudley, and Mr. [Increase] Nowell."[55] For over a year these men and perhaps others assumed the responsibility for nurturing the faith of the church. It was also a common feature of the colony's early life for a lay person to preach to a gathering of saints before a congregation was formed in a town. Sometimes, a visitor from elsewhere would be invited to preach. In 1633 a group of settlers, including John Winthrop Jr., moved to the north of Boston and settled the town of Agawam, soon renamed Ipswich. The new community struggled to find a minister and relied on prophesying. Late in that year John Wilson, "by leave of the congregation of Boston, whereof he was pastor) went to Agawam to teach the people because they had yet no minister."[56] He did so as a private Christian since his ordination only gave him ministerial status inside the Boston church. In the following spring John Winthrop "went on foot to Agawam, and because the people there wanted [lacked] a minister, he spent the Sabbath with them and exercised by way of prophesy."[57]

According to Thomas Lechford, who lived in Massachusetts from 1638 to 1641, "Where farms of villages are, as at Rumney Marsh and Marblehead, there is no minister, a brother of one of the congregations of Boston for the Marsh, and of Salem for Marblehead, preacheth and exerciseth prayer every Lord's day, which is called prophesying in such a place."[58] In the case of Rumney Marsh the inhabitants requested the Boston church to allow John Oliver, a layman of that congregation, to come regularly to teach their servants and be a help to the residents, which the church agreed to.[59] William Walton acted as minister in Marblehead in the late 1630s, though he was not ordained and could not administer the sacraments.[60] John Wheelwright, Anne Hutchinson's brother-in-law, preached as a private Christian by way of prophecy to the settlers of Mount Wollaston while awaiting a call to the ministry.[61] Similar practices were followed elsewhere. And it must be stressed that for reformers who believed that clergy were empowered by the choice of a congregation and not by episcopal ordination, those who hoped to be selected by a congregation, preaching in a trial of their abilities, were necessarily doing so as private Christians.

But preaching by way of prophesying was not the only avenue for lay participation in the shaping of doctrine and practice. It was customary in most of the churches for laymen to ask questions following sermons and to engage in discussion with the clergyman. A noted example of this came on a lecture day in Boston in 1634. John Endecott, in Boston for a meeting of the colony Assistants, was among those present. According to Winthrop, "at the lecture in Boston a question was propounded about veils." Roger Williams had taken the position that women should be covered when they went into public, and particularly to church. Using his own interpretation of 1 Corinthians 11:5–6, "Mr. Cotton concluded that where (by the custom of the place) they were not a sign of women's subjection, they were not commanded by the Apostle. Mr. Endecott opposed, and did maintain it by the general arguments brought by the Apostle." After the debate became heated, John Winthrop intervened to close it off.[62]

Lechford noted that it was also called prophesying "when a brother exerciseth in his own congregation (as at Salem they do sometimes), taking a text of Scripture and handling it according to his ability."[63] This could be during a Sabbath service or at a separate meeting of church member. In *The True Constitution of a Particular Visible Church* (1642), John Cotton laid out one pattern that a session of prophesying during a Sabbath service might take. First, he suggested, the gathering should sing a psalm. The minister would read and preach on a passage of scripture. Then, suitable individuals, two or three, might prophesy. Next, "if the time permit, the elders may call any other of the brethren, whether of the same church or any, to speak a word of exhortation to the people," and finally "for the better edifying of a man's self or others, it may be lawful for any (young or old) save only for women, to ask questions at the mouth of the prophets."[64]

The time provided for this form of prophesying was one in which laymen and laywomen could share their religious experiences. According to Lechford, "the confessions or speeches made by members to be admitted have been by some held prophesying."[65] Following the arrival of John Cotton and his election as teacher of the Boston church, there was an increase in the membership of that church. Many historians have attributed this to the effect of Cotton's preaching, which was likely an important factor. But Winthrop noted that "the Lord gave witness to the exercise of prophesy, so as thereby some were converted, and others much edified."[66] Though he did not experience the same intensity of experience that some did, Roger Clap described the impact of similar accounts given in the Dorchester church at about the same time. Individuals showed "before all the assembly their experiences of the workings of God's Spirit in their hearts to bring them up to Christ...many hearers found very much good by, to help them to try their own hearts, and to consider how it was with them." He described how "many tears...have been shed in Dorchester meeting-house at such times."[67]

Sharing such accounts was a means whereby the believer came to terms with his or her own religious status. It was part also of a process that could help others to put their own struggles into perspective.[68] The accounts served, in part, an evangelical function whereby the laity spoke to the souls of their fellow laymen.[69] And it reinforced the sociability of the godly as they set about creating new societies.[70] The "confessions" gathered by Thomas Shepard in a notebook during the period from roughly 1638 to 1645 are examples of laymen and laywomen sharing religious experiences. The have been viewed by historians as part of the requirements specified by Shepard for those who wished to join his church. But the English Presbyterian William Rathband actually referred to the practices of Thomas Shepard's Cambridge church in a way that suggests that the "confessions" we are familiar with actually had a broader purpose than securing membership in the congregation. According to information Rathband received from a New England correspondent, "the people [in Cambridge] met together privately, at certain times, weekly or fortnightly, each one to hold forth unto the rest the work of God upon his or her soul, from their first conversion unto that present day, that so their pastor might know how they grew in grace."[71] Rathband suggested that this was done to excommunicate the unworthy. Thomas Welde, a former New England clergyman, refuted Rathband's interpretation of why this was done, but acknowledged that such private meetings were held, categorizing them not as admission tests, but as "meetings of the Saints, for such an holy end."[72] Sharing one's spiritual progress nurtured the culture of faith as opposed to being something needed to merit admission or retain membership. And seeing the Shepard "confessions" in this light would help explain the hesitant nature of many of the recorded relations.[73]

Regardless of their function, and it may very well have been that they were part of the church admission process in that congregation, the "confessions" attest to the important role that fellow believers played in each other's progress towards faith and assurance, something demonstrated in the testimonies recorded by Shepard.[74] Edward Collins explained how "by a private meeting of private conference I heard diverse questions propounded and answered... Hence I endeavored to get into private Christian meetings at London." Barbary Cutter told how he had "discovered my estate to some. And so they spake to me as that it was a mercy." Alice Stedman had been changed when she discussed her spiritual state with a neighbor. Henry Dunster enumerated "Holy conferences" as one of the means that had helped him, and said that "by conference the Lord showed me my sins and recovery by Christ." Mr. Haynes told how "several saints would meet with me" and how a female friend "counseled me to speak to others." Richard Cutter attributed help to a friend who counseled him on a lecture day and then on the following day. William Ames (the son of the theologian) likewise credited a Christian friend with assisting him.[75]

Sharing edifying experiences was an important part of the religious life of many churches whether or not they may have also influenced membership decisions. Once the New Haven church was gathered, regular informal Tuesday meetings of church members to discuss and reinforce one another's faith became a venue for such sharing of experience. John Davenport, the pastor of that church, believed that exchanging stories of how God worked in one's soul was an important factor in the ongoing communion of local saints.[76] In a manuscript "Whole Body of Divinity" Hartford's Samuel Stone indicated that those who were able might on occasion speak of "the frame of grace in their hearts," but made the point that such an exercise was to enrich the church, not to gain admission to it. Many saw such sharing as a duty. William Hooke, John Davenport's colleague for a time in the New Haven pulpit, expressed as much after he had returned to England. "There is a duty also incumbent" upon those who were saved, he wrote, "as touching on the transmission of the Truth to the generation to come... You have heard much, and seen much, and known much, and treasured up experiences, and therefore, certainly, you should have much to say to such as are of the younger sort."[77] John Eliot stressed the importance of such statements for those who heard them. Believers in New England, he stated, "open the work of Christ in their hearts, and the relation thereof is an eminent confession of our Lord; experienced saints can gather more than a little from it." It was, he continued, "an ordinance of wonderful benefit... As among the Jews, usually most men did once in their life celebrate a jubilee, thus this confession of Christ is methinks a sort of jubilee; and every good man among us *at least once in his life called to it*" (emphasis added). Such an account not only "gives great glory to the Lord Jesus Christ," but "the souls of devout Christians are hereby very much ingratiated one to another."[78]

Writing at the close of the seventeenth century, one of the first founders of New England, Joshua Scottow, recalled how in the early days of settlement laymen and laywomen shared their "Soul experiences each to other," and found "lively characters of the same grace, line for line appearing, as in those who were made partakers of the same sealing Spirit."[79] As late as 1640, after the controversy that centered on Anne Hutchinson, John Cotton preached that "godly women... may sometimes be more apprehensive of the mysteries of salvation than the best ministers of the gospel."[80]

While clergy played an important part in the shaping of New England's religious culture, a focus on the lay role reveals the important part that zealous Christians, believing themselves empowered by the Holy Spirit, played in creating the region's religious life. It was the self-identified godly who organized autonomous congregations, identified and ordained ministers, and relied on fellow lay saints to guide services when a clergyman was not available. Even in congregations that were served by a pastor or teacher, opportunities existed for the laity to share religious experiences and beliefs. Whether within the structure of a Sabbath service, a public lecture, or a conference, these opportunities provided laymen with an important evangelical role in the life of the church. Over time, the very fact that the laity had such power, and the incidence of some extreme expressions of lay enthusiasm, led some clerical leaders to express concern about the consequences that might stem from such practices.

6
The Free Grace Controversy and Redefining the Role of Lay Believers

Edward Johnson, one of the first settlers of Woburn, had come over with Winthrop in 1630. A few years later he went to England to get his family and bring them to Massachusetts. On his return to Massachusetts he was approached by a group which he categorized as a faction of "ignorant and unlettered men and women, in a posture of preaching to a multitude." "Come along with me," one told him, and "I'll bring you to a woman that preached better gospel than any of your blackcoats who have been at the Ninniversity, a woman of another kind of spirit who hath many revelations of things to come." "For my part," the man who accosted him continued, "I had rather hear such a one that speaks from the merest motion of the Spirit, without any study at all, than one of your learned scholars, although they may be fuller of Scripture." Shortly thereafter he met a "a little nimble tongued woman who said she could bring me acquainted with one of her own sex that would show me a way, if I could attain it, even Revelations, full of such ravishing joy that I should never have cause to worry for sin so long as I live."[1]

Johnson had returned to a colony in the throes of what is often referred to as the Antinomian Controversy, but which Michael Winship more properly calls the Free Grace Controversy. Winship has skillfully dissected the theological issues that were at stake. Rather than covering all of the same ground, in the following pages I want to concentrate on how the controversy illuminated the debate over lay empowerment, the distribution of authority within churches, and the supervision of churches by higher authorities.[2]

Many, perhaps most, puritans lived their lives seeking with John Robinson and John Winthrop further light on the mysteries of faith and God's will. This drove those believers who gathered to pray with Brigit Cooke in Kersey, Suffolk and those who gadded to Dedham to hear John

Rogers preach. In the early days of New England, John Endecott and others engaged with Samuel Fuller and other Plymouth leaders to discuss what those Pilgrims had learned over the previous decade. Early settlers traveled, at times in groups, to hear lectures delivered by the clergy of neighboring towns. Prophesying offered opportunities to clear up doubtful points and to share one's spiritual experiences. Men and women discussed matters of faith as they exchanged goods or drew water from town wells. As they had in England, lay Christians met together in private homes to review sermons, read scripture, and sing psalms. All of this speaks to a religious community that was dynamic and open to discussing new insights into their faith.[3]

Members of the puritan community sought unity but not necessarily uniformity. Fresh ideas, if rooted in scripture and offered with a humility that acknowledged the point might be in error, were welcomed. In fact, it was discussion of new insights that gave vitality to the movement, and lay believers were deeply involved in the process. On occasion, however, notions were advanced with an uncompromising sense of certitude and led to a disruption of the community of believers. This was what happened in London in the quarrels that involved Anthony Wotton, John Etherington, and Peter Shaw that were discussed in Chapter 3. And it was what happened in Massachusetts in the mid-1630s, posing for the colonists the question of how to temper the centrifugal possibilities of lay empowerment with the need to maintain a broad consensus.

Determining the roles of the ministry and laity was a key component in the debate over how to maintain unity. Rejecting the authority of bishops and other superiors to define true doctrine and practice, puritan clergy argued that the Spirit would guide believers to the truth. They encouraged laymen and laywomen to read the scripture, to conference together, and—for Congregationalists at least—to ask questions after sermons and to preach by way of prophesying. Yet at the same time the clergy believed that a combination of grace and university learning suited them to exert leadership in the movement. Reaching consensus with one another was a way ministers further enhanced their influence by allowing individual clergy to present their conclusions as those of a larger body. As the London clergyman Edward Elton explained, "when teachers meet together in one truth... it doth free the teachers from the note and blemish of lightness and newfangled giddiness, and that they teach not opinions of private fancy."[4] Various mechanisms, such as combination lectures, the circulation of manuscripts, and clerical conferences such as that centered on Dedham in the late sixteenth century, provided opportunities to shape common ministerial stances.[5]

While most Congregationalists accepted that clerical conferences and synods had a place so long as their views were only advisory, others were suspicious of any such gatherings. If the clergy saw such cooperative ventures as a way of straining towards symmetry, others viewed them with suspicion as potential interference with the authority of individual congregations. From the earliest days of the settlement of Massachusetts members of the clergy had gathered every other week to discuss the challenges they were facing, each taking a turn in hosting the gatherings. In November 1633 Samuel Skelton and Roger Williams (who was back in Salem but not in a ministerial capacity), "took some exception about it, as fearing it might grow in time to a Presbytery or Superintendency, to the prejudice of the churches' liberties." The clergy rejected the claim, arguing that "the fear was without cause, for they were all clear in that point that no church or person can have power over another church, neither did they in their meetings exercise any such jurisdiction."[6] This was to be the first skirmish over such gatherings in what was to be a battle that continued through the seventeenth century. Within a few years the Free Grace Controversy would bring these issues to the fore again.

For 13 months following John Wilson's voyage in early 1631 to bring his wife to Massachusetts, the Boston church had been led by laymen who preached by way of prophesy, which must have reinforced the concept of lay empowerment in the members of that congregation. Following Wilson's return the ministry of the church was augmented by the addition of John Cotton in September 1633. Many other puritans were flocking to New England at this time, pushed by the more rigorous crackdown on dissent in England and pulled by reports that compared the religious culture of the colony to "the New Heaven and New Earth, wherein dwells righteousness."[7] Among those who arrived in Boston around this time were William and Anne Hutchinson, William and Mary Dyer, and Henry Vane. The church grew, many members drawn by the spiritual experiences shared through the exercise of prophecy. New and old members gathered in private homes to discuss sermons they had heard as well as passages of scripture.

Anne Hutchinson soon stood out as a prominent member of the godly community. She assisted at childbirths. She hosted gatherings of women in her home. John Cotton later recalled that she "readily fell into good discourse with the women about their spiritual estates," and that she "found loving and dear respect from both our church-elders and brethren, and so from myself." Soon men as well as women turned to her for advice. According to John Winthrop "her ordinary talk was about the things of the Kingdom of God," and "her usual conversation was of righteousness and kindness." As noted previously, it was not unknown for women to provide spiritual council and to play a central role in conferences.[8] There were other centers of lay religiosity in the town, but hers was special. Cotton acknowledged that all "the faithful embraced her conference and blessed God for her fruitful discourses."[9] Among those who were drawn to her meetings was Henry Vane, the son of a prominent member of the king's council but a devout puritan who was elected governor of Massachusetts in 1636.

Anne's father, Francis Marbury, had been a puritan clergyman and she was raised reading and discussing the Bible, memorizing scripture passages, joining in family prayers and singing psalms. At some point she developed a form of scriptural interpretation whereby she believed that passages that came to her mind were presented to her consciousness by the Holy Spirit. Following her marriage to William Hutchinson she and her family likely journeyed periodically from their home in Alford to Boston, Lincolnshire to hear John Cotton preach. Possibly a member of Cotton's covenanted inner church she also likely conferenced with other puritans around Alford. She may well have been present when Cotton preached that with the help of the Spirit one might "discern many secret hidden mysteries and meanings of the Holy Ghost in Scripture, more than ever [we] could by any reading or instruction," and that God wished such a saint "to teach others also, to lead on others of their neighbors in the ways of God."[10]

In retrospect it seems clear that some of the religious ideas raised by Hutchinson and other Boston saints in the mid-1630s were testing the limits of orthodox puritan belief (to the extend we can define what was "orthodox"). John Wheelwright, Anne Hutchinson's brother-in-law who arrived in Massachusetts in 1636, later expressed the conviction that "All true believers and saints have received the Spirit as their inward teacher." This was fine if it meant that the Spirit opened to believers the meaning of scripture, but some individuals evidently went beyond this in believing that the Spirit's insight was not limited to the scriptures.[11] As Winship has pointed out, "the Boston church was certainly a potential agent of disorder, yet it was at the same time a striking example and capacity for containing and avoiding doctrinal conflict that gave puritanism its rough, practical coherence."[12] Among the ideas that were being discussed were what happened to the soul after death, whether sanctification provided evidence of salvation, the resurrection of the body, and whether Christ had descended into hell after his death on the cross. Many of these would have been recognized as issues debated in the London underground in the previous decades.

According to John Winthrop the conference that gathered at Hutchinson's home began with a half dozen people but by 1637 met twice weekly and numbered at least ten times that number. There was one meeting for both men and women and another for women only. Hutchinson led the latter but would have participated in the mixed assembly. The structure of the meetings led by Hutchinson was a discussion of John Cotton's sermons, emphasizing the portions with which she agreed and correcting his doctrine on other points, though she would later explain the criticisms as "inquiries." Participants would ask questions to which Hutchinson responded. There would have been lively discussion on various points.

It would be a mistake to underestimate the theological sophistication and charisma of Anne Hutchinson, but it would also be a mistake (which some have made) to depict her as the sole force behind the challenge to the establishment that emerged. There were certainly other laymen and laywomen who engaged vigorously in the discussions that were going on, and some more radical than her. One of the colony's clergy, Giles Firmin, felt that Henry Vane "was the great favorer and maintainer of these errors and did animate that faction."[13] Yet at the same time, those who gathered at Hutchinson's for conference would, according to the clergyman Thomas Welde, "appear very humble, holy, and spiritual Christians, and full of Christ; they would deny themselves far, speak excellently, pray with such soul-ravishing expression and affections."[14] And it should be noted that during the rise in lay engagement and enthusiasm that can be dated from shortly after the arrival of the Hutchinsons, neither of the congregation's ministers—John Cotton and John Wilson—nor its most prominent layman, John Winthrop, saw anything amiss in what was transpiring.[15]

It was Thomas Shepard, the new minister of the church at Newtown (soon to be renamed Cambridge), who first raised questions about what was happening in the Boston church, first in a letter he sent to John Cotton, and then raising his concerns in a ministerial meeting in October 1636. When reports of strange opinions circulating in Boston continued, in December a group of ministers posed a series of questions for Cotton to answer. Shortly thereafter some of the Boston laity met with laymen from Newtown to defend themselves against the rumors circulating about them. Within the Boston congregation, John Winthrop, acting as a fellow lay member of the church and not in his capacity as one of the colony magistrates, sought to find a common ground with some of the more outspoken lay believers by sharing his own story of how he had come to experience God's caress. Winthrop also prepared two theological position papers which Shepard vetted and persuaded him not to circulate.

Toward the end of 1636 the situation became more explosive. An effort to call John Wheelwright, closely affiliated with Hutchinson and Vane, to the ministry of the Boston church so he could formally officiate at its Mount Wollaston parish was defeated. John Wilson then delivered a sermon to the colony's General Court which many in the Boston church felt was a criticism of them and of John Cotton. Members of the Hutchinson circle, branded by others as opinionists, began to publicly assert more extreme positions and to challenge those who questioned them. Of course there had been signs of this in the previous summer, as when Edward Johnson was accosted on his return to Massachusetts. More fuel was added to the fire when John Wheelwright delivered a fast-day sermon in January. The invitation to Wheelwright was striking, since he held no ministerial position at the time. The fast day was intended as an opportunity to cool tempers and heal differences. But Wheelwright lashed out at those who were critical of his faction, calling on those under attack to prepare for spiritual combat and be prepared to suffer martyrdom. Eventually Wheelwright would be banished for what the magistrates viewed as the insurrectionary nature of the sermon.

By wielding his rhetorical axe, Shepard had initiated a process of polarization that developed a life of its own, with individuals of various opinions gradually abandoning dialogue and beginning to hurl negative labels at one another with about as much accuracy as one finds in modern political campaigns. Simplify, exaggerate, and demonize your opponents became the strategy adopted by both emerging camps. As each side came to believe the categorization they had shaped to define their opponents, they hardened their own stance in ways that must have surprised anyone who had observed the dialogue and tolerance that once categorized the affairs of the colony.

Whether the escalation that seems to have occurred early in 1637 was the result of an internal dynamic in the group's discussions or an aggressive defensiveness prompted by the intolerance directed at them by outside clergy is impossible to determine. But there is no questioning the escalation of rhetoric. John Wilson told church members that attending the conference in Hutchinson's home would "rob you of your ordinances, rob you of your souls, rob you of your God," and forbade members of his personal household from participating.[16] Winthrop recorded how laymen disturbed religious services "by public questions and objections to their doctrines which did any way disagree from their opinions."¹⁷ Thomas Welde provided more detail, pointing to how the clergy "must have dung cast on their faces, and be no better than legal preachers, Baal's Priest, Popish factors, Scribes, Pharisees, and Opposers of Christ himself," and that the opinionists would claim that "a church officer is an ignorant man, and knows not Christ;...such a pastor is a proud man, and would make a good persecutor; such a teacher is grossly popish." Opinionists were seeking out clergymen at weekday lectures, and Welde wrote how "after our sermons were ended at our public lectures, you might have seen half a dozen pistols discharged in the face of the preacher, I mean so many objections made by the opinionists in the open assembly against our doctrine delivered." And, in Boston, "you might have seen many of the opinionists rising up, and contemptuously turning their backs upon the faithful pastor [John Wilson] of that church, and going forth from the assembly when he began to pray or preach."¹⁸ According to Giles Firmin, Henry Vane "was the man that did embolden them. When ministers had done preaching, he would find questions to put to them, though they were strangers."¹⁹ The Hutchinsonian faction in the Boston church tried to censure John Wilson for his sermon to the General Court and was prevented only by the fact that the practice of the churches was to act only when there was unanimity.

Following the colony elections in March 1637 the "orthodox" party gained control of the situation. John Winthrop had been elected governor. Henry Vane would soon return to England. The General Court condemned Wheelwright's fast-day sermon as seditious but deferred his sentencing till a later meeting. The Court also issued a call for representatives of the churches of New England to gather to address the controversy. The meeting, generally referred to as a synod, convened in the Newtown meetinghouse at the end of August, 1637. About 25 ministers, including some from Connecticut and Plymouth and the newly arrived John Davenport, were present, as were lay "messengers" representing various churches. Some laymen and laywomen, likely from the Boston-Newtown area, were spectators. Rather than identifying and condemning specific ideas broached in the colony in recent years, the synod discussed and eventually condemned a list of 82 opinions without specifying that they were actually upheld by anyone in the colony. But while the synod refused to be more specific, it was clear that members of the Boston church were seen as culpable of upholding them. When two of the messengers from the Boston church—William Aspinwall and John Coggeshall—sought to debate some of the errors, they were rebuked by Cotton and left the synod. Other laymen, and not just in Boston, were offended by the long list, viewing it, according to Winthrop, as "a reproach laid upon the country without a cause."[20]

At the conclusion of its deliberations the synod approved the list of errors but also adopted non-binding resolutions that sought to curb the type of lay empowerment that many saw as responsible for the controversy. Clergy who had been supportive of those believers who in England had abandoned an inadequate parish preacher to gad off to hear someone more dynamic and who had openly challenged those who used popish ceremonies, were now suddenly aware of the threat that lay activism posed to their own status. The synod criticized the meetings of 60 or more to hear a woman discuss doctrine and expound scripture, and it condemned the practice of using the question period after sermons to do more than seeking an elaboration of points that had been raised.

In November the General Court tried and sentenced to banishment some of Wheelwright's more aggressive supporters and Hutchinson herself. Those trials, while carrying religious overtones, were civil proceedings and, aside from what they demonstrated about Hutchinson's skills as a lay exegete, are not of concern to the themes of this book. But the church trial of Anne Hutchinson, which took place in March 1638, does have much to tell us.

In the months between the civil and church trials a number of things had shifted the popular mood. Concerns were raised when John Wheelwright's farewell sermon in Mount Wollaston was interrupted by one of the listeners rising to attack Wheelwright from a radical perspective that went beyond anything we can associate with Vane or Hutchinson. There are indications that the November trials pushed individuals such as this to cease any efforts to find a common ground and to attack orthodox clergy more vehemently. This new radicalism shocked many who had supported Hutchinson and pushed them back towards a more moderate stance. In other churches firm steps were taken to suppress dangerous opinions. According to Roxbury's Thomas Welde, clergy held lengthy private meetings with opinionists in an effort to persuade them of their errors. Their efforts were not universally successful, for we know some members of the Roxbury congregation moved to Boston (without the required dismissal from Roxbury), while others were censured and a half dozen excommunicated.[21]

The church trial of Anne Hutchinson was held before the Boston congregation with outside ministers also present. It is notable that Hutchinson was allowed to engage in theological discourse with those who had doubts about her positions. John Davenport debated with her the question of the mortality of the soul and after a good deal of discussion, Hutchinson stated that "now Mr. Davenport hath opened it, it is clear to me, or God by him hath given me light."[22] Declining to admit that she had embraced an error, Hutchinson was willing to acknowledge that she had been mistaken. This wasn't enough for some of her clerical critics, who were less interested in reasoning with her than Davenport. Those opponents obtained what they wanted when she espoused other, commonly condemned errors.

After considerable debate over more than one day, it was time to vote. Davenport stated that he believed it proper "that if any of the brethren have any scruples upon their spirits about this or any other point, that they should have free leave to propound it" so that their questions might be resolved. But as for formally admonishing Anne Hutchinson, he reminded them that "admonition is an ordinance of God and sanctified of him for this very end as a special and powerful means to convince the party offending" rather than a final casting off of the individual admonished.[23] In the end, all but a few of Hutchinson's family were willing to cast their votes against her on the points that had been discussed and she was formally excommunicated. But it was the membership that decided. As they reached that point, Davenport had addressed the scruples some in the congregation had as to whether "they may express their judgments by vote or no." This issue of how a congregation was governed was something that Davenport had thought long and hard about in the previous few years. He expressed his belief that there was no other way the members of a church "can bear witness to the truth or against any error but by expressing their assent or dissent, either by silence and lifting up their hands." And for those who asked what the scriptural warrant (in Matthew 18) meant that such matters be dealt with by "the church," he claimed that it was "plain it is the whole church" and not just the officers.[24]

The Free Grace controversy exposed some of the tensions between lay empowerment and clerical authority that had been implicit from the start of the Reformation. In the years that followed some clergy (supported by some laymen) asserted an enhanced view of the ministerial office. Though New England congregations were formed by groups of lay believers and clergy were authorized not on the basis of English episcopal ordination but by lay election, many of the ministers who accepted the role of the laity as God's means for elevating them to office nevertheless believed that their calling itself came from God. John Cotton, for instance, following the lead of continental reformers such as John Calvin and Martin Bucer as well as the English reformer William Perkins, "considered the office of the ministry an 'ordinance' of God, a post established by God's will and filled with men of his appointment."²⁵ This was not a position shared by all lay people, and some of the attacks on clergy during the controversy underlined a different understanding of ministerial authority. Indeed, "Error 54" condemned by the Cambridge Synod was the belief that "No minister can be an instrument to convey more of Christ unto another, than he by his own experience hath come unto."²⁶

It is not surprising that in summarizing the offenses of Anne Hutchinson and her followers, John Wilson would point to "the slighting of God's faithful ministers and condemning and crying them down as nobodies."²⁷ Thomas Shepard painted a similar view of the laity. He described how after a minister "gives reasons strong and answerable for something to be done, a young fellow shall step up and say, without ground or show of it, That is your light, and mine is otherwise." A few years after the controversy Shepard would lash out at the "sons of Korah [who] cast off the Lord's government over them, who will have no rulers or governors in churches."²⁸

In his study of the New England ministry, David D. Hall pointed out that over the course of the seventeenth century "the ministers in new England moved towards a higher definition of their office," and that this was notable by 1643.²⁹ That perspective became the accepted wisdom of the clergy as time went on, and was evident in the judgment of the clergyman William Hubbard, who in his *General History of New England*, written later in the seventeenth century, stated that "In the beginning of times was occasioned much disadvantage to the government of the church by making it too popular."³⁰

When the first churches had been founded in New England, it was widely accepted that episcopal ordination was invalid and that clergy were only empowered to minister to the congregation that elected and ordained them. Though John Cotton had criticized aspects of the church polity of Salem in his letter to Samuel Skelton in 1631, when he came over to New England in 1633 he himself had deferred from baptizing his son Seaborn (born during the voyage) because he then acknowledged no authority to administer the sacraments except in a congregation that had chosen him.³¹ George Phillips had gone so far as to declare that if the Watertown congregation wished him to perform his functions on the basis of his English ordination he would leave them. Not all clergy did so, however. John Wilson had accepted election from the Boston church but at the same time had indicated that he was not renouncing his English ordination. The position taken by those who did renounce their episcopal ordination ran counter to the sacerdotal tradition of a ministerial authority that had been espoused by most Protestants. English critics of colonial practice in the 1630s raised questions about this because it seemed to reduce the status of the clergy to a contractual matter.

Even before the Free Grace Controversy efforts were underway to establish a status for the clergy separate from their selection by the laity. One way was to enhance the ordination ceremony. When John Cotton was ordained the day began with a fast, proceeded with his formal selection, his acceptance, the laying on of hands "in the name of the Holy Ghost," and ending with ministers from neighboring churches extending the right hand of fellowship to Cotton. The visible endorsement of area clergy was intended to enhance his position. Over time it became more common for the actual ordination to be performed by the lay elders of a congregation as opposed to ordinary members, and then in a growing number of cases for neighboring ministers to actually lay on the hands in the ceremony.[32] Newbury's James Noyse criticized any lay involvement in ordination.[33] Those who were committed to lay empowerment fought these developments. In 1642 the members of the Woburn church insisted on ordaining their minister, fearing that involving clergy from neighboring churches "might be an occasion of introducing a dependency of churches, etc. and so a presbytery."[34] John Davenport would continue to insist that the ministerial office was "founded in the relation between the church and its officer," and that "take away the relation and the office and work ceaseth," yet more and more of his peers searched for a more sacerdotal view of their profession.[35]

As part of the effort to further enhance the status of the ministry, some of the clergy began to claim that their authority went beyond the congregation in which they had been ordained. In 1645 John Norton, then the teacher of the Ipswich church, argued that the functions of the ministerial office transcended the individual congregation, with the minister established as an ambassador of God. There was an effort to establish a higher understanding of the ministry at the Cambridge Assembly, where representatives of the regions churches were tasked in 1646 to prepare a statement of the New England Way. Norton was a delegate and was likely one of the members who favored a position advanced by James Noyes that would have authorized an ordained clergyman to minister to any congregation, but opposition from John Davenport and other strict congregationalists prevented that formulation. The Assembly did, however, take a step in that direction by allowing that a minister could minister to another church if specifically invited to do so by that church.[36] And the *Cambridge Platform* further stipulated that a church with a second minister could lend him "for a needful season" to another church that was without a clergyman.[37]

The effort to elevate the ministry increasingly focused on the importance of their education. From the early days of the English Reformation puritan clergy had campaigned for an educated English ministry. William Perkins had echoed many reformers when he emphasized the importance of learning for those who aspired to the ministry, criticizing "Anabaptistical fancies and revelations...[that] condemn both human learning and the study of Scripture."[38] It is not surprising that the Massachusetts General Court chartered Harvard College in 1636, around the time when Edward Johnson was accosted by someone complaining about the clergy trained in "niniversities."[39] Though it was never merely a seminary, close to half of the college's seventeenth-century graduates entered the ministry having been trained in logic, rhetoric, divinity, and ancient languages. Yet, despite the college's concern for the professional training of ministers, the most famous early president of Harvard, Charles Chauncy, emphasized to students that "neither your own study or parts, nor the teaching and instruction of others," no mater how important, could substitute for the gifts of the Spirit.[40] But as time went on the graduates who entered the ministry became more and more inclined to emphasize training as opposed to grace as the key determinant of ministerial qualifications.

If the Free Grace controversy led to efforts to enhance the status of the ministry, did it also produce efforts to reduce the role of the laity? There were significant efforts to do so. In notes that he compiled in the 1630s and 1640s (not published until 1713), John Cotton specified a number of actions that were the responsibility of a congregation's ministers as opposed to the laity.[41] The *Cambridge Platform* stipulated that the members could not refuse a minister's call that they assemble, and that members could only speak in church with the permission of the elders.[42] While the Platform was advisory and not mandated for adoption by individual churches, this indicated the direction that the clergy were moving.

Richard Mather addressed the issue of questions from the congregation in a series of answers to inquiries sent over to the colonies by English ministers. He acknowledged that "in the times a little before the [1637] Synod, divers that were infected with corrupt opinions were very bold & forward in this kind of asking questions after sermons, especially when they heard something delivered publicly that did make against their tenets." But at the time (he was writing in the 1640s), most of those who exercised that freedom in a disorderly manner had been banished or had voluntarily left the colony, so that "a man may now live from one end of the year unto another in these congregations, and not hear any man open his mouth in such kind of asking questions." At the time New Englanders were trying to deflect arguments that their church order spawned and encouraged errors, and Mather desired to downplay instances of lay empowerment. Yet he was forced to acknowledge that

> some think the people have a liberty to ask a question publicly for their better satisfaction upon very urgent and weighty cause, though even this is doubted by others, and all judge the ordinary practice of it not necessary, but (if it be no meekly and wisely carried) to be inconvenient if not utterly unlawful.[43]

But despite the recommendation of the synod and Mather's statement of practice, we know that questions did continue to be asked. For instance, following a sermon preached by John Cotton in December 1640 Francis Lyle, a member of the Boston church, asked a question about whether Christ's grace was limited to those who were among the elect.[44]

Many scholars have concluded that the Free Grace controversy brought an end to the practice of lay prophesying and conferencing. Such was not the case. John Cotton set forth how a session of church prophesying might be conducted in 1642.[45] Despite an interest in downplaying lay empowerment, Richard Mather defended the practice of lay prophesying in his 1643 answer to questions raised by English clerics, though he did so somewhat grudgingly and sought to put limits on it. He contended that

> some private members (to wit such as are eminently fitted with knowledge and utterance, being also men of humble spirits and holy lives, all which qualifications we find but in a few) may without an extraordinary call from God be called forth by the Church upon some occasion (and namely in the absence or bodily weakness of ministers, or for trial of gifts when a man intends the ministry) to speak to edification, exhortation and comfort.

It was, he believed,

> extraordinary that private men and new converts should be so soon, and so suddenly, and so much enlightened and enlarged to be able to prophesy publicly to the edification of a whole church, but this

we conceive to be ordinary, that some private men may be found (at least in some churches) grown Christians of able gifts who may have received a gift of prophesy.[46]

In defending the New England Way against Samuel Rutherford a few years later, Mather again defended the practice of lay prophesying by his analysis of the practices of the early Christian church at Corinth.[47] But it is clear that some clergy sought to put curbs on the practice. Lechford wrote that "some of the most grave and learned" ministers argued that "none should undertake to prophesy in public, unless he intend the work of the ministry, and so in some places, as in schools, and not abroad," arguing that it "requireth good learning, skill in tongues, great fidelity, and good conscience."[48]

While the primary focus in this study is on the relative roles of laity and clergy in the development of puritanism, the role of the civil authorities cannot be ignored. The general Protestant insistence on the importance of Bible reading was part of the motivation for a 1642 Massachusetts law that required the heads of all households to ensure that those in their charge—wives, children, and servants—learn how to read and write for the purpose of being able to read the scriptures and the colony laws. Five years later, in a stated effort to thwart "that old deluder Satan," the General Court required that all towns of 50 or more households employ a teacher to instruct those whose household heads were unable to fulfill the responsibilities set out in the earlier legislation. Larger towns were also to employ a grammar school teacher to prepare suitable boys for college. Other colonies made similar provisions. While the founding of Harvard was designed in part to guarantee an educated ministry, these laws insured that those in the pews would be able to follow clerical references in their Bibles and discuss them intelligently with fellow laity.[49]

Much magisterial intervention in religious affairs took the form of efforts to buttress the authority of the orthodox clergy. When Roger Williams had returned to Salem he had preached as a private Christian and stirred up controversy with his ideas on women wearing veils, the use of the cross in the English ensign, the right of the magistrates to impose laws based on the first table of the Ten Commandments, and other matters. When the Salem church gave signs of electing him to the ministerial role of teacher, the colony magistrates pressured the congregation to dissuade them from that course. Yet Williams as an articulate private Christian still shared his views and was perceived as a continuing threat to the established order. Efforts by clergy and magistrates failed to convince Williams of his errors. Thomas Dudley, whose own daughter commemorated him as being "to sectaries, a whip and maul," was elected governor in place of the more moderate John Winthrop in 1635 and in October of that year the Court of Assistants voted to ship Williams back to England.[50] Warned by John Winthrop of an imminent attempt to carry this out, Williams escaped to Narragansett Bay, where he settled in what would become Providence.

Another step in the efforts of the magistrates to structure the region's religion came in the following year when the Massachusetts General Court sought to put a limit on lay empowerment by stipulating that any new congregation needed to be approved by the magistrates and the ministerial "elders of the greater part of the churches in this jurisdiction."[51] The policy evidently was adopted by the Court at the prompting of some of the clergy, though there were laymen such as Dudley who were determined to impose a single pattern on the colony's religious culture, and fully capable of initiating such a requirement on their own. When Richard Mather sought to organize a church in Dorchester in April of 1636, "the churches by their elders and the magistrates... thought them not meet at present to be the foundation of a church," and the effort was deferred, though subsequently completed with "approbation of the magistrates and elders."[52] Yet the requirement of calling for such approval was not without controversy. When a church was being formed in Dedham in 1638 the organizers did inform the authorities of that fact,

> but in giving notice to the governor hereof we understood by some that the General Court had ordained that no churches should be gathered without the advice of other churches, which we conceived might be prejudicial to the liberty of God's people, and some seeds of usurpation upon liberties of the gospel, wherefore we desired the governor [Winthrop] to inform us of that law and the true intent thereof.

Winthrop, who had been out of office when the measure was passed, responded by professing that "the court or law enacted did no way intend to abridge such a liberty of gathering into Christian fellowship."[53]

While some of the efforts of the magistrates suggested an attempt to become involved themselves in the shaping of religious institutions, in other cases they were content to support the efforts of the clergy to do so. The magistrates had defended the right of the ministers to meet and confer against the complaints of Roger Williams and others, and in 1641 one of the provisions in the colony's *Body of Liberties* confirmed the right for monthly meetings of the clergy.[54] In 1642 the Massachusetts General Court urged ministers to agree on a standard catechism to be used in the colony, though agreement could not be reached. Over the following years the Court expressed concerns about the failure to adequately catechize youth.[55]

When the Massachusetts General Court issued an order for the 1646 Cambridge Assembly, the popular house of that body, the Deputies, insisted that the call be redrafted as a request. Even then the churches of Hingham, Salem, and Boston initially refused to send delegates, the Boston congregation expressing the fear that "this synod was appointed by the elders to the intent to make ecclesiastical laws to bind the churches, and to have the sanction of the civil authority put over them." When the final results of the synod, the *Cambridge Platform*, came before the General Court in 1651, 14 deputies voted not to approve it, and the document came to be seen as a statement of principles rather than binding on the churches.[56]

Just as the magistrates had passed the law in 1636 to regulate how congregations were to be formed, in 1652 the Massachusetts General Court forbade the practice of lay preaching. The court accepted the fact that with the growth of the colony there were communities "destitute of persons fitly qualified to undertake the work of ministry," but was concerned that the result was that some towns, being "necessitated to make use of such help as they have to exercise and preach publicly amongst them," made use of "persons of bolder spirits and erroneous principles," leading to "the infection of their hearers and the disturbance of the peace of the country." Consequently, "it is ordered by this Court that no person shall undertake any constant course of public preaching or prophesying within this jurisdiction without the approbation of the elders of the four neighboring churches, or the county court to which the place belongs."[57] The law not only asserted the authority of the magistrates to govern church practice, but gave a role to neighboring clergy to supervise the actions of a newly forming church.

In Salisbury, then part of Massachusetts but later to be part of the New Hampshire colony, Lieutenant Robert Pike proclaimed that

> such persons as did act in making that law did break their oath to the country...for, he said, it is against the liberty of the country, both ecclesiastical and civil...and further said divers or several churches had called their members to account which did act in that lawmaking.

Stung by this criticism of their involvement in ecclesiastical affairs, the Court quickly responded by calling Pike to appear, judged him "guilty of defaming the Commonwealth," disenfranchised him, and made him post a bond for his future good behavior.[58]

The early history of Boston's Second Church (to become known as the North Church) illustrates both the willingness of laity to allow lay preaching and the new concern of the authorities about the practice. By the late 1640s the population of Boston had grown, with much of the increase in the north end of the town. The meetinghouse of the First Church could not accommodate everyone and the prosperous newcomers wished to have a church closer to their homes in that part of town. In 1649 steps began to build a new meetinghouse in the north end, and in June 1650 the church was gathered with seven laymen serving as "pillars of the church" and uniting in covenant. Samuel Mather, recently graduated from Harvard, preached on the occasion and the congregation invited him to become their minister. Mather did preach for a few months but declined to accept a permanent post, choosing instead to follow his brother Nathaniel to England. The church subsequently invited Ipswich's John Norton and New Haven's John Davenport, but they were not willing to leave their existing posts. In the meantime Michael Powell, who was one of the church pillars, preached by way of prophesying.

According to the church's history, Powell's "services were so satisfactory that the church would have proceeded to ordain him," but under the terms of the recent colony law the Suffolk County Court prevented the call, objecting that

> he was "illiterate as to academical education." They would not suffer an unlearned man to be called to the teaching office "in such a place as Boston." He might have talents and a fine spirit," they argued, "and still not be competent to instruct the educated, explain the Scriptures, and convince the unbelieving. If such men intrude themselves unto the sacred function, there is danger of bringing the profession into contempt."[59]

The church petitioned the colony's General Court, which in October 1652 declared that they did not condemn or discourage "Mr. Powell from exercising in public till it please God to provide better for them," but advised "against proceeding to establish Mr. Powell a teaching elder." The reasons they offered were that

> notwithstanding the judgment of the church concerning Mr. Powell's abilities and fitness, yet the Court are not satisfied of the expediency

of their proceeding in respect of this place of such public resort, and considering the humor of the times in England inclining to discourage learning, against which we have born testimony... in our petition to Parliament, which we should contradict if we should approve of such proceedings among ourselves.

Having said this, the Court then more firmly advised the church and Powell "to desist from any further proceeding" in the matter.[60]

A year later, in September 1653, the General Court again took up the matter. Denying that they had prohibited ordaining Powell to office, the Court clarified that it had only prohibited his call to be pastor or teacher, since for those two offices they found him unfit, not being satisfied that he had "such abilities, learning, qualifications as are requisite and necessary for an able ministry of the gospel, whereby he might be able rightly to divide the word of truth, and be able to convince gainsayers." They cited "the unsuitableness of these times... with such tenets as now abound for the subversion of an able ministry." They did, however, concede that "the church may call Mr. Powell to the office of a ruling elder, and then they may enjoy all the ordinances of Christ among them, save the sacraments" while waiting for "an able minister of the gospel." This, in fact, was to be the case for four years until Joseph Mayo, who was leaving a church at Nosset in Plymouth Colony, was chosen pastor.

The Free Grace controversy demonstrated the extent to which laymen and laywomen were accustomed to discussing matters of faith, bringing their own insights to the debate and demonstrating a willingness to challenge the colony ministers and magistrates. The nature of some of the more extreme lay beliefs and the vehemence with which they were expressed disrupted the harmony of the colony and prompted some clergy and laymen to seek curbs on the liberty of the laity to engage in further pursuit of religious truth. Efforts were undertaken to discourage lay questioning of clergy and lay preaching by way of prophesying. At the same time, steps were taken to enhance the authority of the clergy and to elevate their role as the proper interpreters of God's truth. Those who desired such change would find more justification for their position in reports of the lay enthusiasm that characterized the Civil War period in England.

7
The Role of the Laity in England's Puritan Revolution

The crafting of the New England Way was followed with interest by puritans in England and the Netherlands. John Winthrop's belief that the eyes of all would be upon the puritan New World adventure certainly appeared to be the case in the late 1630s and early 1640s. The Atlantic debate over the nature and value of the colonial system became of even greater relevance as conflict between Charles I and his subjects broke out in England and the Long Parliament called the Westminster Assembly into existence to advise on the restructuring of the English Church. For two decades English laymen would engage in their own efforts to create a godly kingdom, part of which involved discussion of what the lay role itself should be. One result was the fragmentation of the puritan movement and its subsequent restructuring as distinct denominations. This chapter will focus on the various ways in which laymen and laywomen engaged in the efforts to restructure the English church. The following chapters will examine some of the ways in which puritans dealt with the sectarian diversity that resulted from lay explorations of the faith in the 1640s and 1650s.

It should be noted that England's Wars of Religion were precipitated by protests by Scottish laymen over the attempts of King Charles I and Archbishop William Laud to impose a new, English-style prayer book on Scotland.[1] One of the key drivers of the Scottish Reformation of the sixteenth century was the work of groups of Christian believers, meeting in weekly exercises that reached out beyond the parish. That lay fervor was still present when the dean of St. Giles, the newly designated cathedral church of Edinburgh, opened the service on July 23, 1637 in accord with the new Prayer Book. Cries broke out from the congregation. A stool was thrown at the dean and as the service dissolved into a riot the officiating clergy fled. The bishop feared for his life as stones were hurled at his carriage. The riot spread, with one report claiming that "two thousand of the baser sort of people" involved. Petitions and protests followed, with an aristocratic observer noting that there was "great discontentment in all sorts of people both of the best and meanest quality because they all apprehend it will subvert that service of God."[2] Many of the same lay protesters soon were subscribing to a National Covenant that pledged them to defend the nation's Presbyterian kirk (church) against English interference. Prayer Book Rebellion soon became Bishops War.

Charles I's need to finance his effort to restore order in his northern kingdom forced him to call a parliament into session early in 1640. The king had ruled without a parliament for 11 years. The refusal of the new body to grant him funds without addressing the grievances that had accumulated led Charles to dissolve the body after mere weeks, resulting in it becoming known as the Short Parliament. But a deteriorating military situation forced the king's hand, and in November 1640 he summoned what would be known as the Long Parliament. While the initial impetus of that body was directed at redress of accumulated political grievances, religion was also an important concern.

The Scots' defense of their reformed church and the calling of an English parliament appears to have unleashed a torrent of popular lay support for religious reform among Englishmen. Parishioners in the parish of All Hallows Barking, in London, chopped off wooden angels adorning the communion rails ands presented them to the House of Commons as evidence of the sorts of popish innovations perpetuated by the king and his archbishop over the previous years. On December 10, 1640 a crowd of over 1500 gathered in Westminster Yard as a petition calling for religious reform was presented to the Parliament. Nationwide somewhere between 10,000 and 20,000 signatures were obtained for this "Root and Branch Petition," which called for the abolition of the episcopal government of the Church of England. The rule of the bishops was blamed for the decay of preaching in the realm, for the loss of many godly clergy and laity to New England and the Netherlands, and for the advance of popish doctrines and practices in the church. Separate documents were submitted by petitioners from 13 counties.[3]

As the Parliament began to debate the petitions in the Spring of 1641 there were frequent reports of local believers taking reform into their own hands. One of the most common targets was the altar rails that had been ordered reinstated by Archbishop Laud. Altar rails were dismantled in numerous London churches and in parishes throughout the country. Many members of Parliament were alarmed at the evidence of widely based lay dissent. In May a paper was nailed to one of the entrances to the Parliament proclaiming "The voice of God is the cry of the people; bishops the limbs of Antichrist and the plague of the kingdom; destroy them and take away Antichrist." Responding to such pressure, Lord Digby asked, "What can be of greater presumption than for...a multitude to teach a parliament what and what is not the government according to God's word?" Clergymen who found themselves under attack responded. Thomas Chesire preached a sermon at St. Paul's Cross in which he complained about vilification of the prayer book and reported that when he walked the streets he heard complaints that "there goes a Jesuit, a Baal's priest, an abbey lubber, one of Canterbury's whelps."[4]

At the same time there was a proliferation of lay preaching in churches and in the streets of London and other cities. While it had always been difficult for the authorities to fully control such activity, with the bishops under attack it was virtually impossible to do so. The informal mechanisms whereby puritans had tried to regulate the more extreme members of their movement likewise broke down. In June the parliamentarian Denzil Holles reported that "many shopkeepers and others took upon themselves to preach in the City." A sermon by one layman was reported to have lasted for an hour and a half and to have drawn a crowd of 3000.[5] John Taylor attacked the new wave in a pamphlet titled *A Swarme of Sectaries and Schismamtics, Wherein is Discovered the Strange Preaching (or Prating) of such as are by their Trades Cobblers, Tinkers, Pedlers, Weavers, Sowgelders, and Chimney Sweepers* (1641). It was illustrated by a woodcut of Samuel How preaching from atop a tub in the Nag's Head Tavern. In the same year Taylor published a shorter pamphlet denouncing "one Burboone, a leatherseller" who entertained "a whole swarm of Brownists in his house," where he preached for five hours "as the Spirit moved him," and the ranting of "Hunt, a prophet" who disrupted the services at St. Pulcher's church with his message.[6]

In discussing How, Taylor made a point that was to be increasingly important in the years that followed. How, according to Taylor, "did address himself in such a fashion as well befitted such a congregation" as had gathered. "He made some faces, with his hands erected, his eyes (most whitest white) to heaven directed," used various postures, and where "his speech lacked either sense or weight, he made up in measure and conceit."[7] Increasingly lay preachers were described as "enthusiasts," a categorization that would be most evident in the labeling of various groups as "Ranters," "Quakers," and the like. Over time, puritan clergymen would seek to distinguish themselves from such radicals by adopting a more staid preaching style. But the fact is that prior to the 1640s numerous reform ministers were noted for their highly emotional pulpit performances. Dedham's John Rogers had been known as "a Boanerges, a Son of Thunder." He had often played various parts in his preaching, on one occasion taking hold of the pulpit canopy with both hands and "roaring hideously, to represent the torments of the damned." An early biographer of William Perkins wrote that when that divine preached, "he used to pronounce the word damn with such an emphasis as left a doleful echo in his auditors ears a good while after."[8] It was the drama of such sermons that helped draw gadders from great distances. And it likely provided a model for lay preachers.

The debate over the appropriateness of lay preaching became increasingly bitter as the decade went on. Robert Baillie, one of the Scottish representatives at the Westminster Assembly, complained of lay preachers running "without any call, wither from God or man, into every shire of the kingdom." In response to such complaints, John Saltmarsh, one of the New Model Army chaplains, denied that the ability to speak from "the abounding spirit of God," should be "made subject to the Laws and ordinances of men." For Saltmarsh and others, this was simply an expression of the Christian duty to minister to one another. Thus, Walter Cradock asked, "If we see that the Lord fills young men, or tradesmen, etc., and gives them hearts to go and tell the good news to others, why should... your spirits rage at it?"[9]

As was evident from their responses to the New England puritan experiment, English puritan clergy were not united on how the church should be reformed should the episcopal system be torn up root and branch. Some of those who had conducted their own experiments in Congregationalism during their voluntary exile in the Netherlands favored the introduction of that system. Twenty-eight members of the Rotterdam church returned to Norfolk when the new parliament had been called. They began the process of organizing themselves into a gathered church, and eventually called William Bridge to be their pastor.[10] Clergy such as Bridge, Thomas Goodwin, Philip Nye, and Sidrach Simpson became advocates of some form of the New England Way. Other clergymen, such as Simeon Ashe, Daniel Cawdrey, and Edmund Calamy preferred a more hierarchical system such as to be found in Presbyterian Scotland. Much of the lay preaching in London in 1640 and 1641 was deemed radical by the orthodox Calvinist standards of all of these clergy. Consequently, when leading Presbyterians and Congregational clergy agreed in late 1641 to assume a common front in the Calamy House Accord, one of the points of agreement was that since "the preaching of some laymen, tradesmen and mechanics in the public congregations was a great stone of offence in the building of the Temple," ... the Independent clergy (or at least those "judged to be the most gracious and powerful with them") undertook to dissuade the lay preachers from appearing in public pulpits "especially at that time." The implicit assumption that the separatist preachers were amenable to puritan control in the interests of getting rid of the bishops was borne out by the virtual end of lay preaching in public in 1642.[11]

Evidently the leaders of the old puritan underground still held some sway at this time. Prominent preachers who had achieved notoriety in 1641, such as the soap-maker John Durant and the hat-maker John Green, were heard from rarely for the next few years.[12] But the respite was only temporary.

In August of 1641 the king had been presented with the Grand Remonstrance, a compilation of grievances and demands that included a request that Charles agree to "a general synod of the most grave, pious, learned and judicious divines of this island; assisted by some from foreign parts, professing the same religion with us." But Charles would not agree to an assembly, and so, little progress had been made when the king raised his standard at Nottingham in August 1642 and declared the Parliament in rebellion. The English Civil Wars had begun. The following June the two houses of Parliament agreed on a call for a "learned and godly" assembly that was charged to settle the government and liturgy of the church, to reform church government, and to vindicate and clear the doctrines of the church. The membership of the assembly included clergy chosen by members of the two houses of Parliament; two ministers from the French Stranger Church; Joshua Hoyle of Trinity College, Dublin; 30 laymen who were members of the Parliament (though it is not clear if they could vote and only ten generally attended); and (following the signing of the Solemn League and Covenant binding the English Parliament to the Scots), Scottish commissioners. Sir Simond D'Ewes noted that the involvement of Parliament was valuable since laymen were not as influenced by "the great passions clergymen are subject to."[13] The New Englanders John Cotton, John Davenport, and Thomas Hooker were all invited, but declined to participate, preferring to influence the deliberations from afar with their writings.[14]

Early in 1644 divisions between the Assembly majority that favored a more hierarchical church structure and those who advocated for congregational principles came to the fore. On January 17 a committee recommended that only preaching presbyters were to have the power of ordaining clergy. The Congregationalists fought for the right of individual congregations to ordain their own ministers, but were defeated. The following months attention was focused on the role of synods, and here again there was a division. Thomas Goodwin, Philip Nye, and William Bridge led the argument for congregational autonomy. Bridge cited Matthew 18:15 in arguing that "the government which is according to the mind of Christ & his word revealed is this: that every particular congregation should have power in itself."[15] The outcome of these specific debates only reinforced what was already evident, that the Assembly would recommend to the Parliament a Presbyterian-style settlement. Anticipating this, in January 1644 Goodwin, Nye, Bridge, Sidrach Simpson, and Jeremiah Burroughes published *An Apologetical Narration*, which petitioned the Parliament for the accommodation of congregational churches within any national Presbyterian structure that would be proposed. The five authors, along with others who supported them, became known as the Dissenting Brethren. Their position was essentially the New England Way and colonial leaders closely identified with them. The Dissenting Brethren agreed with the Assembly minority on virtually all doctrinal issues, but the majority would not tolerate polity differences.

In the subsequent national debate politics pushed the Dissenting Brethren to ally with others who sought to defeat the Presbyterian thrust.[16] Over the following years the Congregationalists were lumped with all those who dissented from Presbyterianism as "Independents," a categorization which they vigorously rejected, but which has been accepted by most historians.[17] While it is important to recognize the differences (particularly over doctrine) between the Congregationalists and other Independents, the blanket term does have merit in pointing to the common value all these groups placed on congregational autonomy and lay authority within a congregation.

While the Independents had some support in the Parliament, it was their support in the army that forced their opponents to take them seriously. Religious zeal motivated many of those who served in the Parliamentary Army from the start of the war, and this became even more pronounced following a reorganization of the army in 1645.[18] Much of the story of the lay role in the shaping of puritanism at this time centers on the army. According to the foremost scholar on the New Model Army, the officers, and Oliver Cromwell in particular, were the "religious vanguard who set their stamp upon the army." The New Model became known as "the praying army."[19] According to some contemporaries, some of the officers who pushed for religious reform in the New Model Army had previously been among those who gathered in Coleman Street Ward to "study and...to rail against ministers and parish churches, and Presbyterians." Paul Hobson, an army captain and lay preacher, preached to the troops at Newport Pagnell in April 1645, and then later was arrested in Coleman Street along with others accused by the mayor of being members of seditious conventicles. Released, he was soon preaching twice a week in Checker Alley, in the Moorfields district of London. Between 1645 and 1647 Hobson wrote three pamphlets on behalf of Baptist views. Two soldiers who were members of Thomas Lambe's Coleman Street Church—Jeremiah Ives and the weaver Samuel Oates—preached to various groups in the mid-1640s.[20]

Other activist soldiers and officers were former New Englanders. Among the colonists who served in the New Model Army were Francis Willoughby, Daniel Gookin, Hezekiah Haynes, George Fenwick, Stephen Winthrop, Thomas Larkham, and George Cooke. There was a particularly strong representation in the regiment commanded by Thomas Rainsborough, a kinsman of the Winthrops. Israel Stoughton enlisted in the regiment, as did Nehemiah Bourne, who became a major. John Leverett would captain a company in the regiment. William Hudson served as an ensign.[21] In all, somewhere between 80 and one 150 New Englanders served in that regiment.[22] Stephen Winthrop, John Winthrop's son, accepted a commission in the cavalry regiment commanded by Thomas Harrison.[23] Other New Englanders, such as Hugh Peter, would serve as chaplains in the army.

One of the army chaplains, William Dell, recalled "the spirit of prayer" that was found among the rank and file of the army. A critic who was not happy with what he found wrote, "Look at Colonel Fleetwood's regiment, what a cluster of preaching officers and troops there is!"[24] Captain John Hogdgson, walking through the army encampment on the eve of the battle of Naseby, heard a cornet praying aloud extemporaneously. The man "exceedingly carried on in the duty. I met with so much of God in it, as I was satisfied deliverance was at hand."[25] In 1643 the Parliament authorized publication of *The Soldier's Pocket Bible, Containing the Most (if not all) those Places Contained in Holy Scripture, which do show the Qualifications of his Inner Man, that is a fit Soldier to fight the Lord's Battles* (1643). Many spent time around the army campfires discussing the scriptures. A soldier in John Hewson's regiment wrote in 1647 of "the manifest presence of God" that such exercises produced, so that "the sweet union we had with God doth endear us together in love." Two years later a group of 30 army officers and London clergymen addressed their fellow soldiers in a letter praying that through such religious exercises the soldiers might become "burning and shining lights in our generation, to the stopping of the mouths of our enemies, the cheering of the upright in heart, and above all, the glorifying of our father which is in heaven."[26]

In addition to the preaching of chaplains such as Dell, Saltmarsh, and Peter who had ministerial training, lay preaching became widespread in the army. As early as 1643 Colonel John Pickering was preaching to his regiment, prompting anger among some members of Parliament and an order to ban the practice. But the ban was not enforceable. Lucy Hutchinson, who initially was offended by the practices of members of the Nottingham garrison who avoided services in the parish churches of the city and met privately to minister to one another, eventually came to accept their practice and admire their zeal.[27] In June 1645 Pickering's regiment was cited as one of the "chiefest praying and preaching regiments in the army." A short time before, Naseby Richard Beaumont and Paul Hobson aroused the ire of the governor of the Newport Pagnell garrison by their preaching. In February 1646 six or seven soldiers in Colonel Edward Whalley's regiment preached in private houses in Wellingborough, Northamptonshire, prompting a clash with the local rector. Whalley argued that it was the right of soldiers to act as channels for divine revelation, a privilege he was not shy to act upon himself. When the Parliament occupied Oxford, soldiers preached in Christ Church and other venues in the city. In addition to offering their own spiritual messages, officers and common soldiers became noted for interrupting the sermons of ordained clergymen in parish churches to contradict the message being preached or to offer their own insights.[28] When undecided about negotiations with the king in 1647, the army held a series of prayer meetings. Unsure whether to obey orders to cross to Ireland, they held another prayer meeting.[29]

Towering above all the other officers of the New Model Army was Oliver Cromwell, who rose from being a captain of horse in the army of the Eastern Association in the early days of the war to Lieutenant-General in the New Model Army, and then the de facto commander of the army following the execution of Charles I. There is evidence of Cromwell's puritan beliefs as early as the 1630s, when he appears to have preached in gatherings in private homes and also considered emigration to New England. It is likely his preaching at a conventicle in Ely that led to his being made a freeman in 1640 and thus eligible for a seat in Parliament, to which he was chosen in 1640 as an MP for the city of Cambridge. As a member of Parliament and as a military officer he was driven by a godly imperative. He sought recruits who shared his religious zeal regardless of their particular beliefs, welcoming Presbyterians, Congregationalists, and sectaries.[30]

The idea that lay saints received graces that enabled them to understand biblical messages was a key element of the puritan reform movement. Starting in the late 1640s, it was increasingly evident that Cromwell was steering his course by interpretations of scripture passages that he believed were aided by inspiration of the Holy Spirit. While he likely drew on such insights in his lay preaching prior to the Civil Wars, and certainly did so in his letter to his cousin Oliver St. John in 1638, the evidence of him doing so became more evident from the mid-1640s. Hugh Peter reported that Cromwell spent the night of October 13, 1645, prior to storming Basing House, meditating on Psalm 115.[31] It was reported that at a meeting of army officers at Whitehall he prayed for a full hour.[32] In 1652 a German ambassador observed a meeting in what had been the king's chapel in Whitehall. Cromwell and his family were in what formerly was the king's pew. Hugh Peter, dressed as a military officer rather than a clergyman, preached. The ambassador reported that "this is common; anyone may step up, when he wishes, and deliver a sermon."[33] Cromwell's confidence in his ability to comprehend the will of God and his determination to act in accordance with it was central to his military and political efforts throughout his life. In the letters that survive to friends, to family members, and to leaders of opposing forces in Ireland and Scotland, he is constantly citing and interpreting scripture. Similarly, his public speeches during the years of the Protectorate demonstrate how his meditations on the Bible had shaped his positions.

Cromwell on more than one occasion drew upon Numbers 11:29 in stating "would [that] all the Lord's people were prophets," and laymen discussing religious practice and doctrine were never more evident than in the Army Debates of the late 1640s. Despite the defeat of the king's forces in the First Civil War the leaders of Parliament found it difficult to negotiate a settlement with Charles I. London pamphleteers, soon to be known as the Levellers, offered their own ideas as to how the realm should be restructured, and their views gained considerable support in the army. The various options were debated over a period of months in various meetings of the army's officers and representatives of the junior officers and rank-and-file soldiers. One series of such debates occurred in and around the Putney church in late October and early November 1647. One scholar has written of "the extraordinary atmosphere in Putney Church, the mixture of fear and religious exaltation, of logical argument and angry protest."[34]

The Putney sessions were primarily focused on political issues, but the participants attempted to draw upon the guidance of the Spirit, so that the sessions assumed some of the appearance of religious conferencing. Early in the debates, when tempers were running high, Lieutenant-Colonel William Goffe proposed a prayer session "to draw us up to a serious consideration of the weightiness of the work that lies before us, and seriously to set ourselves to seek the Lord." Captain John Clarke urged that everyone "search our own spirits with patience, and look by the light of God within us." On this, as on other similar occasions, those present prayed silently for guidance, studied their Bibles, and shared the insights that they believed the Spirit had led them to. While acknowledging that "we have no record of Cromwell contributing to any of the prayer meetings," John Morrill has suggested that "given his background as a fiery lay preacher, his encouragement of others, and his willingness to deploy exactly the hermeneutics of prophetic preaching in the 1650s...there is little reason to doubt that this is an accident of the fragmentary evidence."[35]

After the prayer session suggested by Goffe was held, on November 1 Cromwell suggested "everyone might speak their experiences as the issue of what God has given in in answer to their prayers." The discussion illustrated both the puritan belief in the ability of individual Christians to profit from the inspiration of the Spirit, but also the moderate puritan concern to test the views that were advanced against both the scripture itself and also against the insights of others in the godly community. John Jubbes shared his belief that "I do not know how to distinguish whether the Spirit of God lives in me or no, but by mercy, love, and peace; and on the contrary whether the Spirit of Antichrist live in me, but by envy, malice and war." Cromwell cautioned about trusting too far in individual revelation. "I shall not be unwilling to hear God speaking in any [man]," he said, but pointed out that "when anything is spoken [as from God], I think the rule is [1 Cor 14:29], let the rest judge," cautioning that testimonies needed to be tested against the scripture and against the testimonies of others. Reflecting on the debates, he said, "I cannot but think that in most that have spoke there has been something of God laid forth to us...And thus far we are agreed, I think it is of God." John Wildman pointed out that

> whatever another man hath received from the Spirit, that man cannot demonstrate [it] to me but by some other way than merely relating to me what he conceives to be the mind of God. [In spiritual

matters he must show its conformity with the scripture, though indeed] it is beyond the power of the reason of all the men on earth to demonstrate the scriptures to be the scriptures written by the Spirit of God, and it must be the spirit of faith [in a man himself] that must finally make him believe whatsoever may be spoken in spiritual matters.[36]

Having agreed on some of the political issues facing them, the army officers turned to some of the issues that divided them regarding a religious settlement. These debates were held in mid-December in Whitehall. Particularly contentious was the question of liberty of conscience, with the tension between clerical guides and godly laymen laid bare. Clergy participating in the deliberations included Thomas Goodwin, Philip Nye, Hugh Peter, and John Goodwin. One of the participants, a Mr. Hewitt, argued against paying particular attention to the clerical representatives, arguing that

> every poor man [that] does understand what he does, and is willing that the commonwealth should flourish, hath as real an hand here as the greatest divine, and for all [the] divinity [you] have had from reading, if you had as many degrees [as there are hours] of time since the creation, learning is but the tradition of men.

The scene was reported by one of the contemporary newsletters, which indicated that when Thomas Goodwin and Nye "requested them not to determine [anything] without advice from some learned divines... the mechanics took snuff, [and] told them they thought themselves as divine as any divines in the kingdom."[37] In the end, voices of moderation prevailed, but the agreement hashed out by the officers was made irrelevant by the decision to put the king on trial.

Arguments over the role of university-trained clergy spilled over into the press wars as well. William Walwyn, a silkman who was a leading spokesman for the Levellers, argued that rather than choosing learned men to be his disciples, Christ had picked "herdsmen, fishermen, tent-makers, toll-gatherers, etc." In his own days men of similar humble origins were capable of understanding the scriptures and interpreting God's will if they would "but take boldness to themselves and not distruct their own understanding."[38]

Less well documented than the debates in the army council were similar exchanges around the campfires. And it is here that New Englanders like Stephen Winthrop were able to share their insights into the colonists struggle to erect a godly kingdom and the workings of the New England Way.[39]

The *Apologetical Narration* had fractured the common front maintained by leading Congregationalists and Presbyterians, and one result was a resurgence of lay preaching and the formation of new congregations. Earlier John Green had attacked clergy for preaching the law and legal preparation instead of the true word of God. His preaching had sparked a riot in Fleet Street and he had fled to Trinidad. By 1643 he was back in London, preaching in Coleman Street, where it was reported that many flocked to hear him.[40] Joel Halcomb's recent University of Cambridge dissertation has catalogued and analyzed close to 200 Congregational churches functioning in England during the 1640s and 1650s. Some were formed by those with clerical backgrounds such as William Greenhill and Nathaniel Holmes, while others were organized by lay preachers such as the soap-boiler Thomas Lambe.[41] Many, however, evolved from groups of ordinary lay believers who came together to pray, fast, and share their experiences, conferencing in voluntary unions of saints. Because the number of members did not make it possible to maintain a minister, some of these churches struggled on without one for many years, with laymen assuming leadership.[42] Although each congregation was independent in terms of its ability to control its own affairs, informal contacts with other churches were employed to maintain a larger communion of the faithful. Churches sent messengers to one another to solicit advice, and occasional regional conferences were held to discuss common concerns. In these cases lay members more often represented congregations than clergymen.[43]

While Parliament did establish a national Presbyterian structure and passed various ordinances to suppress sectarian excesses, the strong opposition of Independents and the latter group's important support in the army, made enforcement virtually impossible. The new presbyteries could do nothing to prevent the emergence of lay believers who drew on what they believed to be the inspiration of the Spirit to advance new doctrinal positions. As David Como has described it, "radical puritans... took ideas, imperatives or cultural presuppositions from within the broader puritan amalgam, accentuated and reshaped those conventions, and then deployed them in ways that were regarded at the time as extreme, unorthodox or particularly corrosive of the status quo."[44] They then attempted to spread their ideas in sermons and writings. Public disputations resembling some of the more open prophesyings and conferences of the Elizabethan era were held throughout the land.

Bernard Capp has observed that "thousands of ordinary people, who would never wade through polemical tracts, heard similar attacks from the pulpit, and large crowds flocked to the public debates that were a striking feature of these years." A debate between Presbyterians and Baptists at Ellesmere in 1656 attracted thousands of laymen, who followed the back and forth for over five hours. When such gatherings did not persuade, they could inspire individuals to new departures. George Fox attended a disputation in Leicester in 1648 between Congregationalists, Presbyterians, Baptists, and supporters of the old Prayer Book. Unconvinced, he went on to develop his own understanding of the believer's relationship to God.[45] In scenes that reminded English critics of the disruptions of services that had accompanied the Free Grace controversy in Massachusetts, believers openly challenged clergy. The Presbyterian Thomas Edwards wrote of how, during a service he was conducting, "up stands one Colonel Washington of Hartfordshire...and spake openly against what I had preached, that I had not rightly given the sense of that parable of the tares, and that I was a false prophet, or, beware of false prophets." In enumerating the dangerous signs of the time, Edwards also offered numerous examples of soldiers disrupting the services of partish churches in the towns where they were garrisoned, in some cases mounting the pulpit and preaching themselves.[46]

For the remainder of the 1640s and into the next decade orthodox clergy warned of and attacked the views of Ranters, Antinomians, Adamites, Familists, Anabaptists, Quakers, Socinians, Libertines, Traskites, Arians, and other such groups. Thomas Edwards was in the forefront of the critics of what he viewed as sectarian excess. In 1641 he had published *Reasons against the Independent Government of Particular Congregations*, and had followed that with *Antapologia* (1644), which was a response to the *Apologetical Narration* of the Congregationalist Dissenting Brethren. A Presbyterian based in London's Christ Church, Newgate, his major work was *Gangraena: Or a Catalogue and Discovery of Many of the Errors, Heresies, Blasphemies and Pernicious Practices of this Time* in three parts, first published in 1646. In it he listed 16 different varieties of sect that he believed had been spawned by the disorder of the times.[47] Throughout the work Edwards related stories that illustrated the dangers of the new prophets and preachers springing up in England. He was particularly critical of mechanic and women preachers, and connected the rise of female preachers to a breakdown of family life and immoral sexual practices.[48] The years 1645–48 saw the largest outpouring of works attacking lay sectaries, another significant one being Ephraim Pagitt's

Heresiography: Or, a Description of the Heretics and Sectaries of these Latter Times (1645).

Women believers in particular benefitted from the breakdown of traditional order, but the groundwork for their participation in religious controversy had been laid earlier. The Protestant emphasis on Bible reading and study had not discriminated on the basis of gender.[49] Following the army debates, while discussions continued on the issues confronting the army, Elizabeth Poole, a lay woman with a reputation as a prophetess, addressed the council of officers of the army. Her argument, that the army had received its power from God and should not surrender it, evidently had an impact on Henry Ireton and some of the other officers.[50] In early January she came before the council again, this time to argue against the king's execution. But when Charles was put to death and none of the consequences she foretold came to pass, she lost her credibility.[51]

The Scot Robert Baillie cited Bastwick and Prynne in asserting that "our London Independents exceed all their brethren, who of late begin to give unto women power of preaching, prophesying, speaking in their congregations."[52] John Goodwin's London congregation allowed women to participate in discussions, though they were not allowed to vote or hold church office.[53] John Bunyan recounted in his spiritual autobiography how a group of women had made a strong impact on his own progress in faith. He had encountered a group of women sitting in a doorway and talking "about a new birth, the work of God on their hearts, and also how they were convinced of their miserable state by nature."[54] Many of the gathered churches had a preponderance of female members. Eight of the twelve founding pillars of the church in Bedford were women. Eighty-three of the 114 members of the Norwich church in 1645 were women.[55] Women shared all of the rights of men (save access to the ministry) in John Rogers's Dublin church. His belief that there was "no warrant" for the power which men did commonly claim was one of the reasons for an eventual split in the congregation.[56]

Edward Reynolds commemorated the life of Mrs. Mary Bewley and praised her spiritual association with others. He commented on

> the joy she took in spiritual conference and the communion of saints, delighting to hear of the experiences of others, and freely communicating her own to those in whom she confided,... evidencing in her Christian conferences knowledge of divine things in a scriptural strain, with holy affections.

"She also," he wrote, "manifested her love to others...with much wisdom, as suiting her words and timing the admonition so that the offender without shame hath known his fault."[57] The New Englander Sarah Keayne, the daughter of Thomas Dudley and daughter-in-law of the merchant Robert Keayne, followed her husband Benjamin to London in the early 1640s. Their marriage fell apart but Sarah remained in England and was caught up in the religious freedom of the time. John Winthrop's son Stephen, also in England at the time, wrote to his father, "my cousin Keayne is grown a great preacher." Shortly thereafter her husband reported that she had "run so fast from that height of error in judgment to extremity of error in practice," applying to her the charge made about other female preachers, that their doctrinal errors led to sexual promiscuity.[58] Some congregations encouraged more participation than all of the female members wished to have. Susanna Parr was urged to speak and participate in the meetings of the Exeter church to the point where she was made uncomfortable.[59]

Accompanying the greater role for women in such churches was an outburst of female preaching during the 1640s and 1650s. There were women preachers in London—including one who preached weekly at the Baptist Church on Bell Alley along Coleman Street—and also in Lincolnshire, Ely, Yorkshire, and other parts of the realm.[60] In an attack on female preachers published in 1641, such individuals were stigmatized as being "ambitious, and...they would have superiority." Another author labeled female preachers as "puffed up with pride," and "arrogance, to preach in mixed congregations of men and women, in an insolent way, so usurping authority over men."[61] The issue of women's roles was controversial even within the sectarian community. Anne Harriman threatened to leave her London Baptist congregation when a male member stated that he could not accept the right of women to speak in church. Even some of the Fifth Monarchists distinguished between the spiritual authority of women and their right to share in the governance of the church.[62]

A Parliamentary committee examining religious disorder noted that women gathered in Coleman Street Ward to preach every Tuesday around four o'clock in the home of a Mrs. Attaway, a lace-seller who lived in Bell Alley. Attaway was one of the preachers and was joined by an unnamed gentlewoman who was a major's wife. The two were Baptists who believed that Christ's sacrifice had redeemed all men. Attaway was said to have preached that the time had come when "God would pour out his spirit on the handmaidens, that they should prophesy." On one occasion Thomas Lambe invited Attaway to preach to his Coleman Street congregation. Samuel Gorton was one of those who heard her preach and they may have preached together on occasion. Women being welcomed as preachers by male colleagues was not unheard of; John Saltmarsh was said to have preached alongside a woman in Brentford around this time.[63] While he denied that charge, there were examples of female preachers in Kent. Joan Banford of Faversham and Susan May of Ashford were accused of public preaching. And their right to do so was defended by Richard Coppin, a preacher in Rochester Cathedral, who wrote that "a woman creature may have freedom to speak and answer as a man." And Francis Cornwell went further, suggesting that women had been allowed to administer communion in the primitive church and should have the right in his time.[64]

Women also took to print. Katherine Chidley composed one of the most effective responses on Thomas Edwards's attacks on the Independent churches.[65] Chidley had been a member of a gathered church in Shrewsbury and had been persecuted for her separatist practices. In her defense of congregational choice of officers against Edwards she emphasized how any deficiency in the minister chosen by a congregation would be made up for by the discernment of ordinary members.[66]

Katherine Sutton published *A Christian Womans Experiences of the glorious working of Gods free grace* in which she claimed to "own a Prophetical voice of Christ, which, if he please to speak, he can make me to hear, yea to believe." She offered "these crumbs which I have gathered from my bountiful Lord's table" in the hope that they would be "savory to... hungry, brokenhearted Christians."[67] Anna Trapnel, in her account of her own experiences, wrote that it was "the desire of all the saints, and of all that wish well to Sion to hear of the experiences each of other, that they have the pourings out of the Spirit."[68]

Lay preaching by mechanics and women was rooted in the historical encouragement of prophesying by various puritan reformers, particularly congregationalists. Consequently, Presbyterian attacks on the more radical expressions of religious enthusiasm were often coupled with criticisms of congregationalism. Robert Baillie was a respected Scottish Presbyterian and one of the Scots attending the Westminster Assembly. His *A Dissuasive from the Errors of the Time* (1645) focused on the Congregationalists. Beginning with the Brownists, he examined separately the New Englanders and the Congregationalists who had been in the Netherlands. One of the practices Baillie was particularly exercised by was the Congregationalist acceptance of lay prophesying. They were, he wrote, of "full agreement, permitting any private man of the flock, or any stranger whom they take to be gifted, publicly to expound and apply the Scripture" after a sermon was preached.[69] But despite what he saw as the evident dangers that prophesying could encourage radical beliefs, many Congregationalists continued to defend the practice. William Bridge asserted that a church was in its "beauty, when the brethren prophesy according to the proportion of faith, and that one by one." Thursday exercises of prophesying in the Yarmouth congregation attracted a "great concourse and throng of people." In a method reminiscent of the Elizabethan prophesyings, sessions of lay prophesying held by the church at Beccles were opened to non-members for their edification, with the exchanges being summed up at the conclusion by clerical elders.[70]

Other churches employed question-and-answer sessions to encourage lay participation in discussion of doctrine and practice. Still others conducted both. The gathered congregation in Canterbury held prophesying exercises on Thursdays and question-and-answer sessions on Tuesdays on a fortnightly basis. That same church held quarterly meetings in which members would share their experiences "of the incomes of Jesus Christ, of their growth in grace, of the temptations and corruptions which they wrestle with, and the strength or victory they have over the same, together with any spiritual experience in any kind."[71] Some churches had sessions which combined questions with prophesying. Members of the Bristol church came together regularly for conference, where

> there was a liberty for any brother (and for any sister by a brother) to propose his doubt of or their desire of understanding any portion of Scripture, and the rest of the brethren (especially the officers of the congregation), one by one, would speak to the answering of the question, according as the Lord did hint upon their spirits, and then be silent, and another speak, and so a third...[72]

The church recorder listed seven ways in which these sessions were edifying, including clarifying darker passages of scripture, bringing shared experience to bear on questions, and revealing the gifts of various members.[73] Rejecting the passive model of lay churchgoing which he associated with Presbyterians, John Saltmarsh argued that "the interest of the people in Christ's kingdom is not only an interest of compliance and obedience and submission, but of consultation, of debating, counseling, prophesying, voting."[74]

While Baillie's charge might have exaggerated the extent of their agreement on prophesying, the English supporters of the New England Way claimed to be following the colonists in this regard. Thomas Goodwin and Philip Nye, in their preface "to the reader" introducing John Cotton's *The Keys of the Kingdom of Heaven*, stated that "we humbly conceive prophesying (as the Scripture terms it) or speaking to the edification of the whole church, may (sometimes) be performed by brethren gifted though not in office as elders of the church," though indicating that it was to be an occasional practice engaged in by those believed to have the gift to do so. And, pointedly, they asserted that it was no more inappropriate for gifted laymen to speak on matters of divinity in a congregation than it was for lay delegates to do so in the Westminster Assembly of Divines.[75]

A group of East Anglian Congregational ministers, in a work entitled *The Preacher Sent: A Vindication of the Liberty of Public Preaching*, asserted that

> Every man...to whomsoever the Spirit hath afforded a gift, either wisely to speak and apply Gospel truths to others...or understandably to give an exposition of the Scriptures, every man that hath such gifts, it belongeth to his place and calling to use those gifts...else he crosseth the end of the Spirit.[76]

They argued that "gifted men may be said to minister in the Gospel" and that "every man that hath that gift of Scripture-interpretation is required to minister unto others." Furthermore, "it is properly preaching to publish, declare, and open or apply Gospel-truths to any persons, whether publicly or privately...preaching not only publicly but also privately in every house."[77]

The strongest defense of the practice came from Sydrach Simpson, one of the original Dissenting Brethren. Simpson had offered a moving account of his own experiences to the Rotterdam church in the mid-1630s. His tract *Wherin the Judgment of the Reformed Churches and Protestant Divines is Showed, Considering Preaching by those who are not Ordained Ministers* was published in 1647. It opened with the bold statement that "A man may lawfully preach the Word, who is not called to be a minister." Simpson claimed scriptural justification—even asserting that women, though not normally allowed to speak in church, might do so if they were "immediately inspired." But it did not take immediate inspiration for men to offer their views. He described how functions that had subsequently become limited to clergy had in the early church been performed by various lay believers, including teaching, reading the scripture, interpreting, offering judgment, praying, leading psalms and speaking in other fashions. Simpson claimed support for his position from the writings of Reformation stalwarts, including Ulrich Zwingli, Peter Martyr, the synods of Emden and Wessel, the early reformed church of Scotland, Thomas Cartwright, Dudley Fenner, and William Ames. He connected preaching with other forms of persuasion, pointing out that "men that are not in the ministry may write commentaries on the Scripture... If they might preach by their pen, they may by their tongue also." It was, he concluded, "lawful for private men to open the Scriptures publicly," and asserted that this "will be no means of error, confusion or heresy, (as it is slandered) but of edification and preservation of the truth."[78]

John Owen began his ministerial career as a support of a Presbyterian order, but became one of the leading exponents of Congregationalism after his exposure to the works of John Cotton. Prior to that change, in 1644 he published a work on *The Duty of Pastors and People Distinguished*. While failing to address the issue of speaking in church, he contended that "the people of God were not only permitted, but enjoined also, to read the Scriptures, and upon all occasions, in their own houses and elsewhere, to talk of them, or communicate their knowledge in them to others," blaming the Council of Trent for forbidding the practice and the canons of the Church of England for condemning such meetings as conventicles.[79]

Owen was a key figure in the gathering of representatives of the Congregational churches in October 1658 that affirmed the legitimacy of lay preaching in the Savoy Declaration. "Although it is incumbent on the pastors and teachers of the churches to be instant in preaching the Word by way of office," the declaration affirmed that "yet the work of Preaching the Word is not so peculiarly confined to them, but that others gifted and fitted by the Holy Ghost for it, and approved (being by lawful ways and means in the Providence of God called thereunto) may publicly, ordinarily, and constantly perform it."[80]

It is hard to deny that encouraging laymen to publicly interpret scripture within congregations contributed to the great explosion of lay preaching in the 1640s.[81] And some Congregational churches expressed concern about the unorthodox ideas that occasionally were expressed. Without rejecting the practice, the Norwich church, which had been accused of consisting of a "rabble of poor mechanics and silly women," decided that no member was to "exercise their gifts in a public way (though but occasionally) without the approbation of the Church first delivered." Others came to adopt similar safeguards, but virtually all Congregationalists remained committed to the principle of lay prophesying.[82]

Along with their commitment to lay prophesying, English Congregationalists and other reformers continued to stress the importance of conferencing, which included sharing religious experiences, and which encouraged the laity to take a greater role in shaping their religious communities. Drawing on the same comparison between the Christian community and the human body that was employed by John Winthrop (among others), Stephen Ford, vicar of Chipping Norton in Oxfordshire, wrote of believers that "it is their duty to teach and to instruct one another; the eye may help the hand; the foot ought to be helpful to the head."[83] John Murcot wrote that it "is doubtless a duty to communicate our experiences, and also to exhort one another while it is called today, as the Apostle hath it; and to reprove one another."[84] Many Congregational churches, including those of Bury and Bristol, came into existence in the 1640s through such conferences of lay believers, and some persisted for a time without having a formal ministerial presence.[85]

John Rogers of Dublin urged that it was "excellent to edification and consolation to tell what God hath done for thy soul. For hereby many receive benefit, and may meet with the like, and other comforts, who have met with the like." He expressed the hope that sharing experiences in the society of saints would become more common.[86] The army officer Richard Lawrence published a tract on gospel fellowship in 1657 in which he stated that "Christ wants his intelligencers to publish and tell of those expressions and passages which would tend to unite and endear differing Christians one to another."[87] The clergyman John Murcot wrote that "the saints may and ought to communicate their experiences to others... You may comfort others with the comforts wherewith yourselves are comforted of God; this is doubtless a duty, to communicate our experiences, and also to exhort one another."[88]

Edward Reynolds, a moderate puritan clergyman who would conform after the Restoration and be elevated to be bishop of Norwich, wrote of the value of sharing experiences. He wrote of how "several particular ingredients make up one cordial, and several instruments concur to the perfecting of one... and the beauty of everything ariseth out of the variety, and order, and mutual serviceableness that the parts thereof have unto one another," and how "so it is in the church too, which Christ hath so tempered together that they might all stand mutually in need of one another." "Therefore," he continued, "we find the saints in Scripture communicating to one another their experiences, temptations, deliverances, comforts, to their mutual edification."[89]

Valuing such experiences, Rogers and others published collections of them to reach and hopefully help a broader audience. Much of the Dublin clergyman's *Ohel, or Beth-shemesh: A Tabernacle for the Sun, or Irenicum Evangelicum* (London, 1653) consisted of narratives offered by members of his congregation.[90] Samuel Petto edited and published a collection of experiences, which he argued was a "means which we may expect the Lord will make successful unto the conversion of sinners," a means, he added, "which for many years have been denied" by the bishops. Beyond being of value for those not yet moved by the spirit, such experiences were, wrote Petto, helpful "for direction and encouragement to such as are in like conditions" to provoke others by showing them "what progress others have made in the ways of God, and what communion they have enjoyed with Christ," and "for confirmation and consolation to such as at great distance may be able to say that as face answereth to face in a glass, so do their experiences to these."[91] Women as well as men, and believers of all classes, shared their experiences. The sharing helped cement the bonds of the communities they were part of, and through the publication of the stories these laymen and laywomen were able to preach to the broader Christian community.[92] Vavasor Powell published a collection of *Spiritual Experiences of Sundry Beleevers held forth by them at severall solemn meetings and conferences* in which he spoke of experience as "one of the chiefest" ways of God's teaching, because "that which cometh from one spiritual heart reacheth another spiritual heart."[93]

The Congregational clergyman Richard Lawrence joined those who argued that "Christ wants his Intelligencers to publish and tell of those expressions and passages which would tend to unite and endear differing Christians one to another." He recognized, however, that the task of doing so was "a very unthankful one, where this spirit of Division hath found entertainment, though there it is most needed; and therefore until you open the door of a free participation of gifts and graces among Saints, expect no union."[94]

Threatening though the nation's drift into war had been, the events of the 1640s and 1650s offered the hope of a new dawn that puritans believed offered a chance to erect a truly godly kingdom. That hope energized many laymen and laywomen as well as clergy. They felt called upon to study the scripture, open their hearts to the promptings of the Spirit, and share their beliefs and experiences with fellow soldiers, churchgoers, and citizens. The conflict also offered such believers greater freedom to act on such callings than had been possible in the previous decades. The result was an unprecedented explosion of lay efforts to shape the nation's religious culture, and explosion celebrated by many while deplored by at least as many.

8
Varieties of Lay Enthusiasm in New England and England

The previous chapters have demonstrated the dynamic nature of lay puritanism, and it is that quality that allowed for the evolution from the movement itself of what most puritans branded heresies.[1] John Coffey has pointed out that "Presbyterians and Congregationalists, General and Particular Baptists, Seekers and Fifth Monarchists, Ranters and Quakers all emerged from the intense religious substructure of the godly."[2] Prophesyings, introspection and self-analysis, the sharing of experiences, and the interpretation of scripture through the grace of the Holy Spirit all drew on a mystical element in puritanism that carried with it a threat that individuals might place their personal understanding before communal understanding of the faith. According to David D. Hall the Free Grace Controversy in Massachusetts in some ways pointed to later controversies since "those who challenged outward behavior as evidence of inner grace could also challenge the practice of infant baptism, and from there move on to deny the objective basis of the ministry. The logic of Anne Hutchinson's spiritism pointed clearly in the direction of the Baptists and Quakers."[3] A similar development can be found in puritanism in England. A review of Baptists and Quakers on both sides of the Atlantic reveals many characteristics that justify identifying them as part of the mainstream puritan movement.

Studies of the Baptist experience in early New England generally depict the Baptists as a distinct religious group in opposition to colonial puritans. But looking at the subject from the point of view of lay empowerment reveals that in many respects Baptists *were* puritans who simply disagreed on the subject of infant baptism. No puritan believed that baptism was essential for salvation, and it was not uncommon for puritan congregations in the Netherlands and in Civil War England to contain a mixture of members who accepted the baptism of infants alongside those who rejected it.

There is little question but that many of those we identify as Baptists began their spiritual progress as puritans and the case can be made that those who opposed infant baptism while retaining Calvinist positions on salvation remained puritan. We have previously noted William Kiffin attending sermons preached by John Davenport and others in London, meeting and discussing matters of faith with a group of fellow apprentices in a puritan conference, and then emerging as a Baptist leader. The Southwark congregation that had been founded by Henry Jacob was led in the late 1630s by Henry Jessey. Jessey had met John Winthrop when he was chaplain to Winthrop's friend Brampton Gurdon in the 1620s. He remained a correspondent of Winthrop and his son John Jr., and became a supporter of the emerging New England Way. In 1638 six members of the congregation Jessey's church left that congregation to join one ed by John Spilsbury which practiced believers baptism. In 1644 one of the members of the Southwark church, Hanserd Knollys, refused to baptize his child. In the ensuing debates, Jessey defended the practice of infant baptism. But as the debate carried on over a period of weeks, the church sought the advice of London area Congregationalists, including Thomas Goodwin, Philip Nye and Sidrach Simpson. Those clergy advised that the church tolerate the members who would not present their children to be baptized—essentially creating a congregation that would accept members who believed in the practice as well as those who rejected it. In the following years many of the members, including Jessey, came to accept believers baptism.[4]

In 1644 seven London churches organized on the principle of adult believers baptism published the first English Baptist *Confession of Faith*. Gradually some of the churches founded on Baptist principles would limit membership to those who accepted believers' baptism. Most English Congregationalists welcomed the support of Baptists so long as they shared a Calvinist theological stance and were willing to join them in the Independent coalition against a Presbyterian state church. Because congregationalists did not see baptism as essential to salvation, they did not view Baptists as heretical. Thomas Edwards, who was a critic of all Independents, argued that toleration of different views on baptism had characterized the Congregational churches in Arnhem and Rotterdam. Speaking of the situation in Suffolk in the 1650s, the Congregationalist Samuel Petto wrote that "there are members in many, if not most, of the churches hereafter mentioned, who are doubtful about infant baptism, yet walk comfortably with their pastors and other members who hold forth in practice what they are dubious about." Henry Jessey and John Tombes were leading Baptists who were proponents of open communion, admitting those who disagreed with them to receive the Lord's Supper in their churches. Consequently, many Congregational churches accepted into their membership both those who believed in the practice and those who rejected it. The Congregationalists' 1658 Savoy *Declaration of Faith* was silent on the matter.[5]

While those referred to as Particular Baptists adhered to a belief in predestination, other Baptists (generally referred to as General Baptists) adopted a belief in universal redemption for those who entered a covenant with Christ through acceptance of believers baptism. This represented an abandonment of Calvinism that was beyond the pale. Baptists also divided over the necessity of a learned ministry. Particular Baptists were more likely to see a value in an educated ministry since many of their leaders, such as Jessey and Tombs, were university trained. Others, especially among General Baptists, saw no value in such training, with some going further and seeing it as a hindrance to grace. In their efforts to define the limits of acceptable belief and practice in the 1650s, English Congregationalists were generally content to view Particular Baptists as fellow puritans, members of the broader godly community, while usually identifying General Baptists as outside the perimeter fence.

Across the Atlantic, the evolution of Baptist views from within the puritan community is easy to trace because it is clear that many New Englanders who became Baptists had been members of puritan churches. Cotton Mather's account of the evolution of the New England Baptist movement located its origin in the effort that some had made to suppress the practice of prophesying. "These men," he wrote, "having privately exercised their gifts in meetings with applause, began to think themselves wronged when their light was put under a bushel, and finding no remedy in our churches, they threw on a cloak of Anabaptism, and so gained the thing that they aimed at in disguise."[6] This analysis might fall short as history, but it does indicate both how many of the second and third generation of New Englanders had come to harbor suspicions about lay prophesying and its consequences, and how central lay prophesying was to how many puritans understood their faith.

One of the first New Englanders to espouse Baptist views was John Clarke, an Englishman who had received some university education and studied medicine for a time, perhaps in Leiden. He emigrated to Massachusetts in November 1637, when the Free Grace controversy was at its height. Clarke sided with the dissidents and moved with them to Rhode Island, settling initially in Portsmouth. Following disruptions in that town he moved to Newport, where he assumed a leadership role. Like other puritan churches without a trained clergyman, the congregations in those towns functioned without an ordained minister. Both churches encouraged lay prophesying and discussion in their services. Thomas Lechford noted in 1642 that in the "town called Portsmouth...there is a meeting of some men, who there teach one another, and call it prophesy."[7] Clarke viewed prophesying as "a plain, and brief declaration of the mind and counsel of God, in words significantly and easily understood...and brought forth for the edification, exhortation, and comfort of the whole." He believed that spiritual discussions in church or separate conferences promoted greater understanding, writing that the Spirit would lead members "from truth to truth, until they be brought to all truth." Clarke maintained that all members of the congregation should be encouraged to prophesy during services. While taking the position that women should not raise questions during services, he did not exclude them from prophesying and accepted their participation in discussions of doctrine. While he did not believe that clergy had to be traditionally educated, he saw university education as desirable.[8]

None of these positions distinguished Clarke from the mainstream of puritan Congregationalism. But by 1644 he and his Newport congregation had come to the conclusion that infant baptism was unscriptural and that adult baptism required total immersion. While Roger Williams had briefly embraced Baptist views in 1639, the Newport church led by Clarke is properly considered the first true Baptist church in America. Over the following decades Clarke would assist other New Englanders seeking to worship as Baptists, and join with English advocates of toleration.

In December 1642 it became evident that Lady Deborah Moody, a well regarded English gentlewoman who had joined the Salem church two years previously, and whom John Winthrop referred to as "a wise and anciently religious woman," had come to doubt the validity of infant baptism, though she did not insist that the practice was clearly wrong. After various individuals failed to persuade her of the validity of the sacrament she decided to leave the colony to avoid further controversy. She ended up settling on Long Island, in the Dutch colony of New Netherland, where she eventually became a Quaker.[9]

While en route to New Netherland, Lady Moody stopped in New Haven to visit her friend, Anne Eaton, the wife of Theophilus Eaton, governor of the New Haven colony. The two women may first have encountered Baptist teaching when they knew each other in London, but they clearly discussed the ideas in New Haven, and Moody lent her friend a copy of Andrew Ritor's *A Treatise of the Vanity of Child-Baptism* (1642). Shortly thereafter, as John Davenport prepared to conduct an infant baptism in the New Haven church, Eaton rose up and left the congregation. Over the following weeks Davenport and his associate, William Hooke, as well as Theophilus Eaton, sought to dissuade her from her position, reviewing with her and (to their mind) refuting Ritor's arguments. While these discussions were ongoing, separate charges were leveled that Anne had treated members of her household—from her mother-in-law to servants—in an abusive fashion. She was eventually censured and excommunicated for that behavior. In the end neither the church nor the civil authorities dealt with her Baptist views and, while excluded from church services for her abusive behavior, she was allowed to continue as a member of the community and provided a seat just outside the meetinghouse where she could listen to sermons and prayers.[10]

The purpose of excommunication is commonly misunderstood. The laity who voted to cast a fellow member out of the church were not consigning them to the outer darkness forever. Indeed, this was generally the last in a series of admonitions that were intended to show the erring brother or sister the error of his or her ways and to lead them back to the church. In the 1640s the Boston church sent messengers to Rhode Island to persuade Anne Hutchinson and those who had left with her to rejoin their communion. Sarah Dudley Keayne, whom Stephen Winthrop had recorded having been a notorious street preacher in London, had returned to New England and been excommunicated from the Boston church for "irregular prophesying in mixed assemblies," but was later reintegrated into the community. Indeed, most laymen who were excommunicated were eventually brought back to the church.

Other individuals, less noteworthy than Lady Moody and Anne Eaton, also embraced Baptist views. Thomas Painter was a laborer and member of the Hingham church when he refused to allow his wife to bring their child to be baptized in 1644. William Witter of Salem was first presented to the county court for claiming that it was sinful to baptize infants and calling the sacrament the "badge of the whore" in February of 1644.[11] In response to the evidence that Baptists views were spreading (or perhaps to its appeal to lower classes), the Massachusetts General Court passed a law in November 1644 against those who maintained the position. Citing how "experience hath plentifully and often proved since the first rising of the Anabaptists about a hundred years since, they have been the incendiaries of commonwealths, and the infectors of persons in the main matters of religion, and the troublemakers of churches in all places where they have been," the court ordered that if any person openly condemned "or oppose the baptizing of infants, or go about secretly to seduce others from the approbation or use thereof, or shall purposely depart the congregation at the administration of the ordinance," should be banished if they do not repent.[12] Implied in the law was the association of Anabaptism with the effort to establish a communal sectarian government in the German city of Munster in the 1530s, which led to a violent rebellion.

The English clergymen Jessey and Tombes, both of whom had strong connections to a number of prominent New Englanders, wrote to the "officers of the churches of Christ in New England" in 1645, arguing that the colonial actions against the Baptists were not the will of God. Jessey also provided his correspondents with a copy of Tombes's response to a 1644 sermon of Stephen Marshall attacking Baptist principles.[13]

It may be noted that New Haven, where John Davenport was more willing to consider Anabaptism something appropriate to be discussed, never passed a law against it. Nor did Connecticut.[14] There is no evidence that Plymouth passed legislation against Baptists and this roused the ire of Massachusetts, the Bay's General Court sending a letter to the Plymouth authorities in 1649 complaining that they had "heard heretofore of divers Anabaptists arisen up in your jurisdiction," and that recently "there have been at Seekonk thirteen or fourteen persons rebaptized" without the authorities doing anything about it. They feared that "the infection of such diseases, being so near us, are likely to spread into our jurisdiction." But there was no action taken by Plymouth.[15]

William Witter evidently traveled from Salem to Newport to be baptized in the church there presided over by John Clarke. In 1651 Clarke, together with two other members of that church, Obadiah Holmes and John Crandall, journeyed to Massachusetts to rebaptize some friends of Witter. Arrested by the authorities after holding a private religious service, and brought to Boston, they were tried before Governor John Endecott and the Council, found guilty of various offenses and sentenced to pay fines or be whipped. The fines were paid for Clarke and Crandall but Holmes was adamant and received thirty lashes.[16]

The remainder of the 26 individuals identified as Anabaptists in Massachusetts for the period between 1639 and 1654 were, like those discussed above, originally members of puritan congregations.[17] In addition, John Cotton contended that he knew of many who silently had doubts about infant baptism but did not espouse them publicly. Some were won back to orthodoxy, while others persisted in their views or went on to embrace more radical positions. Perhaps the most famous of those who did express and retain an opposition to infant baptism was Henry Dunster. A member of the Cambridge, Massachusetts church whose "confession" was carefully recorded by Thomas Shepard, Dunster was the president of Harvard College who put that institution on the right path after a rocky beginning. He was responsible for the building of a new college building at Harvard for the education of Native Americans. His reputation as a Hebrew scholar led to a role in the composition of the *Bay Psalm Book*. But he came to question the practice of infant baptism and consequently refused to present an infant son for the sacrament. Although the Massachusetts General Court had passed a law allowing for the banishment of Baptists, many of New England's puritan leaders were willing to tolerate those who had adopted these views so long as they did not try to proselytize. Dunster's position as head of the college—and thus responsible for theological education— made this difficult, and clerical friends tried to persuade him of the error of his ways, or at least to avoid espousing them, to the point of having someone else discuss the sacrament with the students. Because he was not willing to go that far, he resigned in October 1654. Some of his former students recommended him to Henry Cromwell, who offered him a ministerial post in Ireland, but he declined. After a brief stay in Charlestown he settled in the town of Scituate, in the Plymouth Colony, where he preached on occasion until his death in 1659, though most of the Plymouth churches, as well as those of Massachusetts, espoused infant baptism.[18]

Earlier, in 1638, Charles Chauncy, formerly lecturer in Hebrew and Greek at Trinity College, Cambridge and a respected member of the East Anglian puritan brotherhood, had settled in the town of Plymouth in the colony of that name. Chauncy believed that baptism should be by full immersion, not sprinkling (as most puritans practiced), and that the Lord's Supper should only be celebrated in the evening. While the Plymouth colonists accepted immersion as lawful they were not willing to practice it, believing—as Governor Bradford expressed it—that it was not convenient in the cold climate of New England. In 1641 Chauncy moved on to Scituate, in the same colony, where the church was split over his views.[19] It is interesting that when Dunster resigned as Harvard president he was replaced by Chauncy while Dunster settled in Scituate.

While William McLoughlin, the foremost historian of the early Baptists in Massachusetts, believed that the Baptist doctrine of "further light" distinguished them from other puritans and was the cause of much of the opposition, that distinction is too simple.[20] There were more similarities than differences between the Baptists and the puritan majority, and the fact is that many puritans who believed in infant baptism also believed in the notion of a further light. This is why some New Englanders, and many English Congregationalists were unwilling to unequivocally reject the Baptist position as heretical.

The 1644 law against the Baptists represented the triumph of those Bay colonists who believed in a more rigid definition of what was acceptable to discuss. But it also revealed how conflicted the New Englanders were over how Baptists should be treated. Stephen Winthrop, John's son, who was in England, wrote that there was "great complaint against us for our [New England's] severity against the Baptists," and John Winthrop's nephew George Downing wrote of "the law of banishment for conscience which makes us stink everywhere."[21] In October 1645 a petition by various laymen, including Emmanuel Downing, Nehemiah Bourne, Robert Sedgwick, Thomas Fowle, and others requested that the law be repealed, citing the "offence taken thereat by many godly in England." Many members of the Court, likely including John Winthrop, were in favor of at least suspending the law for a time, but a group of the clergy, protesting the "advantage it would give to the Anabaptists (who began to increase very fast through the country here), and much more in England (where they had gathered divers churches, and taught openly, and published a confession of their faith) petitioned that the law be kept in force." The clergy stated, however, that they "disliked not that all leniency and patience should be used for convincing and reclaiming such Anabaptist erroneous persons." But many others were fearful of any leniency and in May 1646 "seventy seven inhabitants of this colony" petitioned the court, "humbly requesting all due strengthening and keeping in force such laws" against the Anabaptists.[22]

The authorities in the Bay continued to take action against Baptists when faced with challenges that could not be ignored. Christopher Goodwin of Charlestown expressed his opposition to infant baptism by throwing down the basin of water in the meetinghouse. William Witter continued to speak out. He was called before the General Court for stating that the members of the congregation who stayed for a child to be baptized were worshipping the Devil. But there wasn't a great deal of enthusiasm for taking action against the Baptists, perhaps because it was recognized that many colonists were opposed to such actions. Thus, when Witter failed to respond to his summons the magistrates passed over his noncompliance.[23] In the following decades the sect would gradually win acceptance in Massachusetts.

The relationship of Quakerism to puritanism is more complex, though many historians recognize that faith as having roots in the puritan community. At the time, Richard Baxter argued that Quakerism sprang from a variety of sources, including both Grindletonianism but also "in New England Mrs. Hutchinson and Mr. Wheeler [Wheelwright]."[24] But the recognized foundations of the faith were laid in England. Recently, David Como has pointed out that the "features of Quaker worship can be seen to have emerged, sometimes dialectically and as a result of internal dispute, from within the bosom of the godly community over the preceding decades."[25] The description Richard Sibbes gave of puritan conferencing in the 1620s evokes thoughts of the dynamics of Quaker meetings, in which various members would share and build on one another's inspirations from the Inner Light. Sibbes wrote of how "one thing draws on another, and that draws on another, till at length the soul be warmed and kindled with the consideration and meditation of heavenly things."[26] The minister of the parish church where George Fox worshipped as a youth was a supporter of the parliamentary cause and likely a puritan.[27] Individual Quakers—including James Nayler and Francis Howgill—had worshipped in puritan congregations. James Nayler had served in the New Model Army and had been one of the soldier-preachers in that force. He later wrote that up until he had left the army for health reasons in 1651 he had been an Independent.[28] Moving forward, Nayler, like other Quakers from similar backgrounds, had some success in drawing converts from English Congregational churches.

It was George Fox who is regarded as the primary founder of the Quaker movement, although at the time Nayler was equally prominent. In 1643, shortly after his 19th birthday, Fox had left his home and embarked on a search for religious truth. After much seeking and discussing matters of faith with clergy and laymen of various views, in 1647 he heard a voice saying, "there is one, even Jesus Christ, that can speak to thy condition."[29] He came to believe that God was present in all men—an inner light—to guide them through his inspiration. Knowledge of God's will did not require the teaching of ministers or reading the scriptures.

Though powered by the puritan belief in the individual's responsibility to be open and responsive to the inspiration of the Spirit, Quakerism challenged much of what most puritans viewed as orthodoxy and did so with a militancy that seemed particularly dangerous. Perhaps the most critical point separating the Quakers from other puritans was their interpretation of the workings of the Spirit. Whereas the majority of puritans believed that the inspiration of the Spirit was a means to apprehend the truth of the scriptures and could not lead to conclusions that contradicted the scripture, Quakers saw their inner light as the ultimate authority and guide, superseding scripture when there was a clash. Another way to put this is that whereas puritans believed that the guidance of the Spirit provided insight into what God had revealed in the past through the scriptures, Quakers believed that revelation itself continued into their own times. It is true that Fox became concerned about the most anarchic possibilities inherent in these beliefs, and warned his followers to "go not out from the spirit of God." He encouraged Quakers to test their insights against those received by others in meetings of Friends, just as puritans used conferences to share their insights into the meaning of scripture. But the individualism and enthusiasm of the Quakers was hard to control. Quakers were the epitome of lay preachers, with each individual empowered and feeling compelled to spread the message of the inner light that he or she had received. Not only did Quakers reject a formal ministry, they rejected the external sacraments. Reacting to Quaker challenges, English Congregationalists emphasized fundamentals of faith and catechizing their followers in them.

Fox's followers became known as "Quakers" because of their physical trembling and moving as they experienced the light of God. On the basis of the inner light they challenged numerous social conventions of English society, particularly those that were signs of deference to one's betters. This and the efforts of Quaker laity to spread their truth by disrupting the religious services of other groups, led to their persecution and imprisonment. Though Fox met with Oliver Cromwell in 1654 and impressed the Lord Protector with his sincerity, this did little to halt the arrest of Quakers, whose anti-Trinitarian views were considered beyond the pale and whose behavior disrupted public order. They were prosecuted under the Blasphemy Act of 1650, charged with violating the proclamation of 1655 against disrupting public worship and also with refusing to take the oath (oaths being against their beliefs) abjuring papal authority.[30]

For many puritans the threat from the Quakers was spotlighted by the behavior and beliefs of James Nayler. A charismatic leader whose popularity rivaled that of Fox, Nayler gathered strong support, especially among women, some of whom began to disrupt other Quaker meetings. In October 1656, having repudiated Fox's efforts to heal the breech between them, Nayler entered the city of Bristol mounted on a horse, with his companions casting garments before him and chanting "Holy, holy, holy, Lord God of Sabbaoth." To many observers it seemed to be an entrance into the city modeled after that of Christ into Jerusalem. It appeared that his followers were reacting to him as if he was himself divine, that he was in essence moving from believing that Christ was within him to asserting that he was Christ. In the eyes of the orthodox, no more outrageous example could be found of individual inspiration run wild. Though Nayler himself denied that he believed himself to be Christ come again, it does appear that he had not done anything to discourage his followers from treating him as such. He was tried before Parliament, which narrowly defeated a motion to execute him, but sentenced him to be whipped (with three hundred lashes), exposed in the pillory, have his tongue bored, and "B" for blasphemy branded on his head. He was incarcerated and not released till a general amnesty for Quakers in 1659. He died shortly thereafter. The mainstream Quaker movement acted quickly to disassociate itself from the extremes of Nayler and his followers.[31]

The initial reaction of New Englanders to the Quaker movement was to link the movement to troubling incidents in their recent past. Roger Clap was one of the surviving settlers of the first generation who saw a connection between the Hutchinsonian party of the 1630s and the Friends, saying that the earlier Bay dissidents had been "much like the Quakers." The Hutchinsonians would, he remembered, "talk of the Spirit and of revelations of the Spirit without the word."[32] According to Cotton Mather, albeit writing decades later, "most of the Quakers that I have had occasion to converse with were first Anabaptists."[33] This certainly reflected the beliefs of many orthodox puritans, who saw a progression from the one heresy to the other.

Unlike the Baptists, who were, in essence, fellow church members who had become convinced of the error of infant baptism, the early Quakers who came to New England were for the most part strangers.[34] Sarah Gibbons and seven other English Friends arrived in Boston in August 1656. They were questioned, placed in prison, and banished. While Daniel Boorstin's characterization of the Quakers as individuals who had come to Massachusetts "in quest of punishment," is too simple and too harsh, there is no denying that Quakers saw experiencing suffering not only as a witness to Christ but as a means of gaining sympathy and support for their cause.[35] Whereas previous exiles from Massachusetts had stayed away once banished, Quakers came back.

Gibbons and others returned in 1657. There was a steady arrival of Quaker missionaries moving between Barbados, New Amsterdam, Rhode Island, and Massachusetts. As was the case in England, they disrupted church meetings by interrupting sermons and confronting clergymen. One report claimed that Gibbons and Dorothy Waugh confronted John Norton during a service, smashing a bottle as a sign of Norton's spiritual emptiness.[36] If true it is hardly surprising that Norton became one of the most vociferous critics of the Quakers.

Faced with the Quaker refusal to accept simple banishment, the colonial authorities passed further legislation against the sect. Massachusetts enacted a law in 1656 stipulating that Quakers were to be whipped and incarcerated while awaiting deportation. Mary Dyer, who had been a follower of Anne Hutchinson and newly a Quaker, arrived in Boston in 1657. She was not subjected to whipping since she claimed she had not known of the statute, but was banished and returned to Rhode Island, where she had settled. New Haven passed a law in 1657 that "no Quaker, Ranter, or other heretic of that sort be suffered to come into nor abide in this jurisdiction." But this did not mean that colonial clergy did not try to persuade Quakers of the errors of their way. Humphrey Norton, an English Quaker, arrived in the New Haven colony in 1658, disrupted a church service in Southold, and "slandered and reproached" the clergyman, John Youngs, "together with his ministry and all our ministers and ordinances." He was arrested and tried in New Haven, where John Davenport attempted to debate with him. Refusing to engage the clergyman, Norton was convicted, whipped, branded with an "H" for heretic on his hand, and sent out of the colony. But shortly thereafter the colony's General Court moderated its laws, allowing Quakers to come into the colony on business and prohibiting only efforts to proselytize.[37]

Faced with the ongoing Quaker challenge, the Commissioners of the United Colonies of New England had recommended that the individual colonies consider the death penalty for members of the sect who kept returning from banishment. Massachusetts, urged on by John Wilson and John Norton, was the only colony to enact such legislation. In October 1659 Marmaduke Stevenson, William Robinson, Nicholas Davis, and Mary Dyer were sentenced to death, though Dyer was given a reprieve at the last moment. But she too was executed when she challenged the law again in 1660, and William Ledra became the last Quaker hung in the Bay in 1661, following which Charles II ordered a halt to executions. There were some puritans who questioned the harshness employed by Massachusetts. The Boston merchant John Hull observed that "in those parts of the country [New England] where they might with freedom converse (as in Rhode Island...) they take no pleasure to be," whereas in Massachusetts "they seemed to suffer patiently, and take a kind of pleasure in it." Learning of the execution of the three Quaker men in Boston in 1659, John Davenport expressed the wish that the authorities had accepted an offer made by Thomas Temple to carry the Quakers away at his own expense. "The Quakers," he wrote, "would have feared that kind of banishment more than hanging, it being a real cutting themselves off from all opportunities and liberty of doing hurt in the colony by gaining proselytes, which would have been more bitter than death to them."[38]

Despite Hull's observation, Rhode Island became a haven for Quakers. A 1659 Quaker tract referred to Rhode Island as "the habitation of the hunted Christ."[39] And it was there that the sect gained a strong foothold. And it was primarily in Rhode Island that colonists who had been members of the region's churches were won over to the new faith.

The story of the influx of aggressive Quakers into New England and their treatment there accentuates the differences between the two groups. But attention to the external relations between Quakers and puritans can obscure the real inner connections that existed.[40] The evolution of puritanism into Quakerism can be examined in the cases of two members of the colonial establishment. Samuel Winthrop was one of the sons of John and Margaret Winthrop. He attended Harvard but left before graduation, apprenticing briefly with a merchant in the Canary Islands and then settling as a sugar planter and merchant on Antigua. Surrounded by Catholics in the Canary Islands and without an adequate ministry on the Caribbean island, Samuel was accustomed to nurturing his faith through private readings of scripture and then family devotions. He appealed to his brother, John Winthrop Jr., for help in securing a clergyman for the island, but to no avail. At some point in the 1660s Samuel encountered a Quaker missionary, perhaps Jonas Langford, and found in his teachings an expression of the piety and reliance on the Spirit comparable to and compatible with the faith he had been raised in. Winthrop became a leader of the Quaker community in that part of the Caribbean, and met George Fox in Barbados. Despite his embracing of Quakerism he never lost his affection for New England and his ties with his family and friends there remained intact.[41]

William Coddington was a prosperous member of John Cotton's English parish who had gone to prison for refusing to contribute to Charles I's so-called "Forced Loan." He emigrated to Massachusetts and became a prominent merchant, an assistant in the Bay Colony government, and the colonial treasurer. Coddington was a member of the Free Grace party and voluntarily left the Bay when Anne Hutchinson was banished, founding the Rhode Island town of Portsmouth. When religious disputes divided that town he moved on to Newport. After the two settlements were reconciled he became governor of the joint towns. Subsequently he quarreled with Samuel Gorton and resisted uniting with the towns of Providence and Warwick under a charter granted to Roger Williams in 1644. Eventually Coddington was reconciled to Williams and in the 1660s assumed the governorship of Rhode Island. By that time he had, like some others who had followed Hutchinson, become a Quaker. Yet he had reestablished strong relations with some of the puritan leaders of the region, engaging in correspondence with Connecticut's John Winthrop Jr. and others.

Following the harsh treatment of Quakers by the Massachusetts authorities, Coddington in 1672 reflected on how some of the leaders of the Bay colony had departed from their early principles. He wrote a letter to three of his former friends in the Massachusetts leadership—Richard Bellingham, William Hathorne, and Simon Bradstreet—in which he lamented how they, Hathorne and Bradstreet in particular, had ceased to possess the "tenderness in you (for I have known you both long... above this forty five years)" and gone "so far to degenerate from Christianity to hardness and cruelty." He included John Endecott, deceased when he was writing, as another who had abandoned early tenderness towards those whom he might have differences with. He reminded Hathorne of how when they sailed together for America "in the ship I know thou wast tender, serious and retired, as became the Gospel of Christ (for I had speech with thee many times)." "Then and afterward," he recalled, Hathorne had given "testimony against persecution, and stinting or limiting the spirit of prophecy in any, viz., to refrain from preaching but by allowance of certain persons." According to Coddington, at the time Hathorne had argued that "if that should take place in New England thou lookest at it as one of the most horrid acts as ever was done in New England." And yet, now, decades later, it was, Coddington wrote, "the day of God's appearance in his sons and daughters in pouring out his spirit, so they must prophesy, and who could withhold the work of the Lord?" and Hathorne was among those who sought to suppress the prophets.[42]

While reminding his old friends of how John Cotton had spoken of grace and the need to magnify it and draw on it as a teacher, Coddington was harsh in his recollection of how "a persecuting Spirit arose" among the majority of the clergy, whom he referred to as "priests," who demanded that "Anne Hutchinson and John Wheelwright must be banished, and all that stood in their way must remove, and the unclean spirit like frogs came out of the mouth of the false prophet, so that persecution was ushered in." Coddington, "as a man and a Christian...would have no hand in it" and left the colony. He had particularly harsh words for John Norton, whom he saw as a key figure in urging harsh treatment of Quakers in the 1650s and 1660s. Towards the end of his letter he asked his former friends to "consider that forty five years past thou didst own such a suffering people, that now thou dost persecute; they were against Bishops and ceremonies and the conformable priests; they were the seed of God that did serve him in spirit, then called Puritans, now called Quakers."[43] From Coddington's perspective the persecution of Quakers in Massachusetts was a reflection of how leaders of that colony had turned against the expressions of lay piety and enthusiasm upon which New England had been founded. It is hard to see a Humphrey Norton or a Marmaduke Stevenson as part of the New England puritan community. But the lives of Samuel Winthrop and William Coddington serve to remind us of what puritans and Quakers shared.

Rhode Island was the colony in which the diverse nature of puritanism most clearly flourished. In addition to John Clarke and his fellow Baptists, and William Coddington and other Quakers, the story of the multiple possibilities inherent in puritanism can be illustrated by the stories of Samuel Gorton and Roger Williams.

Gorton was one of the more contentious figures to spend time in Rhode Island. Though he never attended university, Gorton knew several languages and had some knowledge of the law. As a London merchant in the 1620s he was influenced by the vital religious culture of the capital, and embraced a mystical version of puritanism. He came to believe in universal redemption, and denied the literal existence of heaven and hell. Gorton emigrated to New England in 1636 and settled in the Plymouth colony, where he was soon banished for his teachings, his disrespect of authority, and his use of force in disciplining one of his servants. He next settled near Portsmouth, in Rhode Island, but there he became embroiled in a controversy with William Coddington, and was again expelled. In 1641 he was living near Providence, where he gathered a following with his lay preaching. Roger Williams asserted that Gorton claimed a direct inspiration from the Holy Spirit independent of scripture. He soon moved again, settling with his followers near Warwick.[44] His followers also expressed themselves forcefully, one female claiming that she was a prophetess and must prophesy in the same words as Ezekiel.[45]

Responding to complaints from natives who claimed Gorton had cheated them of the land on which he settled, the Bay sent an expeditionary force that seized the group and tried them in Massachusetts. Gorton was convicted for blasphemy because of his "dreadful and damnable errors." He and his followers were sentenced to hard labor in scattered Massachusetts towns, but when it was feared that they were spreading their opinions they were released and encouraged to depart the colony. Gorton soon journeyed to England, where he published *Simplicities Defence Against Seven-Headed Policy* (1646), which was an attack on New England intolerance. Edward Winslow, in England representing the colonies, responded in *Hypocrisie Unmasked* (1646), but Gorton won supporters in the radical elements of the London puritan movement and among some members of Parliament. In his response to Winslow, Gorton argued that he held his "call to preach... not inferior to the call of any minister in the country," accusing the educated clergy of "ground[ing] the preaching of the Gospel upon humane principles to the falsifying of the word of God."[46] Through the support of Parliamentary supporters he was able to return to New England in 1648. There he remained till his death in 1677. He continued to write against colonial practices and to advance his own ideas. He was sympathetic to the Quakers. Not only did he preach, but he encouraged prophesying by his followers, writing at one time that they "speak by revelation, by knowledge, by prophecying."

Roger Williams was another puritan who sought his own path. After his departure from Massachusetts in 1635 he founded a settlement that would become Providence, Rhode Island. He briefly embraced Baptist teachings in 1639, but within months concluded that it was impossible to form a pure church till Christ returned. He subsequently did not participate in organized worship for the remainder of his life. This contributed to his willingness to tolerate other groups that sought refuge along the Narragansett Bay, though he quarreled with some, including Samuel Gorton. He journeyed to England on more than one occasion and there befriended some of the more radical members of the Independents, including John Milton. While in England he published attacks on New England intolerance, particularly *The Bloody Tenent of Persecution* (1644) and *The Bloody Tenent, Yet More Bloody* (1652), the latter being a response to John Cotton's answer to the former work. His contacts in England aided him in gaining a charter for Rhode Island. After the Restoration, Williams's ally John Clarke gained a new charter from King Charles II that explicitly guaranteed religious liberty. Williams is often viewed as a clergyman because of his early ministerial career, but his preaching at Salem and Plymouth was as a lay preacher by way of prophesying, and after 1640 he held no church position. In 1672 he emerged from relative obscurity in order to debate and seek to refute Quaker ideas that were popular in Rhode Island.

The antagonism between Williams and the New England puritan establishment is a commonplace in studies of the period, and there is no denying the fact of his banishment from Massachusetts and his published clashes with John Cotton over the issue of toleration. But as in other cases we have examined, the boundaries are not as clear as they might at first appear. In the years after he departed from Massachusetts he retained a friendship and correspondence not only with John Winthrop but with other members of the Winthrop family. And he played a key role as an intermediary between the other colonies and native Americans.

Scholars have long had a difficult time defining exactly what puritanism was. The boundary between dividing non-puritan reformers in the Church of England and those who can best be understood as puritans is a difficult one to establish with certainty. But what is often neglected is that at the other end of the spectrum of beliefs, deciding the boundary between "puritans" and more radical reformers such as Baptists, Quakers, Gortonists, and Fifth Monarchists is no easier. If, as is becoming more common among historians, we focus on the movement as one fueled by the type of temperament and dynamic striving that characterized the individual saint's struggle to reform himself, the church, and the world, it becomes easier to understand a John Clarke, Samuel Winthrop, and Roger Williams as puritans. Similarly, an emphasis on the spiritist or mystical element in the teachings of many whom we call puritans forces us to recognize the continuities between conservative puritanism and the more extreme expressions of the movement. Such considerations explain why the struggle to better define what the movement was about was as much a challenge for those who were puritans as well as those who now study them.

9
Responding to the Challenges of Diversity, 1640–60

If the eyes of all Englishmen, or at least English puritans, had followed the shaping of the New England Way in the 1630s, the eyes of the colonists were focused on the extraordinary expressions of lay involvement in religion during the decades of England's Interregnum. In addition to offering their own advice on how their native land should be reformed, the colonists had to deal with the charge that it was New England that was the source of the heresies of the day, while also dealing with the importation of ideas that many considered threatened the order of the churches that they had established. Meanwhile, English Congregationalists, freed from the threat of a Presbyterian national church, were challenged to develop their own course for advancing a reformed kingdom. If the main focus of earlier puritanism had been defining itself against Roman Catholicism and the remnants of that faith found in the Church of England, the new need was to come to terms with radical puritanism.

Some puritans on both sides of the Atlantic who had embraced the role of the laity in church affairs came to fear that unregulated lay enthusiasm could lead (and to some extent had led) to religious anarchy and the spread of heresy. New Englanders attempted, as previously noted, to set limits on dissent by legislation against Baptists and Quakers, and many English Congregationalists would support measures such as the Blasphemy Act of 1648. But puritans were also concerned with taking steps to prevent such heresies in the future and were divided over the extent to which achieving that goal required formal changes to the nature of congregational practices, or whether the churches could still be relied upon to regulate themselves.

The period of the 1640s and 1650s saw the fragmentation of the old puritan reform movement. It was a time when some, as expressed by

John Morrill, had "an itch to impose their own certainties on others, or rather the godly's involuntary reflex to punish the enemies of God, before God punished the godly for not punishing them."[1] This was an itch felt alike by some conservatives and some radicals. But if some worked to create ways of imposing their certainties, there were also individuals who sought to find accommodation of different views. Emphasizing that perspective, Joel Halcomb has perceptively pointed out that "at the very center of the congregational idea was a belief that walking together despite differences allowed the Spirit to guide the congregation towards further mutual revelation. Congregationalists were anxious to maintain an ongoing conversation between members with different doctrinal understandings."[2]

The Congregationalist clergyman Richard Lawrence (son-in-law of William Bridge) expressed this when he argued that "if Christians would make that which tends most to answer the ends of hearing, (*viz*. the nourishment, edification and comfort of their souls the rule of hearing," divisions would cease to exist. He stated that

> if gracious persons, different-minded, did but sometimes meet to pour out their Souls to the Lord together in prayer, for their joint concernments, and to taste the preciousness of each others experiences, and graces by a mutual communication of spiritual gifts, it would much tend to remove uncharitable jealousies; and endear their hearts one to another.

Citing Acts 11.17, he wrote,

> From which scripture you may clearly gather that it was both Peter's and the believing Jews opinion, that such ought to own and esteem each other as fellow-brethren in the Gospel of Christ, whom God had granted the same precious gifts and graces unto. And I may say, it is impossible for Christians ever to come to an union in things wherein they differ, until they come to a Communion in things wherein they agree.[3]

One of those who agreed with such a stand was Oliver Cromwell, who from the first days of his military career had refused to reject godly soldiers because of particular doctrinal beliefs. His openness to further truths being bestowed on believers and his belief that unity could exist in the cause without uniformity attracted some believers.[4] In his 1653 speech convening the Nominated Parliament, Cromwell beseeched the members to have a care of the whole flock! Love the sheep, love the lambs; love all, tender all, cherish and countenance all, in all things that are good. And if the poorest Christian, the most mistaken Christian, shall desire to live peaceably and quietly under you—I say, if any shall desire but to lead a life in godliness and honesty, let him be protected.[5]

And in what was in essence a defense of lay prophesying and preaching, he stated that "it will be found an unjust and unwise jealousy, to deny a man the liberty he hath by nature [to preach the gospel], upon a supposition he may abuse it. When he doth abuse it, judge."[6]

The Lord Protector was not alone. It was said of John Simpson of All Hallows, London that "He loved no man upon the account of opinion, but upon the account of union with Christ." Thomas Ewins of Bristol wrote that "whether he be Presbyterian, Independent, Baptized, etc., ... wherever I see the image of Christ appear (which is love and holiness) there I desire to love and honor."[7] The Middlesex clergyman William Bartlett wrote that "those of the Congregational Way are content to receive such into communion and church fellowship ... that differ from them in their judgment in things of lesser consequence and moment."[8] John Cook wrote that for the Congregational Independent, it was important that "heads not breed differences in hearts."[9] Statements such as these reflect an openness shared with many but not all puritans to accept that their understanding might yet be enhanced by further light, a position which Baillie had criticized as a "principle of mutability, whereby they profess their readiness to change any of their present tenets."[10] In their *Apologetical Narration*, the Dissenting Brethren had set forth as their "most sacred law" to alter any practices they "discovered to be taken up out of a mis-understanding of the rule."[11]

In his *A Treatise of Justification* (1642), John Goodwin set forth what John Coffey has called "a *progressive Reformation* vision, seeing the Reformation as an ongoing theological adventure that might lead to significant doctrinal and ecclesiastical development."[12] This was similar to the viewpoint of his predecessor at St. Stephen's Coleman Street, the New Haven clergyman John Davenport. Davenport believed that over time, and during his own lifetime, Christians would, with the aid of the Spirit, grow in awareness of the truth. Reform was incremental and only gradually would people move toward perfect understanding. Like his friend and fellow New Englander John Cotton, Davenport anticipated a Middle Advent that would come before the millennium, a time when there would be an explosion of supernatural power that would bring humanity closer to the truth, but not to the final destination.[13] The Middle Advent was an idea that had been advanced by Thomas Brightman in his *Apocalypsis Apocalypeos*, first published in Frankfort in 1609 and available in an English translation in 1611. Thomas Hooker's belief in lay authority in the church was based on a belief, also derived from Brightman, that "these are the times when people shall be fitted to do all that God wished."[14] God was, in the words of one of Samuel Hartlib's correspondents, constantly in "conference with the Spirit of man" with the result being a gradual progress toward perfection as opposed to more dramatic millenarian scenarios.[15] Such puritans were more open to discussion of views that other colonists viewed as beyond the pale. For Davenport this was evident in his willingness to engage Anne Hutchinson leading up to and during her trial, and his treatment of Anne Eaton for her religious views. In later years he would show sympathy for New England's Baptists.

But what happened when ideas that some saw as further light went beyond the limits that others in the group were willing to accept? Minor differences were to be tolerated and discussed in the hope that a common understanding of truth would emerge, but what if the difference was felt to be too significant to live with? Surely some ideas were too dangerous to tolerate.

English critics of Independency complained that Congregationalism was incapable of suppressing dangerous ideas or controlling divisions. The New England Way was blamed for the Free Grace controversy centering on Anne Hutchinson. But it wasn't only the history of the colonies that Presbyterians looked to for signs of the flaws of Congregationalism. Thomas Edwards pointed to the dispute between Sidrach Simpson and William Bridge that had divided the Rotterdam church.[16] And, of course, there were plenty of examples of lay puritans running to extremes in the events transpiring in England itself in the 1640s and 1650s.

Many were drawn to Presbyterianism in the hope that it offered a better means of suppressing dangerous ideas. Such errors were seen as arising from allowing too much power to ordinary lay believers; the greater control over the laity in a Presbyterian order was seen as desirable. Some New England clergy would have welcomed the extension of a Presbyterian national church to America, and reports of sectarian excesses in England gave ammunition for New England clergy who sought to curtail lay power and increase their own authority. James Noyse and Thomas Parker, the Newbury, Massachusetts clergymen, had advocated Presbyterian-style reforms as early as 1643. Noyse expressed his views in *Moses and Aaron*, which was published in 1656, five years after his death. In it he complained that congregationalism was too democratic, and that the colonists had erred in allowing laymen the power of the keys.[17]

While it was useful for such critics to associate Congregationalists with the more extreme views circulating at the time, in point of fact Congregationalists in both England and New England were clear that there were limits to what should be tolerated. They accepted the need for a perimeter fence separating ideas and practices that were tolerable and those that were not.[18] Some puritans, Oliver Cromwell being one such individual whom we have discussed, wished the boundary set wide enough to allow the considerable exercise of different searches for truth. Others, such as some of those who led the campaign against Anne Hutchinson in Massachusetts, believed that their understanding was close enough to the truth—if not actually identical—that little freedom for further explorations was necessary, and that it was appropriate to act against any contrary viewpoints. The diversity of puritanism was reflected not only in the proliferation of sects, but in the disputes within puritan communities over how diverse ideas should be dealt with. It can also be said that the different circumstances that colonial believers and their allies across the Atlantic found themselves in at this time led most New Englanders to set their perimeter fence more closely while English Congregationalists set theirs more broadly.

During these decades those New Englanders who sought to place strict limits on dissent took a variety of steps to strengthen the control of the government over religious affairs and to enhance the authority of the clergy as guardians of orthodoxy. In 1646 the General Court, "seeing that the word is of general and common behoof to all sorts of people, as being the ordinary means to subdue the hearts of hearers, not only to the faith and obedience of the Lord Jesus Christ, but also to civil obedience and allegiance unto magistracy," ordered that every person must attend services on the Lord's Day and on all public fast days and days of thanksgiving, though making clear that it was not compelling individuals to join the churches, nor to force them to participate in the ceremonies of worship. Early in the region's history ministers were supported by the voluntary contributions of church members, something many saw as an essential feature of congregationalism. In 1644 the Commissioners of the United Colonies of New England had called for due maintenance of the clergy in all of the colonies, but it was not until 1654 that the Massachusetts General Court, stating that "it highly tends to the advancement of the gospel that the ministry be comfortably maintained," and that it was "the duty of the civil power to use all lawful means for the attaining of that end," ordered that the County Courts establish what maintenance was to be given to clergy "where towns had not already provided, and that they assess and the local constables collect funds for that purpose."[19] One consequence of this was to make ministerial salaries less dependent on the approval of lay congregants.

In a 1642 law Massachusetts had required all families to provide catechizing for the family members and household servants at least once a week. This reflected traditional puritan concerns for religious instruction in lay households by members of the family, legislating what had been a voluntary expression of lay piety. By the 1650s a movement had begun to place catechizing under the supervision of the clergy. Because heads of households were presumably neglecting their responsibility, clergymen began to take charge. At first they would seek to supplement what was being done in the household. Then, it increasingly became the practice for clergy to hold "public" sessions under the minister's supervision. In the mid-1660s Charles Chauncy recommended that clergy should "catechize every Lord's day in the afternoon, so as to go through the catechism once a year."[20] Regardless of whether this may have resulted from the failure of heads of household to assume their responsibilities, the effect was to shift the shaping of doctrinal truth from lay believers to clerical shepherds.

The Massachusetts authorities were conflicted about the issue of lay preaching, which had been such a key element of puritanism. As noted previously, in May 1653 the Massachusetts General Court required that "no person shall undertake any constant course of preaching or prophesying within this jurisdiction without the approbation of the elders of the four next neighboring churches, or the county court to which the place belongs."[21] Salisbury's Robert Pike protested the law and was found guilty of defaming the General Court by his criticisms. But he was not alone. Ten residents of the town of Woburn submitted a lengthy petition protesting the action. Among the points they raised was that the order "tends to the circumvention of the liberty of the Church of Christ"; that "whatever is acted this way by the civil magistrate to prevent error ... if it be not warranted by God's word, it will not be sanctified by his Spirit for good"; and that the scripture stated that "the prophets prophesy one by one, and the rest judge," indicating that it was "they that hear [that] can best judge of doctrine and person."[22] Faced with such opposition, the Court, acknowledging that the law was "dissatisfactory to divers of the inhabitants whom the Court hath cause to respect," repealed the order, though insisting that "every person that shall publish and maintain any heterodox and erroneous doctrine shall be liable to be questioned and censured by the County Court where he liveth."[23]

Playing against this background was the dispute over Michael Powell's candidacy for the pastorate of Boston's Second Church. Clearly conflicting forces were at play. While some still adhered to the tradition of lay preaching, some clergy and magistrates clearly were seeking to bring the practice under control. Undoubtedly this owed a good deal to works of English writers, like Baillie and Edwards, who had highlighted the extremes to which lay preaching had gone in England. But it also represented a growing effort on the part of some colonists to establish the ministry as a profession and clergy as arbiters of religious truth.

Connecticut had responded more quickly than Massachusetts to the recommendation of the Commissioners of the United Colonies that support be provided for ministers, passing such an order in September 1644. At the same time the Connecticut General Court stipulated that funds be raised for the support of scholars at Harvard. The Code of Laws established for Connecticut in May 1650 included a section on "Ministers Maintenance." Noting how most had come to live in the colony "that they might enjoy Christ in his ordinances without disturbances," the law stipulated that those who were taught the word in the churches should be called together and "voluntarily set down what he is willing to allow" for the support of the clergy, and that if a person refused to pay a proper portion he was to be "rated by authority in some just and equal way." In another move to restructure religious life, in March 1658 the Connecticut General Court ordered that "henceforth no persons in this jurisdiction shall in any way embody themselves into church estate without consent of the General Court and approbation of the neighbor churches." A further measure to control religious affairs came in the same session when the Court ordered

> that there shall be no ministry or Christian administration entertained or attended by the inhabitants of any plantation in this colony, distinct and separate from, and in opposition to that which is openly and publicly observed and dispensed by the settled and approved minister of the place, except it be by approbation of the General Court and neighbor churches.

But at the same time, reflecting the persistence of the tradition of lay conferencing, the court stated that "this order shall not hinder any private meetings of godly persons to attend any duties that Christianity or religion call for, as fasts or conference."[24] There were no similar laws that were passed in New Haven during that colony's existence and there is no evidence to indicate whether the practice in that colony mirrored that in the Bay and Connecticut or not.

David D. Hall has pointed to various factors in the experience of a new generation of clergy that contributed to a growing sense of the ministry as a profession and its consequent assertion of authority. In subtle ways a Harvard education undermined the fervor and charisma that had distinguished the clergy of the founding generation as leaders, and this contributed to the new conception of the ministry. The second-generation clergy aspired to and in most cases achieved a socio-economic status that distinguished them from their flocks. And, unlike the close relationship of religious leaders and followers who had in many cases come to New England together in the 1630s, Harvard graduates rarely had any prior connection with the congregations that ended up hiring them. The very fact that we can talk about them being "hired" and signing contracts is further testament to changes taking place.[25]

A test of the new direction in which some were seeking to steer the colonies was the dispute that broke out in Hartford in the 1650s. Following the death of Thomas Hooker in 1647, Samuel Stone had labored on as the sole minister of the Hartford church. In 1649 the church took steps to fill the vacancy in the ministry (the ideal for puritan churches was two clergyman, a pastor and a teacher). The post was offered to Jonathan Mitchell, recently graduated from Harvard, but he turned it down and shortly thereafter succeeded Thomas Shepard at Cambridge. While this process was going on Stone indicated in a letter to Richard Mather that he was prepared to recognize as members of the church all who had been baptized, regardless of whether they had been considered for membership in their own right upon reaching adulthood. In 1653 the congregation was impressed with the trial preaching of another Harvard graduate, Michael Wigglesworth, but Stone prevented their issuing a call. While he acknowledged that "it is a liberty of the church to declare their apprehensions by vote about the fitness of a person for office upon his trial," he also contended that "it is a received truth that an officer may in some cases lawfully hinder the church from putting forth at this or that time an act of her liberty."[26]

Stone famously is known for having characterized New England church practice as "a speaking aristocracy in the face of a silent democracy," a position which clearly ran counter to the tradition of lay empowerment within congregations. Now he was explicitly placing limits on the rights of the membership, in particular denying them the right to choose their ministers. The church became bitterly split. With the prompting of the Connecticut authorities, both sides initially agreed to submit to arbitration by a group of Connecticut and New Haven clergy. New Englanders accepted the value of such councils for advice on difficult issues, but had traditionally denied them authority. In this case, the advising clergy were asked to serve as arbiters and both sides agreed in advance to abide by the findings. But when the decision was announced, Stone was dissatisfied with it and, according to one of the council members who had heard the case, "rose up in opposition to the council, setting up his own judgment in his own case against the judgment of the council." The dispute continued with Stone's opponents seeking to withdraw from the Hartford church while he and his supporters sought to prevent that by calling on the assistance of Connecticut magistrates and Boston area clergy. Finally, in 1659, the dissidents, together with supporters they had in the neighboring church at Wethersfield, relocated to a new town, Hadley, in Massachusetts.

The Hartford controversy anticipated what would be important developments in the evolution of puritanism in New England. Stone, supported by many other clergy and magistrates, asserted a greater authority for a minister over his congregation than had been envisioned by the founders, a fact that John Davenport and others were quick to point out. This would continue to be a source of conflict in the region in the following decades. Equally significant was the invocation of councils to attempt to resolve disputes. A growing number of clergy wished to establish councils as authoritative—a strong move towards a hierarchical Presbyterian control over congregations. Despite their desires, however, councils, assemblies, associations, and synods would never be recognized as having controlling powers in New England. So while those feeling themselves grieved in the following decades would often call for councils, those who were on the wrong side of the findings would (as had Stone) invariably reject them.

Historians have often contrasted what they see as the stern intolerance of New England with advocacy of religious liberty by English Independents. But the difference was not as great as often portrayed, for English supporters of the New England Way were themselves searching for ways to control excess while allowing for free discussions designed to acquire further light. Even during the 1640s, when the possibility of a powerful Presbyterian national church threatened their liberty and made them hesitant to criticize their Independent allies, English Congregationalists did make clear that there were limits to their advocacy of toleration. Jeremiah Burroughs expressed the views of his fellow Dissenting Brethren when he wrote in *Irenicum* (1645) against those who believed "all things should be tolerated," and the following year he argued against opinions that were "horrid blasphemous things."[27] Addressing the House of Lords, Burroughs stated that "For connivance at Blasphemy or damnable heresies, God forbid any should open his mouth." Thomas Goodwin denied calling for "liberty of all opinions," stating that "I plead only for Saints."[28] Joseph Caryl regretted the errors circulating in the 1640s, "some very dangerous, destructive, and damnable," and wrote that "whatsoever (I say) is an error or heresy, led all the penalties which Christ hath charged upon it be executed to the utmost." Sidrach Simpson's congregation excommunicated Robert Norwood when he could not be persuaded of the error of this ways.[29] Another sign that there were limits to the toleration English Congregationalists were willing to accept was the fact that they continued to endorse the publications of New England clergy. This was a fact recognized by some of the erstwhile allies of the Dissenting Brethren, William Walwyn for one claiming that the Congregationalists were really only interested in toleration for themselves and were in fact close to the Presbyterians in their theology.[30]

There was Congregationalist support for a Blasphemy Act in 1648, and in the early 1650s Congregationalists notably joined with other moderate puritans to curb the more extreme sects. The idea of an English Presbyterian framework had been rejected, but most puritans still hoped for some form of national ecclesiastical framework. *The Humble Proposals of Mr. Owen, Mr. Tho. Goodwin, Mr. Nye, Mr. Simpson, and other Ministers* (1652) sought to provide oversight of parish ministry and public preaching. Though its principal authors were Congregationalists, it was supported by moderate Presbyterians and Baptists. It called for a vetting of candidates for positions in the church by committees of triers, and a parallel system of ejectors who would be authorized to remove scandalous and malignant ministers from their livings. The *Humble Proposals* also set forth a list of 15 "Principles of Christian Religion, without acknowledgment whereof the Scriptures do plainly affirm that Salvation is not to be obtained." The principles reflected the main parts of a broad Calvinist consensus. Anyone who sought to speak in church assemblies, lay preachers as well as clergymen, was to be approved by the Triers.[31]

The *Humble Proposals* reflected the clear break that had developed between the English Congregationalists and some of their former sectarian allies. This was underlined when John Owen and his fellow Congregationalists drafted a list of "fundamentals" which they intended as a basis for a Parliamentary committee draft of "principles of Christian religion." The list was clearly Trinitarian and evangelical Christian, placing many, including former allies, beyond the perimeter fence of acceptable belief.[32] Some of the harshest critics of the fundamentals were men associated with New England dissent. Roger Williams strongly attacked the document in a variety of tracts and also in a letter to Parliament prefaced to John Clarke's *Ill News from New England*. Henry Vane was another vocal critic.[33]

The Humble Proposals demonstrates a willingness of its authors to curb the ultimate authority of congregations to determine their own affairs (in terms of who could preach to them) in order to curb the promulgation of what were seen as dangerous opinions, shifting power from lay members to state regulators and clergy. The system of triers and ejectors was established in 1654, though agreement on the 15 "principles" could not be achieved. Those chosen as triers, however, were Congregationalists, Presbyterians, and Calvinist Baptists whose applications of their own standards of belief guaranteed the approval of orthodox puritans.

Another step to establish order was the organization of regional associations. At least 18 regional ministerial associations were organized in the 1650s. Recognizing the duty of fellowship between individual Christians and also Christian churches, ministers came together, in the words of the Cumberland agreement, "for mutual advice and strengthening of each other." In many ways the associations were similar to the conferences of the Elizabethan era, with clergy cooperating on what they could agree on and tolerating differences while awaiting further light. The movement united a broad spectrum of English clergy. Some of the associations included only Congregationalists, while others were more reflective of the type of Calvinist combination of Congregationalists, moderate Presbyterians, and Particular Baptists that was found among the Triers and Ejectors. A few associations included episcopal clergy. Drawing upon the support of an association gave individual clergymen greater authority in leading their own churches.[34]

The goal of the associations was to keep churches united as they sought to reform religion at the local level. Many associations approved the Westminster Confession of Faith (which New Englanders had also endorsed in their Cambridge Platform) and the Westminster Assembly's *Directory of Public Worship*. Clergy were urged and supported in efforts to properly restrict access to the Lord's Supper. Many of the associations emphasized the importance of catechizing as a means of steering believers from heretical opinions.

The final attempt by English Congregationalists to balance the autonomy of their churches with a national settlement that would control extreme doctrines and practice was the Savoy Conference of 1658. In June of that year Henry Scobell, one of the lay elders of the Congregational church that met at Westminster Abbey, and a clerk to Protector Cromwell's council, sent a letter announcing a meeting of London area Congregational clergy. It was likely at that meeting that the initial plans for a national assembly were laid. The following month some of those clergy met with other Congregational clergy at the Oxford commencement. George Griffith, preacher at the Charter House, then sent out invitations to Congregational churches throughout the realm to come together in September at the Savoy Palace in London. The gathering convened on September 29 with 120 churches represented by slightly fewer than twice that number of messengers, many of them presumably laymen like Scobell. Many leaders of English Congregationalism were all represented, including a number of former New Englanders who had returned to their mother country. The Assembly sought a common ground with moderate Presbyterians by essentially reiterating the Westminster Confession of Faith virtually verbatim. The few changes tightened the language to exclude errors which had arisen or gained greater importance in the 1650s, such as Quakerism and Socinianism. They also altered the wording of the section dealing with the administration of the sacraments from a reference to "a minister of the Word lawfully ordained" to "lawfully called" to represent their congregational principles. Likewise, they removed the implication that church officers could administer the sacraments in congregations other than those that had called them. The Declaration also upheld the right of lay preaching, though allowing for some restrictions.[35]

There is no conclusive evidence that Oliver Cromwell encouraged the Savoy Conference, nor that he would have been willing to seek to implement its recommendations as part of a national religious settlement. As it turned out, the Lord Protector died before the work of the Assembly could be presented to him. But it is not outside the realm of possibility that he would have supported it if he had lived. Many of the clergy who advised him, including John Owen and Thomas Goodwin, were supporters of the New England Way, while others such as Hugh Peter and William Hooke were former colonial clergy. In this regard, it is interesting to note that, according to the New Englander John Leverett, who served for a time as a colonial agent to the Protector's court, when one of Cromwell's advisors complained of "New England's rigidness and persecution... his Highness was pleased to answer very much in favor of them, that they acted like wise men."³⁶

Through the efforts discussed, Congregational puritans in both England and New England sought to curb the centrifugal consequences of lay empowerment and to preserve unity, if not uniformity of belief and practice. The Restoration of 1660 would turn the puritan world upside down and confront puritans on both sides of the Atlantic with new challenges.

10
Clergy and Laity in the Later Seventeenth Century

The latter decades of the seventeenth century saw puritans in the Atlantic world facing new circumstances as they sought to advance God's kingdom. In England, the Restoration of the Stuart monarchy resulted in an effective end to puritan hopes for an English national church reflecting their understanding of godly faith and practice. In New England the Restoration initially had a limited impact. The colonists welcomed Edward Whalley and William Goffe, two of the regicides fleeing from the king's justice. When in Massachusetts, prior to their going into hiding, the two men attended services in Boston area churches and even, exercising the gift of prophesy, "preached and prayed, and gained universal applause and admiration, and were looked upon as men dropped down from heaven."[1] Shortly thereafter the New Haven colony lost its independent identity, in part for its role in sheltering the regicides, but the other Bible Commonwealths retained their constitutional forms. Rhode Island, with its more liberal practices, received a new charter and was relatively untouched. Over the years, however, the ability of the puritan leaders of Plymouth, Massachusetts, and Connecticut were forced to bend to new political realities. One of the first examples came with the royal prohibition on further execution of Quakers, which was sent to the Massachusetts authorities in 1661. A 1664 royal commission was highly critical of the puritan regimes. After decades of skirmishing and failed attempts, the royal courts revoked the Massachusetts charter in 1684. All of the region's colonies were incorporated into the Dominion of New England, bringing puritan autonomy and control to an end where it still existed. The restoration of some of the old order following England's Glorious Revolution—restoration of the Connecticut and Rhode Island charters, and a new charter making Massachusetts (now including Plymouth) a royal colony—did not mean a return of puritanism to political control. And so on both sides of the Atlantic puritans faced new challenges.

In the years following the Restoration puritans in England re-formed in distinct denominations outside the re-established episcopal national church.[2] They did so under persecution that did not proscribe their beliefs, but made the open practice of their faith more difficult. The so-called Clarendon Codes and related legislation excluded them from political office and from admission to Oxford and Cambridge. A Conventicle Act banned the assembly of five or more people meeting for worship except that in accordance with the Church of England. The Five Mile Act prohibited all clergy who refused to take an oath (that they would not seek to alter the government of church or state) from coming within five miles of any place they had previously ministered to or where they had met in a conventicle, as well as any parliamentary town or borough.[3]

The immediate challenge facing puritans after 1660 was posed by the Act of Uniformity of 1662. Re-establishing the Church of England and setting terms for inclusion in it that were unacceptable to most puritans, the Act led to the voluntarily withdrawal of many clergy from posts in the church and universities, and then ejection of more by St. Bartholomew's Day in 1662, the total of those displaced or ejected being by some estimates over 2000.[4] Most went quietly, but there were popular demonstrations in some London parishes by believers angered at losing their spiritual guides.[5] Though some puritans did conform, worshiped in parish churches, and attended private meetings (conventicles in the eyes of authorities) much as they did before, large numbers developed separate religious identities.[6] Congregationalists, Presbyterians, Baptists, and Quakers gradually evolved into distinct denominational bodies, though occasionally they united over common interests. One student of the subject has concluded that "the development of dissent after 1662 was determined by lay rather than by ministerial leadership."[7] The focus here will be on how the lay role changed or remained constant in the Congregational churches.[8]

Groups that had in the 1640s and 1650s worshipped in parish churches reformed by godly clergy, now had to find new places to worship. Not all congregations survived the Restoration since many puritans did conform, at least outwardly, to the new national church. Members of what had been separate congregations came together in some cases under these changed circumstances. Thus, the London Baptist church in Cripplegate included men and women from London, Wantage, and

Exeter.⁹ Similarly, those who heard Oliver Heywood preach in Halifax, Yorkshire came from a wide area.¹⁰ Some congregations proceeded to find meeting places where they could escape official attention, such as in concealed rooms or in the woods. Some met in the middle of the night to reduce the chances of detection. Thomas Jollie preached from a staircase with a specially designed door that could be used as a pulpit during his sermons but dropped to hide him if the meeting was raided.¹¹ An important role played by some laymen was providing meeting places for their congregations. With lay assistance large congregations found places to worship in malthouses, warehouses, and other buildings owned by members.¹² In rural communities a barn would suffice. In 1667 the vicar of Bath reported that 500 dissenters met in a barn, made up into "the formalities of churches, with seats for the convenience of speaking and hearing."¹³ Despite their best efforts, many clergy and laymen were caught, fined, and imprisoned during this period, some dying in prison.

An important way in which the Congregational laity sustained their churches was economic. Cut off from the state support that some had received in previous decades, most clergy were thrown back on the voluntary contributions of laymen and laywomen. Some found support in the households of sympathetic noble families. And just as earlier puritans had done during the Martian persecutions, prosperous farmers provided barns for underground worship and urban merchants made their warehouses available.¹⁴

Though Congregationalists accepted the utility of occasional assemblies or synods so long as they were merely advisory, there were no meetings or any kind of Congregational national assembly between the Savoy Conference of 1658 and the formation of the Congregational Union in 1832. Of course any such efforts prior to the 1689 Toleration Act would have been illegal. This means that individual congregations sustained their identity and beliefs independently, though messengers between congregations allowed a sharing of insights. There is no detailed study of grassroots congregationalism in the decades between the Restoration and the Glorious Revolution comparable to Joel Halcomb's study of the Congregationalists in the 1640s and 1650s, but it appears that the situation faced by these puritans was similar to that which many faced before 1642.¹⁵ Some groups went for periods without a recognized clergyman and met in conference to sustain each other's faith. Official records shed some light on groups that were detected, such as the case of the widow Hester Hooper, who was presented for keeping a private meeting or conventicle in her house.¹⁶ Gifted members might preach to supplement the sermons of a minister in congregations that had attracted a clergyman. In cases where there was no minister or he was in prison, a lay member or members assumed the responsibility of guiding their fellow believers.[17] The Axminster congregation of Bartholomew Ashwood worshipped without him during his imprisonment, often meeting in woods and fields. During Francis Holcroft's imprisonment, members of his Cambridgeshire congregation preached by way of prophesying and some people were converted by these means.[18] Prophesying continued as an important part of Congregational practice. New England's Nathaniel Morton had commented that in speaking of the practice of prophesying, "Dr. Owen, speaking of this exercise, says, "private Christians have a right to make known whatever is revealed to them by the word of God."[19] Owen wrote that "men not solemnly called and set apart to the office of public teaching may yet be endued with useful gifts for edification."[20]

Some of the informal actions of the laity are captured in what Anne Dunan-Page has called the "literary acts of the gathered churches," which record various actions of the saints—"They compose and sing songs, they teach, they name their children, they build monuments, establish commemorative feasts, and commit events to writing." By these means they "charted the intervention of the divine in their lives."[21]

Samuel Thomas has carefully analyzed the various ways in which the members of Oliver Heywood's congregation in Halifax, Yorkshire came together to sustain their faith in these times of persecution. Individuals travelled distances together to hear Heywood preach and often spent hours socializing after the service. As they journeyed home they discussed matters of faith, prayed and sang psalms. Because of the dispersed nature of Heywood's flock it was difficult for everyone to gather regularly, and so many formed small groups that met in different localities to confer and pray. At one such meeting in 1686 Timothy Bancroft prayed aloud, and one of those in attendance commended Bancroft, stating that his prayer had been "an instrument of good to both their souls." Members of the congregation also hosted fasts, which were another occasion when men and women might gather to confess their sinfulness, sing psalms, and pray. Members of the church regularly offered spiritual advice to one another in such groups. Heywood, who had himself been drawn to God by attending such a group as a youth, organized a conference specifically for the youth of his congregation.[22]

During these times of trial many English puritans reiterated the importance of conference in sustaining the faith of the godly. For these puritans each individual bore responsibility for joining with others to sustain a sense of Christian community. In 1682 Thomas Watson complained that "one main reason of the decay of the power of godliness is want of Christian conference." "What makes it a communion of saints," he asked, "but good conference"?[23] In calling for Christian conference John Owen pointed out that "experiences may confirm us against the workings of our unbelief, [and] so may those of others."[24]

Sharing experiences was a vital part of such conferences. As the sun of puritan prominence steadily waned, William Hooke stressed to his fellow believers that "there is a duty also incumbent... touching the transmission of the truth to the generation to come. Make it known therefore by your examples, counsels, encouragements upon all occasions, for you have heard much, seen much, and known much."[25] And Owen listed "frequent spiritual communication for edification" as one of the rules for walking in Christian fellowship.[26] The ejected minister Thomas Vincent urged believers to "communicate the experiences which you have had as you see there is real need... [and] labor in your places to be both shining and burning lights."[27]

Watson urged that those "that have tasted the Lord is gracious, tell others what experiences you have had of God's mercy, that you may encourage them to seek to him for mercy."[28] The Bury St Edmunds congregation recorded a relation in which a new member "related God's dealings with her soul" to the edification of the group.[29] John Flavel likewise reasserted the puritan value in shared experiences, writing that "the experiences of others who have been in the same deeps of trouble are also of great use to keep the soul above water. The experience of another is of great use to prop up a desponding mind."[30] "The transcript of the heart," wrote Richard Baxter, "hath the greatest force upon the heart of others."[31] Elsewhere Baxter referred to the lives of Christian saints as "the true history of exemplary lives."[32]

Samuel Lee harkened back to the call for fellowship and sharing from the earlier period. Advising those who had difficulty in wrestling with difficult points of faith, he told them to "open your soul to some prudent friend and give him leave, nay entreat him to search out the core, and conscientiously follow his advice, and it may prove a happy day to your soul by comparing mutual experiences."[33] Richard Baxter offered a list of ways to spark godly conversation and discussion in his *Christian Directory* (1673). While he enumerated a list of doctrines that were always worthwhile to talk about, he also suggested that the godly individual choose to talk about a recent sermon that impressed, a recent book read, a particular verse of scripture that had lodged in his mind, or a providence the individual had experienced.[34] On occasion the members of a conference would review and discuss a sermon that one of the members had heard in a parish church.[35]

An anonymous tract titled *Stated Christian Conference Asserted to be a Christian Duty* called for more zealous use of the tool. "Philalethes" (lover of truth) noted that "conference is practiced in and about London, and also in New England, and elsewhere by some serious Christians." He denied that the practice represented an infringement of ministerial authority and argued that it was "the duty of gracious souls to convene together as often as conveniency will permit, to stir up and exhort each other, to adhere to the cause and truth of Christ in so declining an age, and to give each other a lift heavenward." He complained that "gospel ministers do not intermix their discourses more with their own experiences," and asserted that it was "granted by ministers and others that some private Christians have a richer stock of experiences than ministers generally have." He insisted that those laymen who participated in conferences should prepare themselves—"it is every Christian's duty to labor after a full knowledge of the Scripture." Believers should test clerical teaching by comparing it to the scriptures, using "annotations, expositions, learned commentaries, and successive preaching." Concluding his arguments for lay engagement, he asked, "why may not my soul be profited by a layman as well as by a clergyman"?[36]

By far the most influential work of English literature during this period was John Bunyan's religious allegory, *The Pilgrim's Progress from this World to that which is to come* (1678). While some have viewed Christian's *Pilgrim's Progress* as a lonely journey, Bunyan describes edifying conversations in which his pilgrim engages on his journey. Joining up with Faithful, for instance, Christian engages his companion in "sweet discourse of all things that had happened to them in their pilgrimage."[37]

Family devotions were domestic forms of the practice of conferencing long urged upon the faithful. The English puritan Samuel Clarke memorialized his wife's concern for all in their household, servants as well as children. "She would," he wrote, "take all occasions and opportunities to manifest her love and care of their souls by frequent dropping in good counsel and wholesome instructions, by catechizing, enquiring of what they remembered of the sermons they heard, [and] reading her notes to them."[38] Clarke was noted for recording the lives of many exemplary saints in addition to that of his wife. During the latter part of the seventeenth century there was a new proliferation of spiritual biographies that taught, by way of exemplary lives, the way to faith and salvation.[39]

In the last decades of the seventeenth century the campaign in New England to enhance clerical authority at the expense of lay power and congregational autonomy continued. But while considerable progress was made in accomplishing this, other voices continued to advocate for laymen and laywomen exercising grace in their lived religion. A significant milestone in the changing of the New England Way came with the Synod of 1662. That assembly is best remembered for its strong recommendation for the adoption of what became known as the Half-Way Covenant. But equally important was its strong recommendation of consociation of churches.

The Half-Way covenant was an idea, first broached by Richard Mather in the late 1640s, to expand membership in the churches by admitting individuals who, as children of members, had been baptized as infants but who, on reaching maturity, had not undergone the test for membership in their own right. Mather's proposal was to allow such individuals a partial membership that would entitle them to have their own children baptized but not give them access to the Lord's Supper. It would also place them under the supervision of the church. No conclusion was reached when the idea was raised at the assembly that drafted the Cambridge Platform in the late 1640s. A 1657 synod in Boston recommended the innovation, but few churches adopted it at that time. One of the reasons for this was strong lay opposition. While Salem's pastor Francis Higginson believed extending baptism was "clear to him to be his duty," he recognized that this was possible only "if he might do it with the consent of the church in a peaceable way."[40]

Because the synod of 1657 had not settled the issue, in December 1661 the Massachusetts General Court called for another assembly to meet in March 1662. Only Massachusetts churches responded, with more than 80 delegates from the Bay churches, most of them laymen, gathered in Boston for the meeting. Overriding opposition that came from Increase and Eleazar Mather, Charles Chauncy, and the absent John Davenport, the Synod recommended the Half-Way Covenant and also called for consociations of area churches that would have the ability to excommunicate an offending congregation. The Massachusetts General Court officially recommended that the findings be adopted in all of the churches.[41]

Regardless of the General Court's recommendation, the decision to adopt the findings of the synod had to be approved one church at a time by the lay membership. Over the following years many congregations became bitterly divided over the proposals. James F. Cooper has pointed out that the findings "forced the churches of the Bay to reassess and, in some cases, to revise their stances toward Congregational autonomy, unanimous consent, church councils, and the rights of dissenters."[42] In church after church laymen debated the issue. While most clergy supported the proposal, those opposed provided arguments against it, largely branding the recommendations as a departure from the system created by the founders of New England. John Davenport, identified by Cooper as "a strong defender of lay liberties," was particularly forceful in making that case. Laymen were, of course, divided, just as the clergy were, but the fact that they rejected a passive role to actively argue their cases against both other laymen and clergy on the opposite side is demonstration of how strongly the tradition of lay empowerment remained.[43] In the course of the debates, clergy appealed to the authority of the Synod of 1662 and to the endorsement of the proposals by the General Court to buttress their cause, in the process making clear their acceptance of the role of authorities beyond the individual congregation.[44]

While treatments of the Synod of 1662 focus on the Half-Way Covenant, for many New Englanders the more serious issue was the recommendation of consociations. One of those concerned about this was John Davenport. Davenport accepted the value of a fellowship of churches with responsibility for advising one another, and even the legitimacy of a church voluntarily deciding on its own to withdraw the right hand of fellowship from a congregation that had adopted beliefs or practices deemed beyond the pale. But he rejected the idea put forth in the synod recommendations that a consociation or council could pronounce a judgment of non-communion on an erring congregation. This was, he asserted, "to establish a new form of church [in New England], having power of church government, and exercising it over particular churches in classical or synodical assembles—[in short], a Presbyterian church." "Particular churches," he stated, "are sisters to one another...and there is a brotherhood of visible saints throughout the world," but "the manner of their communion must be *social*, as between equals, none exercising jurisdiction and authority over another." And he reminded New Englanders that a similar quest for uniformity had "brought great persecution under the prelacy upon the godly part in our native country, whereby sundry of us were driven into this wilderness."[45] Consistent with this, while he personally opposed the Half-Way Covenant, Davenport accepted the right of individual congregations to adopt it, and believed that this was the type of disagreement that should not sunder relations between churches.

As Davenport feared, as the proposals of the Synod of 1662 slowly gained footing throughout the region the nature of New England puritanism clearly changed. The individual who recorded an admission of a non-member's child to the Dorchester, Massachusetts congregation called the event "a corruption creeping in as an harbinger to old English practice viz. to make all members (which God prevent in mercy)."[46] Nathaniel Mather was one of the sons of Richard Mather. Following his graduation from Harvard he had emigrated to England, where he became an important member of the Congregational movement there. He viewed the changes occurring in New England with disappointment. Writing in 1681 to his brother Increase on the changes brought about by the Synod of 1662, he warned that he saw on both sides of the Atlantic "a departure... of late in congregational men from old principles and practices," and that Philip "Nye not long before his death saw and much laid to heart what he saw of that kind."[47] Three years later Nathaniel wrote to his brother Increase that in England it was "said... that you in New England, and yourself in particular, are turned Presbyterian," referring to the growing move toward geographical parishes and clerical authority within the church.[48]

As Davenport had warned, and Nathaniel Mather pointed out, the expansion of membership authorized by the Half-Way Covenant was a major step in the drift from Congregationalism and toward Presbyterian principles, eroding the concept of a gathered church of saints and moving toward an inclusive, geographical-style parish. Lay empowerment to a large degree rested on the notion that those who were gathered together were indeed saints and that as such what they had to share was likely inspired by the Spirit. Once the congregation included those who were not presumed saints, the dynamic was changed. It might be appropriate to listen to someone prophesy if that person was sharing thoughts inspired by the Spirit. Listening to what was no more than the opinion of a neighbor was a different matter. Admission to the Lord's table was still limited to full members, but over the following decades that policy too was abandoned by some churches, following the lead of clergy who viewed it a means of grace. This was another change that ministers officiating over the sacrament may have seen as a way of enhancing their own status.

Some of the issues at stake in these debates were illustrated when First Church Boston called John Davenport to be its pastor in 1667. Following the death of John Cotton in 1652, the church had eventually settled on

Ipswich's John Norton to join John Wilson in the ministry. The Boston church had always been noted for strong lay involvement in church affairs, and in particular for suspicion of synods. But in the early 1660s Norton and Wilson favored a greater role for such assemblies. Both of those clergymen tried but failed to bring the congregation to accept modifications in baptismal practices. The two clergymen held a narrow view of acceptable beliefs and had been vocal in urging harsh treatment of Baptists and Quakers. Leading lay members of the congregation were on the side of greater toleration. These divisions prevented the congregation from agreeing on a replacement when John Norton died in 1663. The situation became critical when Wilson died in the summer of 1667. On his deathbed the elderly minister, who years before had faced the lay revolt identified with Anne Hutchinson, complained that once again the "people rise up as Corah against their ministers, as if they [the ministers] took too much upon them." He lamented that "it is nothing for a brother to stand up and oppose, without scripture or reason, the word of an elder, saying I am not satisfied." He believed that God was provoked by "our neglect of baptizing the children of the church, those that some call grandchildren," and "not subjecting to the authority of Synods, without which churches cannot long subsist."[49]

The church majority that had thwarted Wilson on these issues voted to call Davenport to the pastorate. Because I have discussed the resultant controversy in great detail elsewhere, I wish to focus on the elements that speak to the issues of lay empowerment and congregational autonomy. One of these was a difference over how unanimous church actions had to be. In the first decades of the colony, decisions made by the members were expected to be unanimous, or nearly so. Since God's truth was single, achieving unanimity was a way of feeling confident that indeed the Spirit had led the members to that truth. But over time unanimity became more and more difficult to achieve, and gradually congregations proceeded on the basis of majority opinion, which was a significant change from the former practice.

In the case of the First Church Boston's call to John Davenport, a minority of the church, recognizing that the clergyman represented positions that they strongly opposed, sought to prevent the election on the basis that the call was not unanimous. When this failed, they petitioned neighboring churches for the right to withdraw from First Church and establish their own congregation, currying support with area clergy by expressing support for the findings of the synod of 1662. In the process they raised questions about the legitimacy of Davenport's release from the New Haven church that he had served since its establishment in 1638. After an initial council failed to resolve the dispute, a second council of 15 churches determined in April 1669 that the First Church minority should be dismissed from their existing membership and be allowed to form a new church. First Church strongly objected to this infringement of their liberties, but to no avail, with the dissidents organizing the Third Church in Boston (later to be known as Old South) in 1669. In his own dealings in the dispute, Davenport consistently presented his opinions as representing the judgment of his congregation, and while it would be naïve to suggest that he did not influence the positions the church took, there is ample evidence that the actions taken by the First Church majority against their dissenting brethren were most forcefully advanced by powerful laymen such as Edward Hutchinson, Edward Tyng, James Penn, and John Leverett.[50]

The final chapter of this controversy unfolded before the Massachusetts General Court in May 1669. The deputies of that body, generally the house most sympathetic to lay rights, invited Davenport to give the annual election sermon. The clergyman minced no words. He warned the magistrates not to "deprive any instituted Christian church, walking according to Gospel rules, of the power and privileges which Christ hath purchased for them by his precious blood." He indirectly criticized the council that had authorized the formation of the Third Church for having "countenance[d] and upheld others to exercise power over the churches in such things, to whom Christ never gave such power." He rejected empowering councils or synods which, "under a pretense of helping the church with their light, bereave them of their powers." He reminded those assembled of the foundations that he and others had laid in the 1630s, and warned that if the principles of the original New England Way were eroded then the Lord would "remove the golden candlesticks and the burning and shining lights in them."[51]

Inspired by Davenport's words, in 1670 the deputies appointed a committee to inquire into what they saw as God's controversy with New England. The resulting report identified a number of causes for God's displeasure, including declension from the original principles of congregationalism, innovations in doctrine and worship, "an invasion of the rights, liberties, and privileges of churches, [and] an usurpation of a lordly and prelatical power over God's heritage," all resulting in "turning the pleasant gardens of Christ into a wilderness, and the inevitable and total extirpation of the principles and pillars of the congregational way." The report also labeled the formation of the Third Church as irregular, illegal, and disorderly. Davenport, who had died earlier that year, would have approved.[52]

The ministers and the magistrates who had supported the recent changes clearly did not agree. Fifteen clergy supportive of the policies being attacked responded to the General Court in 1671, defending their positions and accusing the deputies of fostering "an antiministerial spirit." The clergy and their supporters had been active in the election of that year's court so that 30 of the deputies from the previous year had lost their seats. The new Court embraced the ministers' complaint, and determined that the deputies' report of the previous year "should be accounted useless" and that there was "no just cause of those scandalizing reflections."[53]

Complaints of lay actions and demands for more clerical power, which had been evident in the 1650s, became more pronounced over the following years. Samuel Willard, pastor of the frontier Massachusetts town of Groton, complained in 1673 that throughout New England one could see "ministers despised, their office questioned, their authority cast off and trampled upon, their persons undervalued and vilified, their comfortable supply and maintenance neglected." John Woodbridge, an advocate of Presbyterian reforms, complained to an English correspondent "that the people are grown so rude, insolent, and coltish (Independency has so fatted them) that the ministers that have the most authority have not enough to stamp a judgment and sentence of good metal to make it current with them."[54] As summarized by David D. Hall, Woodbridge argued that "'Congregationalists' wanted the brethren of the church to have equal authority with the minister, rejected the authority of councils, and declared for a gathered membership. 'Presbyterians' stood for comprehensive baptizing, greater power in the ministry, and authoritative synods."[55] On his deathbed, John Wilson had complained of the failure of the Boston First Church to adopt the Half-Way Covenant, New England's failure in "not subjecting to the authority of synods, without which churches cannot long subsist," and the disrespect of the clergy by laymen who think it "nothing for a brother to stand up and oppose, without scripture or reason, the word of an elder."[56] What is striking about this controversy is the extent to which these clergy presented the argument for lay authority as an innovation and as a sign of anti-ministerial bias, when it was essential to the church polity of early New England.

The frustration expressed by Willard and Wilson was the consequence of the fact that the clergy's struggle to impose their will on the laity was always limited by the determination of lay members of individual congregations to defend their liberties. One response to their frustration was to look to the civil authorities for support, seeking a role for the magistrates beyond merely punishing heresies branded as illegal. Increase Mather, who had shifted from his previous opposition to the proposals of the Synod of 1662, took the lead in campaigning for more aggressive government actions to punish heretics, expand church membership, legislate against "provoking evils" such as long hair and immodest dress, and recognize the clergy as arbiters of the New England Way.[57] His efforts to achieve these ends were thwarted for a time by John Leverett. Leverett had served in the New Model Army, was one of the First Church members responsible for the call of John Davenport, and had himself earned a reputation as a proponent of lay rights and congregational autonomy. He was elected governor of Massachusetts in 1673 and re-elected each year until his death in 1679. On more than one occasion he clashed with Mather, who complained in his diary that "magistrates have no heart to do what they might in order to [further] reformation, especially the governor." Preaching the election day sermon in 1677, Mather attacked the magistrates for failing to live up to the standards of predecessors such as Winthrop, Dudley, and Endecott, and warned them against becoming "cold and indifferent in things of God."[58]

Having initially failed to enlist the government in his crusade, Mather worked to persuade the churches of New England to each observe a day of fast and humiliation that would acknowledge the backsliding of the times. Each congregation was then to renew its covenant. He was able to persuade the Plymouth Colony government to recommend this path to the churches in their jurisdiction and had some success in persuading individual churches in Massachusetts and Connecticut to do so. But his greatest success came following the death of Leverett in March 1679. The General Court elected that year called for a synod that met in the Boston townhouse in September. The so-called "Reforming Synod" not only issued its own call for covenant renewals, but took other measures to strengthen the hierarchical elements of the New England Way.[59] It was suggested at the synod that the Cambridge Platform's sections on church government be revised to limit lay power.[60] While no full revision was undertaken, the Propositions assembled in the second session of the synod were more explicit than previous church statements in asserting a minister's authority in his congregation, stating that "the pastor of a church may by himself authoritatively suspend from the Lord's table a brother accused or suspected of a scandal," and explicitly asserted the clerical elder's "negative on the votes of the brethren."[61]

The consequences of this would be evident in the ability of numerous clergymen to establish greater authority in their churches over the following years. Thus, for instance, in 1697 Samuel Willard, who had moved on to ministry in the Third Church Boston, rejected the individual most members of the congregation wished to choose as his colleague. Echoing the position taken earlier by Hartford's Samuel Stone, Willard insisted "that he had a negative voice and was not only a moderator." This was in keeping not only with the results of the Reforming Synod but also with an agreement reached earlier in the decade by Boston area ministers that while a congregation must concur in such a choice, ministers had "a negative on the votes of the fraternity."[62]

During these years New Englanders were also coming to terms with dissenting groups, with those colonists most protective of lay authority demonstrating the greater sympathy for the dissenters. In 1665 nine individuals met in the Charlestown home of Thomas Goold, a wheelwright and farmer, re-baptized themselves by immersion, and signed a covenant forming themselves into the first Baptist church in Massachusetts. Goold had previously been censured by the Charlestown Church for holding private meetings in which Baptist and even Quaker ideas appear to have been discussed. Now he and four of the members of his congregation were excommunicated in the hope that this would shock them into a return to the orthodox fold. When they proved unbowed the General Court convicted them for violating the law against Baptists, disenfranchised them, and threatened them with imprisonment if they persisted. Over the next few years Goold was dragged into court and fined on several occasions. Members of the congregation held services on Noddles Island in the harbor of East Boston. The Court of Assistants threatened them with banishment, but the deputies (the lower house of the General Court) refused to acquiesce in that penalty.[63]

In March 1668 the Governor and Council ordered "a full and free debate" be held between Goold and his associates and six leading clergy appointed by the council. The purpose was to reduce the Baptists "from the error of their ways." The debate was held in the meetinghouse of the First Church of Boston. Both sides agreed on Calvinist theological principles, including predestination, which is not surprising since the Baptists involved had been members of New England churches. Goold and one of his fellow Baptists took the position that differences over infant baptism should not be sufficient to cause a meaningful rift with the colony's other churches and that members of both should be able to worship and pray together. At the other extreme, two of the other Baptist spokesmen, John Crandall and Benanual Bowers, maintained that the orthodox churches in the colonies were corrupt if not antichristian and that only the Baptist position was true to the scriptures. Others took a mediating position, arguing for toleration of separate Baptist churches within the structure of the New England way. In the course of the debates the Baptists raised the importance of lay prophesying and the growing effort to restrict it, and questioned the legitimacy of a salaried ministry as opposed to one supported by free contributions. While it was not a major part of the debate it was clear that the Baptists did not require an educated ministry.[64]

Following the debate the orthodox clergy who had been involved informed the General Court that the Baptist church was "an enemy in the habitation of the Lord; and anti-New England in New England." The Court pronounced a sentence of banishment on Goold and two of his brethren, but the men made no effort to leave the colony and were imprisoned while awaiting forcible ejection. But within a week of the Court publishing its order, 66 inhabitants of the colony petitioned that the Baptists be freed and tolerated. Released temporarily from prison in March 1669, Goold appeared to have removed to Noddle's Island, where he conducted worship for the next five years while the magistrates overlooked the existence of a Baptist church there.[65] Influencing the Court may have been a letter criticizing the colony's treatment of Baptists which leading English Congregationalists, including Thomas Goodwin and Philip Nye, sent to the Massachusetts authorities in March 1669.[66]

During this ongoing debate, Boston's First Church was the center of the local support for extending toleration to the Baptists. Some of the congregation's members were among the signers of the 1645 petition seeking the repeal of the law against Baptists. Stephen Winthrop, who had written from England against the treatment of the Baptists, had been a member of First Church. In the aftermath of the 1668 debate with Baptist spokesmen that had been held in the First Church meetinghouse, the church received a letter from a former member, Nehemiah Bourne, who had fought in the Parliamentary forces in England. In the letter Bourne criticized the Massachusetts "government and their proceedings against some Anabaptists." John Davenport, whose sympathy for the Baptists was one of the things that led the First Church laity to call him to their ministry, made the letter public, drawing down upon himself to criticism from the magistrates. A large number of the 66 inhabitants who petitioned for freeing Goold in 1668 were members of the church.[67]

In October of 1669 the First Church Boston invited John Oxenbridge to be an assistant to the aging John Davenport and James Allen in the ministry of the church. Oxenbridge had served a congregation in Bermuda for a time, following his deprivation as a college tutor by William Laud, but had then returned to England and briefly served as assistant to William Bridge in the Congregational church in Great Yarmouth, Norfolk. Following the Restoration, he preached briefly in Surinam and Barbados before the call to Boston. Oxenbridge was known for his sympathy toward Baptists, possibly due to his experience with Baptists who were members of the Great Yarmouth church.[68] This likely was one of the factors that made him attractive to the Boston church. In an election sermon he delivered in 1671 he was critical of the Half-Way Covenant and advocated the toleration of Baptists. Furthermore, he warned the colonists not to "backslide and to fashion yourselves to the flaunting mode of England in worship or walking," whereby they would "forget...your errand of planting this wilderness," and that if "you have a mind to turn your churches into parishes and your ministers into priests, I cannot think the Lord will ever endure it."[69]

Given this, it is not surprising that John Leverett, a member of First Church and elected governor in 1673, allowed the Baptist church to leave Noddles Island and worship in a Boston home in 1674. Like many who had lived through the turmoil of the 1640s and 1650s in England, Leverett was tolerant of Baptists, and was recognized by them as a friend.[70]

While there were clergymen such as Davenport and Oxenbridge who were sympathetic to the Baptists and who wished them to be tolerated within the perimeter fence of orthodoxy, most of New England's clergy sought to restrict their liberty and suppress their churches. Seen in this context it is not surprising that much of the support for the Baptists came from laymen who were noted for defending lay authority against overreaching clergy, and defending congregational autonomy against the efforts of clerical gatherings and their magisterial allies to define orthodoxy.[71]

The revocation of the Massachusetts charter in 1684, followed by the establishment of the Dominion of New England, which implicitly vacated all other regional charters for the time being, and the redrafting of the region's colonial institutions after the Glorious Revolution of 1689 all contributed to changing the relationship of the colonial governments to the churches. In Massachusetts, recognizing that they could no longer enlist the magistrates on their behalf as they had before, the Boston area clergy met in October 1690 and formed a ministerial association. This was intended as a professional body that could exert clerical authority over the churches of the area.[72] One of the policies adopted by the group was to "not allow the rites of this order to be regularly and conveniently performed by any but such as were themselves of the same order."[73] This was an explicit rejection of the practice of lay ordination. Furthermore, as Cotton Mather explained it, ordination was a ceremony of "consecration to their ministry, and by this consecration they were to be owned, as admitted into the order of pastors, through the whole church of God."[74] Ordination, in essence, bestowed upon them powers that derived from God, not just their congregants. When Benjamin Colman accepted the call to the ministry of the Brattle Street Church in Boston in 1699 he sought and received ordination from English Presbyterians, which he considered sufficient without any ordination required in the congregation to which he would minister. In keeping with this, and reversing the judgment of the Cambridge Platform, the association of Boston area clergy asserted the right of an ordained clergymen to administer the sacraments at a neighboring church.[75] The Association also expressed support of a 1691 agreement between English Congregationalists and Presbyterians which embraced broad-based church membership and Presbyterian-style views on ordination.[76]

The move toward Presbyterian principles which has been traced for Massachusetts was even more pronounced in the Connecticut Valley. Samuel Stone's assertion of his right to deny the congregation a vote on Michael Wigglesworth's candidacy for the church's ministry, and the support he received, was indicative of a desire by some to change the traditional relationship between pastor and members. Support for the Half-Way Covenant in the Valley can be seen as an effort to broaden membership to a more geographical basis likewise was viewed by its opponents as a move toward Presbyterian principles. Noting that those who advanced these positions did not initially embrace synods, the historian Robert G. Pope identified these men as holding an ecclesiastical position between Presbyterianism and Congregationalism and labeled them "presbyterialists."[77] Paul R. Lucas disputed the label, arguing that Pope's definition of Presbyterianism was too rigid, and that many of the Connecticut clergy and laymen resembled English Presbyterians of the time. Both Pope and Lucas might be trying to make distinctions that are too fine. While some members of the faction pushing for such reforms may have sought an elaborate system of classes or associations, others like Samuel Stone did not go so far, primarily focusing on the affairs of the local church. Lucas also argues that the Connecticut General Court's "Act of Toleration of 1669" gave freedom not only to congregations of orthodox doctrinal beliefs that adopted or rejected the Half-Way Covenant, but also to Presbyterians.[78]

Connecticut became, as Lucas elsewhere referred to it, a *Valley of Discord*, but over time those seeking a more Presbyterian system gained the upper hand.[79] Clerical associations were organized along the valley, and by the 1670s the authority of one such group was illustrated at the formation of the Westfield, Massachusetts church. Visiting elders, led by Northampton's Solomon Stoddard, did not approve of the planned order of the day's business, and forced the proposed pastor, Edward Taylor, to write out some form of creedal statement before they would proceed.[80]

The ultimate triumph in Connecticut for those pushing for greater ministerial autonomy and authority can be seen in the Saybrook Platform of 1708. Called by the colony's assembly and agreed to by Governor Gurdon Saltonstall, himself a former clergyman, the Saybrook Synod adopted the 1658 Savoy Confession of faith of English Congregationalists. It endorsed the 1691 *Heads of Agreement* between English Congregationalists and Presbyterians which embraced broad-based church membership and Presbyterian-style views on ordination. And it called for the establishment both of ecclesiastical consociations in each county (with lay and clerical members) which would have the responsibility of overseeing local congregations, and ministerial associations which would exercise the task of approving ministerial candidates. The Saybrook Platform was adopted by the Connecticut General Assembly. Though churches were not required to accept it, many did, and the called-for bodies were established in Hartford, New London, Fairfield, and New Haven counties.[81]

Toward the end of the seventeenth century, Joshua Scottow, one of the last surviving members of New England's first generation, worried about the growing authority of the clergy, who were asserting greater religious authority at the expense of the founders' belief that "all the Lord's People might be Prophets, and that he would put his Spirit upon them." "New England," he judged, "is not to be found in New-England."[82] There was a good deal of truth in Scottow's observation. But his concerns overlooked the fact that laymen, including himself, continued to labor to be as candles that would shed light on others and guide them to a deeper faith.

Conference was still valued in New England. John Davenport told his listeners at a fast-day sermon that God "requireth reading, hearing, meditating, praying, conference, etc."[83] Samuel Wakeman, pastor of the congregation in Fairfield, Connecticut, listed it among the things that distinguished New Englanders as godly—"we read, we hear, we pray, we receive sacraments, we have our conference meetings, our lectures, fasts, and other solemnities."[84] Conferencing was even encouraged by clergy such as Jonathan Mitchell, someone who sought to increase the authority of clergy within churches and over the churches. Mitchell saw the coming together of the saints on earth as a precursor of what could be expected in heaven. "Consider," he urged his listeners, "how sweet is the communion, company, and converse of gracious saints here on earth: How do your hearts burn in Godly conference?" He urged them to spend time with a godly friend and "be much in quickening conference, giving and taking mutual encouragements and directions in the matters of heaven."[85]

Cotton Mather argued in 1702 that it was "the indisposition to religious conference" that was a reason for what he perceived as the decline of godliness in New England. There were too many church members who were like dead coals. But, he stated, "if the dead coal were lying among the living ones, it would be no longer so dead. Lively Christians in like manner (say I) keep one another alive by being together. The company and the conference of lively Christians has a mighty tendency to keep Christianity alive among them."[86] He encouraged such efforts among the members of his congregation, and went so far as to help organize a conference of the more than 30 black members of the church as well as other slaves in Boston. As outlined in his publication of *Rules for the Society of Negroes* (1693), the members pledged to meet together every Sunday evening, to "pray together by turns, one to begin, and another to conclude the meeting." The society was limited to those who had "sensibly reformed their lives from all manner of wickedness," and provided a mechanism for these laity to develop their faith that was no different from conferences that had long been part of the puritan movement.[87]

Conferencing was not merely a recommendation of the clergy. There is ample evidence that it was a practice embraced by many of the laity. The diary of the prominent merchant and judge Samuel Sewall documents his involvement in one such group. "We have," he recorded, "our private meetings, wherein we pray and sing, and repeat sermons, and confer together about the things of God." The members took turns hosting the meetings. Typically, a scripture verse would be read by one of the laymen, and everyone would engage in a discussion of its meaning. "The exercise," Sewall wrote on one occasion, "was such, preaching and praying, as if God did intend it for me." In addition to engaging in conferencing, Sewall also worked to advance the faith in other ways. He carried a number of catechisms in his pockets and gave them away to those whom he believed could benefit from them. He published his own religious speculations, and arranged for the publication of works he thought would help believers grow in faith. Thus, it was Sewall who arranged for the Boston publication of Bunyan's *Pilgrim's Progress*.

The events that followed upon the Restoration of the monarchy in 1660 posed new challenges for puritans on both sides of the Atlantic. In England, many simply conformed to the re-established national church. The puritan communities that persisted depended on lay efforts in providing venues for worship, supporting clergy, and sustaining one another's faith by sharing experiences and beliefs in formal and informal settings. In New England, puritans labored under a growing threat of royal intervention in their affairs, the decades between 1660 and 1690. That period witnessed a struggle between those who viewed the society's purpose as resting on a strong lay engagement in the life of the churches and those who looked to the ministers and magistrates to guide the churches.

Epilogue:
Looking Backwards, and Ahead

Puritanism began with the beliefs of zealous men and women who were convinced that they had a responsibility to serve God by perfecting the Church of England, and, eventually, all of Christendom. Puritans were inspired by access to the Bible in their own tongue, and possessed of a belief that God would provide them through his Holy Spirit with grace that would enable them to see the truth in the Bible. They sought each other out to share their insights and experiences, creating dynamic communities of godly believers. They were to be lights to lead others to the biblical truths. They valued the insights of clergymen who had superior education, but were divided over how important that was, many believing that the experience of grace, more than book learning, was the essential means that enabled a Christian to recognize and edify fellow believers.

Recognizing their frailties as fallen creatures, many puritans saw both themselves personally and their godly communities collectively embarked on a journey in search of further light. Some of the questions they wrestled with dealt with doctrines. Others focused on ceremonial practices. Still others concerned church order. They debated what constituted a true church, how one could be formed, how church leaders were to be chosen and empowered, and what the role of the laity should be in a reformed church. The fact that there was no one person or body laying out the central meaning of puritanism but that the movement resulted from a multitude of interactions between individuals and groups of believers helps to explain the varieties of puritanism. One of the answers to the questions about church order evolved into Congregationalism, an emphasis on autonomous churches of visible saints that would be espoused by some puritans in the Netherlands, the vast majority of those who settled in New England, and by an important element in England in the 1640s and 1650s. It is this variety of puritanism that has been my primary focus in this study. How one understands puritanism has a lot to do with what one sees as its characteristic emphasis. Viewed along the axis of lay participation, Congregationalists had more in common with Baptists, and perhaps even Quakers, than they did with Presbyterians.

The relationship between the laity and the clergy in the Congregational pursuit of religious truth and order was generally one of partnership rather than opposition. There is no denying that the articulation of these positions was generally written and defended by university-trained clergymen such as John Cotton and Thomas Goodwin. But there was always some tension, even if it could be a creative tension. At times in England during the sixteenth and early seventeenth centuries it was the laity that drove the movement forward, insisting on reforms where some clergymen were willing to temporize. And if some clergy were not willing to tarry for the magistrate, some lay believers were not willing to wait for clerical leadership. Laymen and laywomen journeyed together to hear a noted clergyman preach and thus "get a little fire," singing psalms and discussing his message on their journey home. Families gathered with neighbors to study scripture and share their insights. Laymen entered pulpits to preach on the frontier of New England where a minister was unavailable. Laymen and even laywomen took to the streets of London and other cities to proclaim their insights. Around the campfires of the New Model Army soldiers debated the reforms necessary to make England God's kingdom. Out of the dynamics of Congregational empowerment of the laity evolved the Baptists, Quakers, and other sects.

Over time the very clergy who labored to stimulate such enthusiasm also came to worry about it, and the explosion of sectarianism heightened their concerns. Were the clergy merely the first among equals in a community of believers, or were they leaders to whom deference should be due? Clergy who did not need the support of their flocks in a contest with an oppositional hierarchy were attracted to a higher definition of their role. They pointed to their education as something that gave them better tools than their lay supporters with which to discern the meaning of scripture.

If the relationship between clergy and laity could be a source of tension, so could the relationship between communities of saints. On a practical level, puritan separatists and non-separatists on both sides of the Atlantic had to negotiate what if any contacts they should have with one another. On a theoretical level the reformers had to decide if individual congregations were totally autonomous, or if local churches should be subject to the supervision of church councils or magistrates, or both. These were questions that concerned the nature of the church order being erected, but also had implication for the power exercised by the laity over their spiritual affairs.

One of the things that makes it so difficult for scholars to agree on what exactly puritanism was, is the fact that it was constantly evolving during the sixteenth and early seventeenth centuries. As believers embarked on a journey to comprehend the will of God the puritans valued unity but did not insist on uniformity. As a community they wrestled with the question of where to draw the perimeter fence separating ideas and practices that were clearly false from those that might offer hope of further light. How that boundary was drawn owed something to the temperament of those making the decisions and the circumstances in which they found themselves. Fluctuations in the boundary reflected changes in what might be called puritanism.

In the early decades of New England settlement, some laymen and clergy sought to narrowly define the "New England Way," while others were open to new ideas so long as they were offered as possibilities to be explored and not (as Anne Hutchinson did) as certitudes. It was laymen—Vane, Hutchinson, Witter, Clarke, Gorton—who were challenging the boundaries and precipitating the debate, but it was also laymen such as Endecott, Winthrop, Dudley, and Leverett who played key roles in determining how the challenges were to be dealt with—albeit often with the advice of clergymen. Some formal boundaries were set, but we must avoid the temptation of exaggerating how divided the society became. There is no doubting that the puritan governor of Connecticut, John Winthrop Jr., and his brother, the Quaker governor of Antigua Samuel Winthrop, recognized the root of the matter in each other. In England the realities of Civil War pushed Congregationalists to be more open to dissent, and close relations were maintained with Baptists and others who were seen as part of the godly community. Oliver Cromwell emerged as a layman who was able to impose a degree of toleration that allowed for puritans to continue to engage in debates over the future that reform should take.

In the last decades of the seventeenth century things seem to have changed. We don't have enough close studies of English dissenters from the Restoration to the Glorious Revolution to enable us to identify and make sense of how the religious situation evolved from the perspective of the laity. But in New England we have been able to trace a number of significant changes. An elevated sense of the meaning of the ministry began to develop, and the distinction between laity and clergy became more pronounced. While still chosen by their congregations, ministers were increasingly ordained by fellow ministers. Clergy sought a greater role in the congregational decision-making process, and generally achieved it. When they failed they were likely to complain about the disorderly and ill-informed laity. Clergymen such as Increase Mather increasingly called upon the magistrates to enforce what they saw as the religious needs of the society. Increasingly, particularly after political power ceased to be in the hands of puritans, clergymen came together in ministerial associations which they would attempt to call upon to reinforce their local authority.

Whether from a sense of complacency or a certitude that what had evolved was ideal, many laymen acquiesced in these changes. While puritanism had its roots in the experience of God's caress, as time went more attention was paid to forms and structures. Puritans have been described as the "hotter sort of Protestants," and at one time the faith of each believer was likened to a burning ember, which, piled up one next to another, would produce a powerful flame. As Cotton Mather complained at the turn of the century, there were too many dead coals. I haven't found evidence of lay prophesying or asking questions in church services during this period. While conferences such as the one that Samuel Sewall attended still existed, they seem to have focused on cultivating individual spiritual growth rather than serving as a driving force in the affairs of the church. Enthusiasm, once a badge of puritanism, became an object of suspicion in an increasingly enlightened rational world.

In the years that followed the story set forth in this study, the religious situation in New England continued to change. Religion became more rational, the appeal to the mind replacing the appeal to the heart in many pulpits. Clergy focused more on addressing issues of morality and the benefits of doing good, an emphasis seen as Arminian by some who clung to the old beliefs. Yale was founded because Harvard's faculty was perceived by conservatives as having drifted too far from orthodox Calvinism, but the new college's reputation was dealt a serious blow when the college president and leading tutors converted to Anglicanism.

There is no denying the fact that the effort to elevate the role of the clergy and of clerical associations was supported in late seventeenth-century New England by many laymen. And it is likely that many of those individuals were less energized personally and thus more willing than their predecessors to trust to the authority of church leaders. It is plausible to think that the clerical assumption of greater authority, such as an expanded role in catechizing youth, was due in large part to the lay neglect of that responsibility. There were, as time went on, fewer burning coals and shining lights. The active faith of the hotter sort of Protestants was being replaced by a more passive, easier, and traditional faith.

And then, in 1734, the preaching of Jonathan Edwards sparked a revival of religion that would be called the Great Awakening. In churches throughout New England men and women had the fire of grace kindled in their hearts. Preachers such as Edwards, the English revivalist George Whitefield, and John Davenport's grandson James attacked the rational religion of their time and lay believers responded with enthusiasm. Issues that had been debated in the seventeenth century were debated again—how did grace enable the saints to see and apprehend God's truth? What was the use of a clergyman's education if he had not experienced a new birth? Who should be allowed access to the sacraments? Godly laity seized control in many churches, while where the godly were in the minority lay believers seceded and formed their own congregations. All of this is a different story, but one that might be better understood if placed in the historical context of the role the laity played in the original development of puritanism.

Finally, it is worth speculating how the religious developments discussed in this book may have influenced the political culture of New England. Years ago the English scholar Geoffrey F. Nuttall wrote of "the democratic form of church-meeting being not an end in itself but a means of discovering 'the government of the Spirit; and... it was the church-meeting which gave birth, in England, to political democracy, not vice versa."[1] And what is true of England is true also of New England, where strong connections also existed between religious and political culture.[2] On both sides of the Atlantic, lay people who believed they could comprehend God's plan for the church believed themselves capable of choosing the forms and leaders of secular society as well.

Notes

Introduction

1. Diarmaid MacCulloch, *Silence: A Christian History* (London: Allen Lane, 2013), 191.
2. William Hubbard, *A General History of New England*, second edition (Boston, 1848), 184.
3. Francis J. Bremer, *Shaping New Englands: Puritan Clergymen in Seventeenth Century England and New England* (Boston: Twayne, 1994).
4. Darrett B. Rutman, *American Puritanism* (Philadelphia: Lippincott, 1977).
5. The literature on radical laymen and laywomen is vast. Their story will be discussed in the chapters that follow.
6. See especially Christopher Hill, *The World Turned Upside Down: Radical Ideas during the English Revolution* (New York: Penguin, 1972).
7. The essay was later published in Collinson's collection of essays, *Godly People: Essays on English Protestantism and Puritanism* (London: Hambledon, 1983).
8. James Fulton Maclear, "'The Heart of New England Rent': The Mystical Element in Early Puritan History," *The Mississippi Valley Historical Review*, 42 (1956), 621–52.
9. Abram C. Van Engen, *Sympathetic Puritans: Calvinist Fellow Feeling in Early New England* (New York: Oxford, 2014).

1 The Experience and Meaning of God's Caress

1. For a discussion of some of these alternative visions of Christianity see Elaine Pagels, *The Gnostic Gospels* (New York: Random House, 1979).
2. Diarmaid MacCulloch, *A History of Christianity: The First Three Thousand Years* (London: Penguin, 2009), 130.
3. Richard L. Greaves, "The Ordination Controversy and the Spirit of Reform in Puritan England," *Journal of Ecclesiastical History*, 21 (1970), 225.
4. Andrew Cambers has provided an excellent discussion of the relationship between puritanism and reading in *Godly Reading: Print, Manuscript and Puritanism in England, 1580–1720* (Cambridge University Press, 2011).
5. Christopher Hill, *Society & Puritanism in Pre-Revolutionary England* (New York: Schocken, 1964), 487–8. David D. Hall points out that in his early writings Luther took the position that "the whole body of the faithful were priests: all who were believers could offer the 'spiritual' sacrifice of faith," but that by the 1530s he had retreated from this position as he came to see a greater need for order. David D. Hall, *The Faithful Shepherd: A History of the New England Ministry in the Seventeenth Century* (Chapel Hill: University of North Carolina Press, 1972), 7–8.
6. MacCulloch, *History of Christianity*, 574–603.

7. John White, *Direction for the Profitable Reading of the Scriptures* (London, 1647), 80.
8. Geoffrey F. Nuttall, *The Holy Spirit in Puritan Faith and Experience*, with a new introduction by Peter Lake (University of Chicago Press, 1992), 22.
9. Sibbes, quoted in Nuttall, *Holy Spirit*, 23–4.
10. Goodwin, quoted in Nuttall, *Holy Spirit*, 38.
11. Francis J. Bremer, *Building a New Jerusalem: John Davenport, a Puritan in Three Worlds* (New Haven: Yale University Press, 2012), 185–7.
12. John Davenport, *The Saints Anchor-Hold, in All Storms and Tempests, Preached in Sundry Sermons, and Published for the Support and Comfort of Gods People in All Times of Tryall* (London, 1661), 67.
13. Robinson, quoted in Nuttall, *Holy Spirit*, 24.
14. John Winthrop, "A Model of Christian Charity," in *Winthrop Papers, II*, 294.
15. Baillie quoted in Nuttall, *Holy Spirit*, 107, where Nuttall discusses this aspect of Congregational thinking.
16. Patrick Collinson, "Sects and the Evolution of Puritanism," in Collinson, *From Cranmer to Sandcroft* (London: Hambledon, 2006), 131.
17. Lynn Baird Tipson, "The Development of a Puritan Understanding of Conversion" (Yale University PhD, 1972), 8.
18. Thomas Hooker, *The Application of Redemption by the Effectual Work of the Word and Spirit of Christ* (London, 1656), bks 9–10, 395. See also Ian H. Murray, "Thomas Hooker and the Doctrine of Conversion," *Banner of Truth Magazine*, 195 (1979), 10–29.
19. Stephen Brachlow, *The Communion of the Saints: Radical Puritan and Separatist Ecclesiology, 1570–1625* (Oxford University Press, 1988), 3. Some of these issues are discussed in Marilyn J. Westerkamp, "Puritan Patriarchy and the Problem of Revelation," *Journal of Interdisciplinary History*, 23 (1993), 571–95.

2 Thinking of the Laity in the English Reformation

1. The title and thrust of this chapter owes much to Peter Iver Kaufman, *Thinking of the Laity in Late Tudor England* (University of Notre Dame Press, 2004).
2. For the early English Reformation see Richard Rex, *Henry VIII and the English Reformation* (2nd edn, Basingstoke: Macmillan, 2006) and Diarmaid MacCulloch, *Thomas Cranmer* (New Haven: Yale University Press, 1996). For a valuable perspective on Thomas Cromwell see Diarmaid MacCulloch, "Heinrich Bullinger and the English Speaking World," in P. Opitz and E. Campi, eds, *Heinrich Bullinger: Life–Thought–Influence*, 2 vols (Leiden: Brill, 2006), II, 892–909.
3. Diarmaid MacCulloch, *A History of Christianity: The First Three Thousand Years* (London: Penguin, 2009), 375–6.
4. See Gabriel Andiso, *The Waldensian Dissent* (Cambridge University Press 1999) and Richard Wunderli, *Peasant Fires: The Drummer of Niklashausen* (Bloomington: Indiana University Press, 1992).
5. Kaufman, *Laity*, 31
6. Christopher Marsh, *Popular Religion in Sixteenth-Century England* (Basingstoke: Macmillan, 1998), 169.

7. Claire Cross, *Church and People, 1450–1660: The Triumph of the Laity in the English Church* (Hassocks: Harvester, 1976), 9–10.
8. Quoted in Cross, *Church and People*, 21.
9. Keith Thomas, "Women and the Civil War Sects," *Past & Present*, 13 (1958), 46.
10. Cross, *Church and People*, 16.
11. Cross, *Church and People*, 33–40.
12. Kaufman, *Laity*, 40.
13. William Tyndale, *The Whole Works of W. Tyndall, John Frith, and Doct. Barnes* (1573), 285–6.
14. Alec Ryrie, *Being Protestant in Reformation Britain* (Oxford University Press, 2013), 395.
15. Kaufman, *Laity*, 38, 39.
16. Kaufman, *Laity*, 42–3.
17. The story of these communities is best treated in Andrew Pettegree, *Foreign Protestant Communities in Sixteenth-Century London* (Oxford University Press, 1986).
18. See A. G. Dickens, *The English Reformation* (London: Collins, 1967), 84. I do not wish to create the impression that only the Protestant laity were active in the struggle to define the nation's faith and practice. There were many laymen who were deeply committed to Catholic practice and resisted orders to make changes in their beliefs. See in particular Eamon Duffy, *The Stripping of the Altars: Traditional Religion in England, 1400–1580* (New Haven: Yale University Press, 1992) and idem, *The Voices of Morebath: Reformation and Rebellion in an English Village* (New Haven: Yale University Press, 2001).
19. Brett Usher, "Backing Protestantism: The London Godly, the Exchequer and the Foxe Circle," in David Loades, ed., *John Foxe: an Historical Perspective* (Aldershot: Ashgate, 1999), 105–34.
20. Francis J. Bremer, "William Winthrop and Religious Reform in London, 1529–1582," *The London Journal*, 24 (1999), 9–10.
21. Diarmaid MacCulloch, "The Impact of the Reformation on Suffolk Parish Life," *Suffolk Review*, n.s., 15 (1990), 7.
22. See Duffy, *Stripping of the Altars*, 453ff.
23. Diarmaid MacCulloch, *Tudor Church Militant: Edward VI and the Protestant Reformation* (London: Allen Lane, 1999), 106–7.
24. Cross, *Church and People*, 139.
25. The phrase, honoring those who refused to accept Catholic practices (compared to the idol Baal in the Old Testament), is found in a variety of sources, including William Winthrop to John Foxe, 18 November 1560, *Winthrop Papers: I*, 15–16, and Edward Underhill, "Anecdotes of Underhill," in John Gough Nichols, *Narratives of the Days of the Reformation* (Camden Society Publications, O.S. 77, 1859), 149.
26. Diarmaid MacCulloch, "Catholic and Puritans in Elizabethan Suffolk: A County Community Polarizes," *Archiv fur Reformationsgeschichte*, 72 (1981), 263–4.
27. Cross, *Church and People*, 97.
28. Alcock, Allerton, and Allen are discussed in Kaufman, *Laity*, 54–6. The quote from Allen is on page 56.

29. To the Reader by R. H., in John Bradford, *The Good Old Way, or, An excellent and profitable treatise on repentance made by John Bradford in the year 1553* (1652).
30. Mark Greengrass, "Scribal Networks and Sustainers in Protestant Martyrology," in Anne Dunan-Page and Clotilde Prunier, eds, *Debating the Faith: Religion and Letter Writing in Great Britain, 1550–1800* (Dordrecht: Springer, 2013), 29–30, 33.
31. David D. Hall, *The Faithful Shepherd: A History of the New England Ministry in the Seventeenth Century* (Chapel Hill: University of North Carolina Press, 1972), 28–9.
32. Hooper quoted in Ryrie, *Being Protestant*, 393–4, 395.
33. Francis J. Bremer, "William Winthrop and Religious Reform in London, 1529–1582," *London Journal* 24 (1999), 1–17.
34. Kaufman, *Laity*, 57. See also Brett Usher, "In a Time of Persecution: New Light on the Secret Protestant Congregation in Marian London," in David Loades, ed., *John Foxe and the English Reformation* (Aldershot: Ashgate, 1997), 233–51; and J. W. Martin, "The Protestant Underground Congregations of Mary's Reign," *Journal of Ecclesiastical History*, 35 (1984), 319–38.
35. "Anecdotes of Underhill," 149, 171.
36. Cross, *Church and People*, 116–18.
37. Patrick Collinson, *The Elizabethan Puritan Movement* (Oxford University Press, 1967) remains the foundational work on the subject, though its focus is largely on the clergy who shaped the movement.
38. Kaufman, *Laity*, 78–9. It should be noted that university training had not been a requisite for entry to the Roman Catholic priesthood and that it was a mainstream Protestant aspiration that would never in this period be fully realized.
39. Francis J. Bremer, *John Winthrop: America's Forgotten Founding Father* (New York: Oxford University Press, 2003), 35.
40. Patrick Collinson, *Archbishop Grindal, 1519–1583: The Struggle for a Reformed Church* (Berkeley: University of California Press, 1979), 114.
41. Patrick Collinson, *The Religion of Protestants: The Church in English Society 1559–1625* (Oxford University Press, 1982), 157.
42. Bremer, *John Winthrop*, 37–8.
43. There is an extensive literature on lectureships from the time of Elizabeth till the outbreak of the Puritan Revolution. These include Paul Seaver, *The Puritan Lectureships: The Politics of Religious Dissent, 1560–1662* (Stanford University Press, 1970), which deals mostly with London; Patrick Collinson, "Lectures by Combination: Structures and Characteristics of Church Life in 17th Century England," in Collinson, *Godly People: Essays on English Protestantism and Puritanism* (London: Hambeldon, 1983), 467–98.
44. Collinson, *Religion of Protestants*, 172–5.
45. Ian Green, "Varieties of Domestic Devotion in Early Modern English Protestantism," in Jessica Martin and Alec Ryrie, eds, *Private and Domestic Devotion in Early Modern Britain* (Farnham: Ashgate, 2012), 9–11.
46. Huntingdon, quoted in Stephen Brachlow, *The Communion of the Saints: Radical Puritan and Separatist Ecclesiology, 1570–1625* (Oxford University Press, 1988), 121.
47. Collinson, *Religion of Protestants*, 243.

48. Alexander Top, *St. Peters rocke under which title is deciphered the faith of Peter* (London, 1597), 98.
49. Ryrie, *Being Protestant*, 394.
50. Whitaker, quoted in Robert Ork Stuart, "The Breaking of the Elizabethan Settlement of Religion: Puritan Spiritual Experience and the Theological Division of the English Church" (Yale University PhD, 1976), 96.
51. Kate Narveson, "'Their Practice bringeth little profit': Clerical Anxieties about Lay Scripture Reading in Early Modern England," in Martin and Ryrie, eds, *Private and Domestic Devotion*, 165–6.
52. Kate Narveson, *Bible Readers and Lay Writers in Early Modern England: Gender and Self-Definition in an Emergent Writing Culture* (Farnham: Ashgate, 2012), 5–6.
53. Kaufman, *Laity*, 95.
54. Kaufman, *Laity*, 103.
55. Kaufman, *Laity*, 107.
56. Kaufman, *Laity*, 123–4. For the Stranger Churches see Pettegree, *Foreign Protestant Communities*. For the French Church in particular see Charles Littleton, "Geneva on Threadneedle Street: The French Church of London and Its Congregation, 1560–1625" (University of Michigan PhD, 1996).
57. Bremer, "William Winthrop," 8. His involvement in the Italian Church can be followed in Owe Boersma and A. Jelsma, eds, "Unity in Multiformity: The Minutes of the Coetus of London, 1575 and the Consistory Minutes of the Italian Church of London, 1570–1591," *Publications of the Huguenot Society of Great Britain and Ireland*, 59 (1997).
58. Collinson, *Archbishop Grindal*, 234.
59. Joanne J. Jung, *Godly Conversation: Rediscovering the Puritan Practice of Conference* (Grand Rapids: Reformation Heritage Books, 2011), 37.
60. Kaufman, *Laity*, 131, where Harrison is quoted.
61. Kaufman, *Laity*, 121–2.
62. Queen Elizabeth's order quoted in John Gwynfor Jones, "The Growth of Puritanism c. 1559–1662," in Alan P. F. Sell, ed., *The Great Ejectment of 1662: Its Antecedents, Aftermath, and Ecumenical Significance* (Eugene, OR: Pickwick, 2012), 13–14.
63. Collinson, *Grindal*, 232–45.
64. Thomas Paynall, *A fruitfull booke of the common places of all S. Pauls Epistles right necessary for all sortes of people* (London, 1562), chapter 41.
65. Ian Green, *Print and Protestantism in Early Modern England* (Oxford University Press, 2000), 45, 50.
66. Cranmer, quoted in Green, *Print*, 43.
67. Green, *Print*, 74–5. Historians have rightly pointed to the Calvinist commentary in the Geneva Bible for puritans, but have overstated their reliance on that text. While those reformers often did learn from the Geneva commentary, their first priority was the accuracy of the translation. Puritans agitated for the superior translation that was authorized by King James I, and a number of the assigned translators for that project were themselves puritans. Following its publication, the King James version became the preferred translation of many puritans.
68. Basil Morgan, "Crowley, Robert (1517–1588)," *Oxford Dictionary of National Biography*.

69. Ryrie, *Being Protestant*, 394. These dialogues have been used by many scholars analyzing the ideas of the clergy who wrote them. But it is also significant that the authors placed the religious arguments in the mouths of laymen.
70. Seymour Baker House, "Becon, Thomas (1512/13–1567)," *Oxford Dictionary of National Biography*.
71. Timothy Scott McGinnis, "Swingebreeches and Schollers: Images of Pastoral Leadership in Elizabethan Puritan Dialogues," in Peter Iver Kaufman, ed., *Leadership and Elizabethan Culture* (New York: Macmillan, 2013), 145–6.
72. McGinnis, "Swingebreeches and Schollers," 147–8.
73. Stuart, "Breaking of the Elizabethan Settlement," 99.
74. Perkins quoted in Jung, *Godly Conversation*, 64–5.
75. William Perkins, *The Art of Prophesying* (Edinburgh, 1986 reprint), 74.
76. An excellent analysis of Dent's work is to be found in Christopher Haigh, *The Plaine Man's Pathways to Heaven: Kinds of Christianity in Post-Reformation England* (Oxford University Press, 2007).
77. Both quoted in Brachlow, *Communion of the Saints*, 119, 120.
78. Kaufman, *Laity*, 107–9; Fulke quoted on p. 109.
79. Kaufman, *Laity*, 155–6, where Kaufman makes the case for Fulke's authorship, acknowledging that others believe Walter Travers or John Field composed the work. See also Joseph L. Black, ed., *The Martin Marprelate Tracts: A Modernized and Annotated Edition* (Cambridge University Press, 2008), xxii–xxiii.
80. Fulke quoted in Black, *Marprelate Tracts*, xxiii.
81. Brachlow, *Communion of the Saints*, 167–8.
82. Both quoted in Brachlow, *Communion of the Saints*, 121–2.
83. This is discussed and Fletcher quoted in Brachlow, *Communion of the Saints*, 122. See also Patrick Collinson, "Cranbrook and the Fletchers: Popular and Unpopular Religion in the Kentish Weald," in Collinson, *Godly People*, 417–20.
84. A. Peel and L. H. Carlson, eds, *The Writings of Robert Harrison and Robert Browne* (London?, 1953), 52–3.
85. Harrison, quoted in Patrick Collinson, "Sects and the Evolution of Puritanism," in Collinson, *From Cranmer to Sandcroft* (London: Hambledon, 2006), 135.
86. Godly clergy also sought to reach lay audiences through the written word. Published treatises expounding Calvinist doctrine and suggesting ways of leading a good life could spread the reform message and could be published in England for official positions of the church.
87. Patrick Collinson, "The Godly: Aspects of Popular Puritanism," in Collinson, *Godly People*, 2–3, 13.
88. John Craig, "The Growth of English Puritanism," in John Coffey and Paul Lim, eds, *The Cambridge Companion to Puritanism* (Cambridge University Press, 2008), 37.
89. Thomas Woodham, quoted in Collinson, "Godly," 8.
90. Patrick Collinson, *Richard Bancroft and Elizabethan Anti-Puritanism* (Cambridge University Press, 2013), 83–4.
91. Quoted in David D. Hall, *The Faithful Shepherd: A History of the New England Ministry in the Seventeenth Century* (Chapel Hill: University of North Carolina Press, 1972), 31.

92. Hall, *Faithful Shepherd*, 33.
93. Collinson, *Bancroft*, 100.
94. Collinson, *Religion of Protestants*, 266.
95. Collinson, *Bancroft*, 131.
96. Wilson, quoted in Collinson, *Religion of Protestants*, 265.
97. Collinson, *Bancroft*, 131–3.
98. Collinson, *Religion of Protestants*, 261.

3 Lay Puritans in Stuart England

1. Patrick Collinson, *Richard Bancroft and Elizabethan Anti-Puritanism* (Cambridge University Press, 2013), 33.
2. Francis J. Bremer, *First Founders: American Puritans and Puritanism in an Atlantic World* (Hanover, NH: University Press of New England, 2012), 47.
3. Francis J. Bremer, *Building a New Jerusalem: John Davenport, a Puritan in Three Worlds* (New Haven: Yale University Press, 2012), 57–9.
4. Jeremy Dupertius Bangs, *Strangers and Pilgrims, Travellers and Sojourners: Leiden and the Foundations of Plymouth Plantation* (Plymouth, MA: General Society of Mayflower Descendants, 2009), 212.
5. For lectureship see Francis J. Bremer, *Congregational Communion: Clerical Friendship in the Anglo-American Puritan Community, 1610–1692* (Boston: Northeastern University Press, 1994), esp. 48ff., and Paul Seaver, *The Puritan Lectureships: The Politics of Religious Dissent, 1560–1660* (Stanford University Press, 1970).
6. Claire Cross, *Church and People, 1450–1660: The Triumph of the Laity in the English Church* (Hassocks: Harvester, 1976), 184.
7. Bremer, *Building a New Jerusalem*, 85–6. The story of the Feoffees is fully examined in Isabel M. Calder, ed., *The Activities of the Puritan Faction of the Church of England, 1625–1633* (London: Church Historical Society, 1957).
8. Samuel Clarke, quoted in Patrick Collinson, *The Religion of Protestants: Church in English Society, 1559–1625* (Oxford University Press, 1983), 259.
9. Alexandra Walsham, "The Godly and Popular Culture," in John Coffey and Paul C. H. Lim, eds, *The Cambridge Companion to Puritanism* (Cambridge University Press, 2008), 287.
10. The importance of preaching and the ways in which believers absorbed the message is the subject of Arnold Hunt's *The Art of Hearing: English Preachers and Their Audiences, 1590–1640* (Cambridge University Press, 2010.
11. Oliver Heywood, quoted in Bremer, *Congregational Communion*, 39. For a discussion of Rogers's preaching style and that of other puritan preachers see Francis J. Bremer and Ellen Rydell, "Performance Art? Puritans in the Pulpit," *History Today*, 45 (September 1995), 50–4.
12. Margaret Winthrop to John Winthrop (c. 25 May 1629), *Winthrop Papers*, six volumes (Boston: Massachusetts Historical Society, 1929–) II, 93.
13. John Angier, as quoted in Collinson, *Religion of Protestants*, 244.
14. Bremer, *Building a New Jerusalem*, 77.
15. Quoted in Peter Iver Kaufman, *Thinking of the Laity in Late Tudor England* (University of Notre Dame Press, 2004), 6.

16. Bownd, quoted in Patrick Collinson, *The Religion of Protestants: The Church in English Society 1559–1625* (Oxford University Press, 1982), 265.
17. John Cotton, quoted in Charles Hambrick-Stowe, "Christ the Fountain of Life by John Cotton," in Kelly M. Kapic and Randall C. Gleason, eds, *The Devoted Life: An Invitation to the Puritan Classics* (Downers Grove, IL: IVP Academic, 2004), 77.
18. Samuel Hartlib, "Ephemerides," 1634 part 5, Hartlib Papers, Sheffield University, 29/2/50A.
19. Rogers, quoted in Jung, *Godly Conversation*, 114, 143.
20. Hooker, quoted in Baird Tipson, *Hartford Puritanism: Thomas Hooker, Samuel Stone, Their Terrible God, and the Roots of Evangelicalism in America* (forthcoming from Manchester University Press), chapter 3. I thank Dr. Tipson for providing me a copy of this work prior to its publication.
21. Richard Bernard, *Joshua's Resolution for the Well-Ordering of His Household* (1629), 51–2.
22. Tipson, *Hartford Puritanism*, chapter 3.
23. Thomas Watson, *Religion our true interest* (London, 1682), 92.
24. Richard Sibbes, *The Soules Conflict with itself, and victory over itself* (London, 1635), 312–13.
25. Rogers, quoted in Diane Willen, "'Communion of the Saints': Spiritual Reciprocity and the Godly Community in Early Modern England," *Albion*, 27 (1995), 19.
26. The issue of the legality of such meetings is explored in Patrick Collinson, "The English Conventicle," reprinted in Collinson, *From Cranmer to Sandcroft* (London: Hambledon, 2006), 145–72.
27. Quoted in Bangs, *Strangers and Pilgrims*, 11–12.
28. Canons 11, 71, 72, and 73 in Gerald Bray, ed., *The Anglican Canons 1529–1947* (Woodbridge: Boydell, 1998), 279, 363–5.
29. John Winthrop, "Common Grievances Groaning for Reformation," in *Winthrop Papers. Volume I*, 297.
30. John Craig, "The Growth of English Puritanism," in Coffey and Lim, eds, *Companion to Puritanism*, 34.
31. Cotton, quoted in Jesper Rosenmeir, *'Spiritual Concupiscence': John Cotton's English Years, 1584–1633* (Boston, UK: Richard Kay, 2012), 111, where he discusses the covenanted group in some detail.
32. The phrase is from Baird Tipson, who discusses Hooker's time in Chelmsford in *Hartford Puritanism*.
33. Eliot, quoted in Geoffrey Nuttall, *Visible Saints: The Congregational Way, 1640–1660*, 2nd edn (Weston Rhyn, UK: Quinta Press, 2001), 83.
34. Quoted in Collinson, "Sects," 143.
35. The actual visitation articles are collected in Kenneth Fincham, ed., *Visitation Articles and Injunctions of the Early Stuart Church, Volume I* (Woodbridge: Boydell 1994). See pp. 6–7, 34, 38.
36. Fincham, *Visitation Articles, I*, 40.
37. Fincham, *Visitation Articles, I*, 59, 103, 144.
38. Fincham, *Visitation Articles, I*, 157.
39. Kenneth Fincham, ed., *Visitation Articles and Injunctions of the Early Stuart Church, Volume II* (Woodbridge: Boydell, 1998), 24.

40. See, for example, Fincham, *Visitation Articles, I*, 181, 195 and Fincham, *Visitation Articles, II*, 16, 52, 58, 92, 129, 138, 199, 206, 214.
41. Two laymen who compiled sermon notebooks at this period were John Winthrop and Robert Keayne. Both manuscript notebooks are in the collections of the Massachusetts Historical Society. For Winthrop see Francis J. Bremer, *John Winthrop: America's Forgotten Founding Father* (New York: Oxford University Press, 2003), 119. A transcription of his sermon notebook will be part of Francis J. Bremer, ed., *Winthrop Papers: Religious Manuscripts*, to be published by the Massachusetts Historical Society. Keayne's notes on sermons in England are discussed in Bremer, *Building a New Jerusalem*, 81. A transcription of Keayne's English notes is included in Susan B. Ortman, "Gadding about London in Search of a Proper Sermon: How Robert Keayne's Sermon Notes from 1627-28 Inform Us about the Religious and Political Issues Facing the London Puritan Community" (Millersville University of Pennsylvania MA thesis, 2004). For sermon notes see also Meredith Marie Neuman, *Jeremiah's Scribes: Creating Sermon Literature in Puritan New England* (Philadelphia: University of Pennsylvania Press, 2013).
42. Udall, quoted in Collinson, *Religion of Protestants*, 265.
43. Collinson, "Godly," 10-11, where the church records are quoted.
44. Collinson, *Religion of Protestants*, 266.
45. See David R. Como, "Radical Puritanism, c. 1558–1660," in Coffey and Lim, eds, *Companion to Puritanism*.
46. Richard Rogers, *Seven Treatises containing such direction as is gathered out of the holie Scriptures, leading and guiding to true happiness, both in this life and in the life to come* (London, 1603), 477–490.
47. Rogers, *Seven Treatises*, 489–90.
48. Ezekiel Culverwell, *Time Well Spent in Sacred Meditations* (1635), 209.
49. Culverwell, *Time Well Spent*, 208.
50. Bremer, *Winthrop*, 96–97, 102.
51. Heywood, quoted in Stephen Foster, "New England and the Challenge of Heresy: 1630–1660: The Puritan Crisis in Transatlantic Perspective," *The William and Mary Quarterly*, 3rd series, 38 (1981), 627.
52. Quartermayne, quoted in David Cressy, *England on Edge: Crisis and Revolution, 1640–1642* (Oxford University Press, 2006), 145.
53. Thomas Goodwin, *The Trial of a Christian's Growth* (London, 1650), 49.
54. Thomas Taylor, *Davids learning, or, The way to true happiness* (London, 1617), 271.
55. Taylor, quoted in Collinson, *Religion of Protestants*, 268.
56. Rogers, quoted in Alec Ryrie, *Being Protestant in Reformation Britain* (Oxford University Press), 393.
57. Rogers, quoted in Robert Ork Stuart, "The Breaking of the Elizabethan Settlement of Religion: Puritan Spiritual Experience and the Theological Division of the English Church" (Yale University PhD, 1976), 66.
58. Vavasor Powel, *Spiritual Experiences of Sundry Believers Held Forth by them at severall solemne meetings and Conferences to that End* (London, 1651/2), 173.
59. Samuel Petto, *Roses from Sharon, or Sweet Experiences Gathered Up by some precious hearts, whilst they followed on to know the Lord. Published for public soul-advantage* (London, 1654), epistle to the reader.

60. Richard Sibbes, *The Glorious Feast of the Gospel* (London, 1650), 157.
61. John Rogers, *Ohel, or Beth-shemesh: A Tabernacle for the Sun, or Irenicum Evangelicum. An Idea of Church Discipline* (London, 1653), 366–7.
62. Richard Gilpin, *Demonologia sacra, or, A treatise of Satan's temptations* ((London, 1677), 15.
63. Robert Bolton, *Mr. Boltons last and learned worke of the foure last things, death, judgment, hell, and heaven* (London, 1632), 48–9.
64. Richard Vines, *Gods drawing, and mans coming to Christ discovered* (1662), 320.
65. Alec Ryrie, "Congregations, Conventicles, and the Nature of Early Scottish Protestantism," *Past & Present*, 191 (2006), 53. The main thrust of the article is to cast doubt on John Knox's reconstruction of more institutional origins of the Scottish Reformation and to emphasize more lay-driven, informal processes. Margo Todd points to the role of the laity in *The Culture of Protestantism in Early Modern Scotland* (New Haven: Yale University Press, 2002), especially 361, 363. The lay involvement in the religion of Edinburgh is discussed in depth in Laura A. M. Stewart, *Urban Politics and British Civil Wars: Edinburgh, 1617–53* (Leiden: Brill, 2006). I thank Dr. Todd for pointing me to this study.
66. Samuel Rutherford, *A peaceable and temperate plea for Pauls presbyterie in Scotland* (London, 1642), 326.
67. Samuel Rutherford, *Influences of the Life of Grace* (London, 1659), 308.
68. Robert Rollock, *Lectures upon the History of the Passion, Resurrection, and Ascension of our Lord Jesus Christ* (Edinburgh, 1616), 395.
69. Thomas Gouge, *Christian Directions, Showing how to walk with God all the day long* (London, 1661), 45.
70. John Owen, *Eschol: a cluster of the fruit of Canaan . . . or, Rules for Direction for the Walking of Saints in Fellowship* (London, 1648), 58–60.
71. Sibbes, quoted in Geoffrey F. Nuttall, *The Holy Spirit in Puritan Faith and Experience*, with a new introduction by Peter Lake (University of Chicago Press, 1992), 39.
72. Ward, quoted in John Craig, "Bodies at Prayer in Early Modern England," in Natalie Mears and Alec Ryrie, *Worship and the Parish Church in Early Modern Britain* (Farnham: Ashgate, 2013), 181.
73. D'Ewes, quoted in Ryrie, *Being Protestant*, 391.
74. James Janeway, *Heaven upon Earth, or, The Best Friend in the Worst of Times* (London, 1671), 311–12.
75. David George Mullan, *Narratives of the Religious Self in Early-Modern Scotland* (Farnham: Ashgate, 2010), 13, 18.
76. Tom Webster writes about how puritans could "take on the model [of godliness] themselves and also recognize their like-minded kindred spirits, such recognition always dependent upon continual observation of the criteria for godliness." Tom Webster, "Early Stuart Puritanism," in Coffey and Lim, eds, *Companion to Puritanism*, 62.
77. John Saltmarsh, *Sparkles of Glory, or Some of beams of the morning-star* (London, 1647), 142, 144.
78. Quoted in Nuttall, *Holy Spirit*, 142.
79. Quoted in Nuttall, *Holy Spirit*, 143.
80. Byfield, quoted in Ryrie, *Being Protestant*, 391.

81. This is discussed in Kathleen Lynch, *Protestant Autobiography in the Seventeenth Century Anglophone World* (Oxford University Press, 2012), 185. The fact that so-called "conversion narratives" were a report from the battlefield and not a statement of final victory has often been overlooked by those who focus on the use of these narratives in New England.
82. See, for example, Daniel Featley, *Threnoikos the House of Mourning... delivered in sermons preached at the funerals of divers faithful servants of Christ* (London, 1660).
83. James Janeway, *Invisibles, Realities Demonstrated in the holy life and triumphant death of Mr. John Janeway* (London, 1674), 83.
84. Rogers, *Seven Treatises*, 477.
85. Kate Narveson, *Bible Readers and Lay Writers in Early Modern England: Gender and Self-Definition in an Emergent Writing Culture* (Farnham: Ashgate, 2012), 201.
86. Narveson, "Their Practice," 181–3.
87. For discussion of this work see Michael P. Winship, *Godly Republicanism: Puritans, Pilgrims, and a City on a Hill* (Cambridge, MA: Harvard University Press), 89–91.
88. Quoted and discussed in Diane Willen, "'Communion of Saints'," 26.
89. Narveson, *Bible Readers*, 115, 177.
90. Collinson, "Godly," 12–13.
91. Christopher Cob, *The Sect Everywhere Spoken Against: or, the Reproached Doctrine of Ely* (1651).
92. Bangs, *Strangers and Pilgrims*, 13–14.
93. John Morrill, "Cromwell, Oliver (1599–1658)," *Oxford Dictionary of National Biography*.
94. Quoted in Kate Narveson, "'Their practice bringeth little profit': Clerical Anxieties about Lay Scripture Reading in Early Modern England," in Jessica Martin and Alec Ryrie, eds, *Private and Domestic Devotion in Early Modern Britain* (Farnham: Ashgate, 2012), 179.
95. Narveson, *Bible Reading*, 127.
96. Narveson, "Their Practice," 171.
97. Stephen Geree, *The Ornament of Women, Or, A Description of the True Excellency of Women* (London, 1639), 2, 20 as quoted in Diane Willen, "Godly Women in Early Modern England, Puritanism and Gender," *Journal of Ecclesiastical History*, 43 (1992), 567.
98. Collinson, *Religion of Protestants*, 266–7.
99. Ryrie, *Being Protestant*, 370.
100. Ryrie, *Being Protestant*, 395; Jung, *Godly Conversation*, 149, 150.
101. Ryrie, *Being Protestant*, 371.
102. Ryrie, *Being Protestant*, 391.
103. John Ley's account, quoted in Ryrie, *Being Protestant*, 390. For more on Radcliffe see Peter Lake, "Feminine Piety and Personal Potency: The 'Emancipation' of Mrs. Jane Radcliffe," *The Seventeenth Century*, 2 (1987), 143–65. For the broader picture see Willen, "Godly Women," 561–80.
104. Heywood, quoted in Foster, "Heresy in New England," 627.
105. Michael Winship provides an excellent discussion of her activities in "Brigit Cooke and the Art of Female Self-Advancement," *The Sixteenth Century Journal*, 33 (2002), 1045–59.

106. Michael Winship discusses what little we know of her years in England, including her fasting and methods of reading scripture, in *Making Heretics: Militant Protestantism and Free Grace in Massachusetts, 1636–1641* (Princeton University Press, 2002), 38–40. Anne clearly was a product of the puritan belief that the individual could gain insight into scripture from the grace of the Spirit. Michael Ditmore explores her method of understanding scripture in "A Prophetess in her own Country: An Exegesis of Anne Hutchinson's 'Immediate Revelation'," *The William and Mary Quarterly*, third series, 57 (2000), 349–392.
107. Jenison, quoted in David R. Como, "Women, Prophecy, and Authority in Early Stuart Puritanism," *Huntington Library Quarterly*, 61 (1998), 205.
108. Como, "Women," 207.
109. Fenwick, quoted in David Como, introduction, *The Early Modern Englishwoman: A Facsimile Library of Essential Works. Series I: Printed Writings, 1500–1640: Part 4, Volume 5: Anne Phoenix* (Farnham: Ashgate, 2006), ix.
110. Collings, quoted in Willen, "'Communion of Saints'," 27–8. Willen discusses her life in more detail in her article.
111. Marilyn J. Westerkamp, "Anne Hutchinson, Sectarian Mysticism, and the Puritan Order," *Church History*, 59 (1990), 488.
112. Como, "Women," 210–17.
113. Anna Trapnell, *A legacy for saints; being several experiences of the dealings of God with Anna Trapnell* (London, 1654), to the reader, 7.
114. Katherine Sutton, *A Christian Womans Experiences of the glorious working of Gods free grace* (London, 1663), 40.
115. Brachlow, *Communion of the Saints*, 160.
116. Collinson, *Religion of Protestants*, 267.
117. John Morrill, "Renaming England's Wars of Religion," in Charles A. Prior and Glenn Burgess, eds, *England's Wars of Religion, Revisited* (Farnham: Ashgate, 2013), 321.
118. Bremer, *Building a New Jerusalem*, chapter 4.
119. Bremer, *Building a New Jerusalem*, 60–1.
120. Bremer, *Building a New Jerusalem*, 78–9.
121. William Orme, ed., *Remarkable Passages in the Life of William Kiffin* (London, 1823), 4–5.
122. These activities are discussed in Bremer, *Building a New Jerusalem*. Diane Willen documents the importance of links that bound reformers together in "Communion of the Saints," 19–41, but to my mind does not distinguish sufficiently between the local and trans-local sense in which individuals experienced and promoted the communion of saints.
123. Henry Scudder, *The Christian's Daily Walk* (London, 1635 edition), 787, 243–4.
124. Bremer, *Building a New Jerusalem*, 68–9.
125. Bremer, *Building a New Jerusalem*, 100–1.
126. Thomas Taylor, *A Commentary Upon the Epistle of Paul Written to Titus* (London, 1612), 688–9.
127. Richard Sibbes, *Bowels Opened, or, A Discovery of the Near and Dear Love, Union, and Communion Betwixt Christ and the Church* (London, 1639), 289.
128. Orme, *Life of William Kiffin*, 11–12.

194 Notes

129. Peter Lake, "Puritanism, Familism, and Heresy in Early Stuart England: The Case of John Etherington Revisited," in David Lowenstein and John Marshall, eds, *Heresy, Lityerature, and Politics in Early Modern English Culture* (Cambridge University Press, 2006), 95–6.
130. Patrick Collinson, *The Religion of Protestants: The Church in English Society 1559–1625* (Oxford University Press, 1982), 168.
131. Narveson, "Their Practice," 179–80.
132. Murray Tolmie, *The Triumph of the Saints: The Separate Churches of London 1616–1649* (Cambridge University Press, 1977), 36.
133. Peter Lake and David Como, "'Orthodoxy' and Its Discontents: Dispute Settlement and the Production of 'Consensus' in the London (Puritan) Underground," *Journal of British Studies*, 39 (2000), 45.
134. Lake, "Etherington Revisited," 100.
135. The three cases are discussed in Lake and Como, "'Orthodoxy' and Its Discontents," 34–70.
136. Lake and Como, "'Orthodoxy' and Its Discontents," 64, 68.
137. David Como provides an excellent treatment of this in *"Blown by the Spirit": Puritanism and the Emergence of an Antinomian Underground in Pre-Civil-War England* (Stanford University Press, 2004).
138. Como, *Blown by the Spirit*, 57, and Taylor quoted 57, n. 53.
139. See the discussion of How in John Donoghue, *Fire Under the Ashes: An Atlantic History of the English Revolution* (University of Chicago Press, 2013), 39–42.
140. Samuel How, *The Sufficiency of the Spirits Teaching without Humane Learning* (London, 1640), unpaginated.
141. Donoghue, *Fire Under the Ashes*, 89.

4 Gatherings of the Saints in England and the Netherlands

1. Michael P. Winship, *Godly Republicanism: Puritans, Pilgrims, and a City on a Hill* (Cambridge, MA: Harvard University Press, 2012), 42.
2. Browne, quoted in Williston Walker, ed., *The Creeds and Platforms of Congregationalism* (Boston: Pilgrim, 1960), 13–14.
3. Browne, quoted in Peter Iver Kaufman, *Thinking of the Laity in Late Tudor England* (University of Notre Dame Press, 2004), 149.
4. Robert Browne, *A Booke which Sheweth the Life and Manners of All True Christians* (Middelburgh, 1582), 30.
5. Michael E. Moody, "Browne, Robert (1550?–1633)," *Oxford Dictionary of National Biography*. The development of tests to limit church membership to the godly has been explored in Edmund S. Morgan's *Visible Saints: The History of a Puritan Idea* (Ithaca: Cornell University Press, 1963).
6. Stephen Wright, *The Early English Baptists, 1603–1649* (Woodbridge: Boydell, 2006), 21.
7. William Bradshaw, *English Puritanism, Containing the Main Opinions of the Rigidist Sort of Those that are Called Puritans* (1605), 5.
8. For Bradshaw see Victoria Gregory, "Bradshaw, William (*bap.* 1570, *d.* 1618)," *Oxford Dictionary of National Biography*. Polly Ha discusses the English Presbyterian response to the views of Jacob in *English Presbyterianism, 1580–1640* (Stanford University Press, 2011).

9. Francis J. Bremer, *Building a New Jerusalem: John Davenport, A Puritan in Three Worlds* (New Haven: Yale University Press, 2012), 24–5.
10. Winship, *Godly Republicanism*, 48.
11. Winship, *Godly Republicanism*, 49.
12. Patrick Collinson, "Barrow, Henry (c.1550–1593)," *Oxford Dictionary of National Biography*.
13. Barrow, quoted in Winship, *Godly Republicanism*, 56.
14. David D. Hall, *The Faithful Shepherd: A History of the New England Ministry in the Seventeenth Century* (Chapel Hill: University of North Carolina Press, 1972), 30.
15. Michael E. Moody, "Johnson, Francis (*bap.* 1562, *d.* 1617)," *Oxford Dictionary of National Biography*, which includes the Middleburg covenant.
16. Stephen Brachlow, *The Communion of the Saints: Radical Puritan and Separatist Ecclesiology, 1570–1625* (Oxford University Press, 1988), 132, where Johnson is quoted.
17. Stephen Wright, "Smyth, John (*d.* 1612)," *Oxford Dictionary of National Biography*.
18. Brachlow, *Communion of Saints*, 129.
19. Smyth, quoted in Wright, *Early English Baptists*, 25.
20. The best study of this group is Jeremy Dupertuis Bangs, *Strangers and Pilgrims, Travellers and Sojourners: Leiden and the Foundations of Plymouth Plantation* (Plymouth, MA: General Society of Mayflower Descendants, 2009).
21. Keith L. Sprunger, *Dutch Puritanism: A History of English and Scottish Churches of the Netherlands in the Sixteenth and Seventeenth Centuries* (Leiden: Brill, 1982), 5–9, 102.
22. Keith L. Sprunger, "Parker, Robert (c.1564–1614)," *Oxford Dictionary of National Biography*.
23. Brachlow, *Communion of the Saints*, 125.
24. The best study of Ames is Keith Sprunger, *The Learned Doctor William Ames: Dutch Backgrounds of English and American Puritanism* (Urbana: University of Illinois Press, 1972).
25. Brachlow, *Communion of Saints*, 125–6.
26. Stephen Wright, "Jacob, Henry (1562/3–1624)," *Oxford Dictionary of National Biography*.
27. Brachlow, *Communion of Saints*, 137, where Jacobs is quoted.
28. Brachlow, *Communion of the Saints*, 186–7; Jacobs quoted on 186.
29. Quoted in Sprunger, *Dutch Puritanism*, 60.
30. Brachlow, *Communion of the Saints*, 211, where Bradshaw is quoted.
31. John Cotton, *The Keys of the Kingdom of Heaven* (1644), in Larzer Ziff, ed., *John Cotton on the Churches of New England* (Cambridge, MA: Harvard University Press, 1968), 70.
32. Brachlow, *Communion of the Saints*, 169.
33. Brachlow, *Communion of the Saints*, 171, where Parker is quoted.
34. Brachlow, *Communion of the Saints*, 186–7.
35. Baillie, quoted in Brachlow, *Communion of the Saints*, 174.
36. See Hunter Powell's conclusion in *The Crisis of British Protestantism, 1638–1644* (forthcoming from Manchester University Press). I wish to thank Dr. Powell for sharing the book manuscript with me.
37. Murray Tolmie, *The Triumph of the Saints: The Separate Churches of London 1616–1649* (Cambridge University Press, 1977), 14.

38. Tolmie, *Triumph of the Saints*, 15.
39. Brachlow, *Communion of the Saints*, 181.
40. Sprunger, *Dutch Puritanism*, 340.
41. Ainsworth, quoted in Brachlow, *Communion of Saints*, 135.
42. Wright, *Early English Baptists*, 33.
43. David D. Hall, *Faithful Shepherd*, 41.
44. John Robinson, *The Peoples Plea for the Exercise of Prophesie* (1618), 4–5.
45. Robinson, *Prophesie*, 39, 61.
46. Bangs, *Strangers and Pilgrims*, 269.
47. Quoted in Bangs, *Strangers and Pilgrims*, 266.
48. Synod conclusions quoted in Geoffrey F. Nuttall, *The Holy Spirit in Puritan Faith and Experience*, with a new introduction by Peter Lake (University of Chicago Press, 1992), 77.
49. Bangs, *Strangers and Pilgrims*, 227.
50. Bangs, *Strangers and Pilgrims*, 266.
51. Bangs, *Strangers and Pilgrims*, 228.
52. Robinson, quoted in Bangs, *Strangers and Pilgrims*, 267.
53. Henry Ainsworth, *The Confession of faith of certain English people living in exile* (1607), 54–5.
54. Henry Ainsworth, *A Defence of the Holy Scriptures, worship, and ministerie, used in the Christian Churches separated from Antichrist* (Amsterdam, 1609), 36.
55. Ainsworth, *Defence*, 59–60.
56. Smyth, quoted in Wright, *Early English Baptists*, 25.
57. Sprunger, *Dutch Puritanism*, 64–5.
58. Stephen Wright, "Helwys, Thomas (*c*.1575–*c*.1614)," *Oxford Dictionary of National Biography*.
59. Helwys, quoted in Wright, *Early English Baptists*, 53.
60. Sprunger, *Dutch Puritanism*, 68.
61. Sprunger, *Dutch Puritanism*, 139–40.
62. "Selected documents from the Gould Manuscript," in Champlin Burrage, ed., *The Early English Dissenters in the Light of Recent Research (1550–1641)*, two vols (Cambridge University Press, 1912), II, 296.
63. Tolmie, *Triumph of the Saints*, 21–2.
64. John Coffey, *John Goodwin and the Puritan Revolution: Religion and Intellectual Change in Seventeenth-Century England* (Woodbridge: Boydell, 2006), 60.
65. Tolmie, *Triumph of the Saints*, 36–7.
66. Brachlow, *Communion of the Saints*, 190–1.
67. Brachlow, *Communion of the Saints*, 195.
68. Ger van Dijk, *History of the Beguinage in Amsterdam from 1307 to the Present* (Amsterdam, 2005), 6–12.
69. For detail on Paget's life see Keith L. Sprunger, "Paget, John (*d*. 1638)," in *Oxford Dictionary of National Biography*.
70. Alice C. Carter, *The English Reformed Church in Amsterdam in the Seventeenth Century* (Amsterdam, 1964), 53–66.
71. Interestingly, this would foreshadow a similar controversy in the 1650s triggered when Samuel Stone, as the sole minister of the Hartford, Connecticut congregation asserted his right to override his congregation's choice of a clergyman to succeed the deceased Thomas Hooker.

72. William Best, *A Just Complaint Against an Unjust Doer, wherein is declared the miserable slavery and bondage that the English Church of Amsterdam is now in by reason of the tyrannical government and corrupt doctrine of Mr. John Paget* (1634), preface.
73. Davenport, *Reply*, 226.
74. Samuel Eaton, *Defence of Sundry Positions* (1645), 84–5. John Coffey, *John Goodwin*, 108–9, quotes another source, *M. S. to A. S with a Plea for Liberty of Conscience* (1644), 9–19, as claiming that "John Davenport had remarked 'in his way to New England,' a classical presbytery was 'but thirteen Bishops, for one.'"
75. Stephen Goffe in the Hague April 26 [1633] to William Laud, SP 16/286/202.
76. A copy of the articles is to be found in the Boswell Papers, British Library Add Ms 6394, f154.
77. Stephen Goffe in the Hague April 26 [1633] to William Laud (?), SP 16/286/202.
78. "Transcript of the Journal of Daniel Bradford of Norwich, 1636–48," Norwich Record Office, MC64/4, 508x8. I would like to thank Joel Halcomb for providing me with a copy of this manuscript.
79. W. H. D. Longstaffe, ed., *Memoirs of the Life of Mr. Ambrose Barnes*, Surtees Society, *Publications*, 50 (Durham, 1866), 131–3. Stephen Foster, *The Long Argument: English Puritanism and the Shaping of New England Culture, 1500–1700* (Chapel Hill: University of North Carolina Press, 1991), 163, states that the congregation at Arnhem in the Netherlands, under the ministry of Thomas Goodwin and Philip Nye, used such a test of membership but the sources he cites are (1) the account of Simpson's relation, which was in Rotterdam, and (2) a mere list of who some of the members of the Arnhem church were.
80. Sprunger, *Dutch Puritanism*, 167–70, 229.
81. Sprunger, *Dutch Puritanism*, 173.
82. Robinson, quoted in Keith Thomas, "Women and the Civil War Sects," *Past & Present*, 13 (1958), 44.
83. Thomas, "Women," 46, where Robinson is quoted. See also Bangs, *Strangers and Pilgrims*, 227–8.
84. Sprunger, *Dutch Puritanism*, 173.

5 Shaping the New England Way

1. John Davenport, recalling a report from John Cotton in the 1630s; quoted in Francis J. Bremer, *Building a New Jerusalem: John Davenport, a Puritan in Three Worlds* (New Haven: Yale University Press, 2012), 339.
2. Hinton, quoted in Bangs, *Strangers and Pilgrims*, 647.
3. William Bradford, *History of Plymouth Plantation, 1620–1647*, two volumes (Boston: Massachusetts Historical Society, 1912), I, 402–3.
4. Bradford, *Plymouth Plantation*, II, 348–51.
5. William Hubbard, *A General History of New England*, 2nd edn (Boston, 1848), 65. Hubbard argued that the practice of lay prophesying was not a custom in any other churches in New England, but as we will see this was clearly not

the case for the early seventeenth century and is an example of early clerical historians writing out the role of the laity.
6. Bradford, *Plymouth Plantation*, I, 213.
7. Mark A. Peterson, "The Plymouth Church and the Evolution of Puritan Religious Culture," *The New England Quarterly*, 66 (December 1993), 575–6. Peterson provides an excellent analysis of the church, stressing the extent to which it was dominated by the laity in its early years.
8. For Endecott see Francis J. Bremer, *First Founders: American Puritans and Puritanism in the Atlantic World* (Hanover, NH: University Press of New England, 2012), 29–44.
9. Raymond Phineas Stearns and David Holmes Brawner, "New England Church 'Relations' and Continuity in Early Congregational History," *Proceedings of the American Antiquarian Society*, 75 (1965), 24.
10. Thomas Hooker, *A Comment upon Christ's Last Prayer* (1656), 80.
11. Quoted in Geoffrey F. Nuttall, *The Holy Spirit in Puritan Faith and Experience*, with a new introduction by Peter Lake (University of Chicago Press, 1992), 142.
12. Quoted in Nuttall, *Holy Spirit*, 142.
13. Quoted in John Morrill, "Cromwell, Oliver (1599–1658)," *Oxford Dictionary of National Biography*.
14. Endecott to Bradford, in Bradford, *Plymouth Plantation*, II, 90–2.
15. Winship, *Godly Republicanism*, 141.
16. Endecott to Bradford, in Bradford, *Plymouth Plantation*, II, 90–2.
17. Charles Gott to William Bradford in *Governor William Bradford's Letter Book* (Bedford, MA; 2001 reprint), 47–9.
18. Historians have generally attributed the formation of the church to the efforts of Higginson and Skelton, but the evidence is unclear and if the date we have for their arrival is accurate, it is more likely that the process was at least underway when they arrived.
19. The task of forming a church was one that normally took place over time as those self-identified as godly came together, discussed their faith, and prepared a covenant. While formation of a church at Salem could conceivably have been the first order of business on July 20, it is unlikely, and made more so by the fact that the surviving description of the day's events makes no mention of such a momentous event.
20. Williston Walker makes the case for why the formation of the church had to have come before the selection of Higginson and Skelton as officers in Williston Walker, *The Creeds and Platforms of Congregationalism* (Boston: Pilgrim, 1960), 104–7.
21. The traditional story of the formation of the Salem church places the official formation as August 6. But, as Williston Walker pointed out, the contemporary documents refer to the "members" of the church choosing Higginson and Skelton to office on July 20. Following congregational theory and practice, a church had to be organized by individuals subscribing to a covenant before ministers could be chosen. See Walker, *Creeds and Platforms*, 104–5. Another possibility is that prior to the arrival of the ministers, John Endecott, with the help of Fuller, had drawn up a covenant which individuals had subscribed to and that Higginson later revised that statement, which members then committed to on August 6.

22. The description of these events was set forth by Charles Gott in a letter to William Bradford. The letter is found in Bradford, *Plymouth Plantation*, 93–6. A fuller version in *Governor William Bradford's Letter Book*, 47–9 indicates that Bradford had entertained Gott and his wife on a previous visit to Plymouth.
23. The office of ruling elder was often seen as distinct from that of the preaching elders. Whether the office was *jure divino* or not, and whether it existed in terms of its relationship to the lay congregants and the clergy were matters of debate in both New England and in England during the 1640s and 1650s. While some scholars have argued that in New England the ruling elder, like the deacon, was a lay officer, John Cotton and others appear to have viewed the office as clerical. I am not going to explore this particular theme in the role of the laity in puritanism, but an excellent review of the issues can be found in William M. Abbott, "Ruling Eldership in Civil War England, the Scottish Kirk, and Early New England: A Comparative Study of Secular and Spiritual Aspects," *Church History*, 75 (2006), 38–68.
24. Nathaniel Morton, *New England's Memorial...with Special Reference to the first colony thereof, called New-Plimouth* (Cambridge, MA; 1669), 75. Morton's account was written many years after the event, but he had access to Bradford's papers. Despite this, there are some aspects of his account that are open to question.
25. Michael Winship reviews some of this, including my own previous marginalization of the Pilgrim influence in *Godly Republicanism*, 288–9, note 2.
26. Foster, *The Long Argument*, 154.
27. A similar process of forming a congregation, unaided by any contact with Plymouth, took place in Bermuda, where the puritan clergyman Lewis Hughes organized a church sometime before 1617, having members of the church signify their choice of elders by a show of hands. See A. C. Hollis Hallett, *Chronicle of a Colonial Church; 1612–1826, Bermuda* (Bermuda: Juniper Hill, 1993), 19–20.
28. Winship, *Godly Republicanism*, 143.
29. Morton, *General History*, 77–8.
30. I owe this suggestion to Michael P. Winship in an e-mail communication in March 2014.
31. Richard Gildrie, *Salem, Massachusetts 1626–1683: A Covenanted Community* (Charlottesville, VA: University of Virginia Press, 1975), 5–8.
32. Francis J. Bremer, *John Winthrop: America's Forgotten Founding Father* (New York: Oxford University Press, 2004), 166–7.
33. Bremer, *John Winthrop*, 167. The company eventually reimbursed the Brownes for the financial loss they had suffered as a result of Endecott's actions.
34. I have set forth the reasons for believing that this was the time and venue of Wingthrop's sermon in Bremer, *John Winthrop*, 173–4.
35. Bremer, *John Winthrop*, 173–84.
36. The only source for these events is a letter complaining about them from John Cotton to Samuel Skelton, June 13, 1631 in Sargent Bush, Jr., ed., *The Correspondence of John Cotton* (Chapel Hill: University of North Carolina Press, 2001), 15–41, 149. A slightly different transcription, with its own commentary, is in David D. Hall, "John Cotton's Letter to Samuel Skelton," *William and Mary Quarterly*, 3rd s., 22 (1965), 478–85.

37. Cotton to Skelton, 144.
38. Cotton to Skelton, 145–6.
39. Winthrop, quoted in Bremer, *John Winthrop*, 179.
40. Winthrop's openness to further light is similar to that of John Robinson, who, according to Geoffrey Nuttall believed that although the Lutherans and Calvinists "were precious shining lights in their own times, yet God had not revealed his whole will to them; and were they now living, saith he, they would be as ready and willing to embrace further light as that they had received... It is not possible that the Christian world should come so lately out of such thick antichristian darkness, and that perfection of knowledge should break forth at once." Nuttall, *Holy Spirit*, 113.
41. Philip F. Gura, *A Glimpse of Sion's Glory: Puritan Radicalism in New England, 1620–1660* (Middletown, CT: Wesleyan University Press, 1984), 37.
42. Fuller to Bradford, 28 June 1630, in *Bradford's Letter Book*, 56–7.
43. Edward Winslow and Samuel Fuller to William Bradford, 26 July 1630, in *Bradford's Letter Book*, 57–8.
44. Samuel Fuller to William Bradford, 2 August 1630, in *Bradford's Letter Book*, 58–9.
45. Walker, *Creeds and Platforms*, 128–9.
46. Stephen Foster, "New England and the Challenge of Heresy, 1630–1660: The Puritan Crisis in Transatlantic Perspective," *The William and Mary Quarterly*, 3rd s., 38 (1981), 628.
47. Don Gleason Hill, ed., *The Record of Baptisms, Marriages, and Deaths... Transcribed from the Church Records in the Town of Dedham, Massachusetts, 1638–1845* (Dedham, 1888), 1–6.
48. I have examined the issue of church membership requirements in Francis J. Bremer, "'To tell what God hath done for thy soul': Puritan Spiritual Testimonies as Admission Tests and Means of Edification," *New England Quarterly* (scheduled for December 2014). In it I take issue with the assumption that "conversion narratives" were the norm in the colonies.
49. Bremer, *John Winthrop*, 175.
50. Richard S. Dunn, James Savage, and Laetitia Yeandle, eds, *The Journal of John Winthrop, 1630–1649* (Cambridge, MA: Harvard University Press, 1996), 44.
51. *Journal of John Winthrop*, 50.
52. There are various possible explanations for the decision not to call Williams to office in Salem at this time. Endecott and others may have felt that it was important for the colony to maintain a united front on such matters. Williams may have found that the separatism practiced by Skelton was not as thorough as he was comfortable with. Or it may have been that at a time when churches sought unanimity in major decisions. the remaining Old Planters who were part of the church may have wielded enough influence to block the call. The last possibility is presented in Gildrie, *Salem*, 24–5.
53. The quote is from Cotton Mather's *Magnalia*, as in Baird Tipson, *Hartford Puritanism: Thomas Hooker, Samuel Stone, Their Terrible God, and the Roots of Evangelicalism in America* (forthcoming from Manchester University Press), chapter 3.
54. *Journal of John Winthrop*, 82.
55. *Journal of John Winthrop*, 48.
56. *Journal of John Winthrop*, 105.

57. *Journal of John Winthrop*, 114.
58. Thomas Lechford, *Plain Dealing, or, News from New England* (London, 1642).
59. J. Hammon Trumbull, ed., *Plain Dealing by Thomas Lechford* (Boston, 1867), 40 n. 40. For Rumney Marsh see James F. Cooper, Jr., and Kenneth P. Minkema, eds, *The Colonial Church Records of the First Church of Reading (Wakefield) and the First Church of Rumney Marsh (Revere)* (Boston: Colonial Society of Massachusetts, 2006).
60. *Bicentennial History of the First Congregational Church, Marblehead, Massachusetts* (Marblehead, 1884), 6.
61. Michael P. Winship, *Making Heretics: Militant Protestantism and Free Grace in Massachusetts, 1636–1641* (Princeton, 2002), 49.
62. *Journal of John Winthrop*, 111.
63. Lechford, *Plain Dealing*, 42.
64. John Cotton, *The True Constitution of a Particular Visible Church* (1642), 6.
65. Lechford, *Plain Dealing*, 42.
66. *Journal of John Winthrop*, 106.
67. Roger Clap, *Memoirs of Capt. Roger Clap* (Boston, 1731), 5.
68. It might be instructive to compare the role of such narratives to the "conversion narratives" by criminals awaiting execution, accounts that were also designed to impact the audience. As for England, see Peter Lake with Michael Questier, *The Antichrist's Lewd Hat: Protestants, Papists & Players in Post-Reformation England* (New Haven: Yale University Press, 2002), 131ff. For colonial New England see Daniel E. Williams, "'Behold a Tragic Scene Strangely Changed into a Theater of Mercy': The Structure and Significance of Criminal Conversion Narratives in Early New England," *American Quarterly*, 38 (1986), 827–47; and Daniel A. Cohen, *Pillars of Salt, Monuments of Grace: New England Crime Literature and the Origins of American Popular Culture* (Amherst, MA: University of Massachusetts Press, 2006).
69. See the discussion in Lewis R. Rambo, *Understanding Religious Conversion* (New Haven: Yale University Press, 1993), especially 137–8 and 158.
70. Michael McGiffert, ed., *God's Plot: Puritan Spirituality in Thomas Shepard's Cambridge* (Amherst: University of Massachusetts Press, 1994), 147.
71. [William Rathband], *A briefe narration of some church courses held in opinion and practise in the churches lately erected in New England. Collected out of sundry of their own printed papers and manuscripts with other good intelligences. Together with some short hints (given by the way) of their correspondence with the like tenents and practises of the separatists churches. And some short animadversions upon some principall passages for the benefit of the vulgar reader. Presented to publike view for the good of the church of God by W. R.* (London, 1644), 39
72. Thomas Welde, *An Answer to W. E., His Narration* (London, 1644), 54. In light of this it is striking that the modern editors of the "confessions" point out that "Unfortunately, there is little evidence in the *Confessions* to indicate that the relations of faith were actually given in public." George Selement and Bruce C. Wooley, eds, *Thomas Shepard's Confessions*, Publications of the Colonial Society of Massachusetts, 58 (Boston: Colonial Society of Massachusetts), 22, note 42.
73. I have argued elsewhere that the paradigm established by Edmund S. Morgan in *Visible Saints: The History of Puritan Idea* (Ithaca: Cornell University Press,

1963) is flawed and that many if not most New England churches did not require such a statement of personal experience for admission. See Francis J. Bremer, "To tell what God hath done for thy soul." Writing of the Shepherd confessions, David D. Hall has commented that the "uncertainty about assurance of salvation that runs through them is at odds with a persistent stereotype of the Puritans as excessively self-confident." Hall, "Review Essay: What is the Place of 'Experience' in Religious History?," *Religion and American Culture: A Journal of Interpretation*, 13 (2003), 242.
74. A new perspective on these "confessions" is provided by Andy Dorsey in "A Rhetoric of American Experience: Thomas Shepard's Cambridge Confessions and the Discourse of Spiritual Hypocrisy," *Early American Literature*, 49 (2014), 629–62, but like others Dorsey focuses on how clergy shaped these accounts rather than on what they meant to the laymen who delivered them and heard them.
75. Selement and Wooley, *Thomas Shepard's Confessions*, 83, 92, 104, 156–61, 165–7, 180, 211.
76. John Davenport, *The Profession of Faith of That Reverend and Worthy Mr. J. D., Sometimes Preacher of Stevens Coleman-Street, London Made Publiquely Before the Congregation at His Admission into One of the Churches of God in New England* (London, 1642), 6–7.
77. William Hooke, *The Priviledge of the Saints on Earth Beyond Those in Heaven in Respect of Gifts and Graces Exercised* (London, 1673), 77–8.
78. Cotton Mather, *Magnalia Christi Americana: The Ecclesiastical History of New England*, 2 vols (Hartford, CT, 1853), I, 554.
79. Winship, *Godly Republicanism*, 48.
80. Cotton, quoted in Ann Hughes, "Puritanism and Gender," in John Coffey and Paul Lim, eds, *The Cambridge Companion to Puritanism* (Cambridge University Press, 2008), 298.

6 The Free Grace Controversy and Redefining the Role of Lay Believers

1. Edward Johnson, *A History of New-England* (London, 1654), 95–6, 102.
2. Michael P. Winship, *Making Heretics: Militant Protestantism and Free Grace in Massachusetts, 1636–1641* (Princeton University Press, 2002). In the pages that follow I am drawing heavily from Winship's work, which is my source except where other material is specifically cited.
3. An excellent discussion of this is to be found in Michael P. Winship, " 'The Most Glorious Church in the World': The Unity of the Godly in Boston, Massachusetts, in the 1630s," *Journal of British Studies*, 39 (2005), 71–98.
4. Elton, quoted in Winship, *Making Heretics*, 66.
5. For a discussion of these networks and how they were used to achieve agreement see Francis J. Bremer, *Congregational Communion: Clerical Friendship in the Anglo-American Puritan Community, 1610–1690* (Boston: Northeastern University Press, 1994).
6. Richard S. Dunn, James Savage, and Laetitia Yeandle, eds, *The Journal of John Winthrop, 1630–1649* (Cambridge, MA: Harvard University Press, 1996), 102–3.

7. John Davenport, quoting a report from John Cotton that he received in the mid-1630s; John Davenport, *A Sermon Preached at the Election of the Governor at Boston, in New England, May 19th, 1669* (1670), 11.
8. Marilyn Westerkamp discusses Hutchinson in this context in "Anne Hutchinson: Sectarian Mysticism and the Puritan Order," *Church History*, 59 (1990), 487–8.
9. Quotes in Winship, 41–3.
10. Cotton, quoted in Charles Hambrick-Stowe, "Christ the Fountain of Life by John Cotton," in Kelly M. Kapic and Randall C. Gleason, eds, *The Devoted Life: An Invitation to the Puritan Classics* (Downers Grove, IL: IVP Academic, 2004), 74. Though the sermon containing these statements was not published until 1651, Hambrick-Stowe argues persuasively that it was first preached in Boston, Lincolnshire before 1630.
11. Wheelwright, quoted in Winship, *Making Heretics*, 47.
12. Winship, *Making Heretics*, 44.
13. Firmin, quoted in Winship, *Making Heretics*, 51.
14. Welde, quoted in Winship, *Making Heretics*, 59.
15. Winship, *Making Heretics*, 62.
16. quoted in Winship, *Making Heretics*, 117.
17. Winthrop, quoted in Winship, *Making Heretics*, 116.
18. Welde, quoted in Winship, *Making Heretics*, 116.
19. Firmin, quoted in Winship, *Making Heretics*, 116.
20. Winthrop, quoted in Winship, *Making Heretics*, 157.
21. It is important to note that excommunication was not intended to be a permanent judgment, but a final way to bring an erring member to his or her senses. In many cases that we can trace through the seventeenth century, the member confessed their error and was readmitted to the congregation.
22. "A Report of the Trial of Anne Hutchinson before the Church in Boston," in David D. Hall, ed., *The Antinomian Controversy, 1636–1638: A Documentary History* (Middletown, CT: Wesleyan University Press, 1968), 358–61. Hereafter "Trial."
23. "Trial," 366–7.
24. "Trial," 358–9.
25. David D. Hall, *The Faithful Shepherd: A History of the New England Ministry in the Seventeenth Century* (Chapel Hill: University of North Carolina Press, 1972), 5.
26. Hall, *Antinomian Controversy*, 233–4.
27. Wilson, quoted in Hall, *Faithful Shepherd*, 91.
28. Shepard, quoted in Hall, *Faithful Shepard*, 111. Korah was Izhar's son who rebelled against Moses in Exodus 6.
29. Hall, *Faithful Shepherd*, x, 115.
30. William Hubbard, *A General History of New England*, 2nd edn (Boston, 1848), 184.
31. Hall, *Faithful Shepherd*, 102.
32. Hall, *Faithful Shepherd*, 102–6. Not surprisingly, Hall suggests that the pattern of lay ordination may have persisted in Plymouth longer than elsewhere.
33. Hall, *Faithful Shepard*, 103.
34. Foster, *The Long Argument*, 171.
35. Hall, *Faithful Shepherd*, 102.

36. Bremer, *Building a New Jerusalem*, 258.
37. Hall, *Faithful Shepard*, 107.
38. Perkins, quoted in Hall, *Faithful Shepherd*, 54.
39. See Samuel Eliot Morison, *The Founding of Harvard College* (Cambridge, MA: Harvard University Press, 1935) and *Harvard College in the Seventeenth Century* (Cambridge, MA: Harvard University Press, 1936).
40. Hall, *Faithful Shepard*, 179.
41. *A Treatise I. of Faith...IV. Questions and Answers Upon Church Government Taken from Written Copies long since delivered by the late Reverend Mr. John Cotton* (Boston, 1713), 21–3.
42. Hall, *Faithful Shepard*, 111.
43. [Richard Mather], *Church-Government and Church-Covenant Discussed, in an Answer of the Elders of the Several Churches in New England* (1643), 78–9.
44. Winship, *Making Heretics*, 218.
45. John Cotton, *The True Constitution of a Particular Visible Church* (1642), 6.
46. [Mather], *Church-Government*, 78.
47. Richard Mather, *A Reply to Mr. Rutherford, or, A defence of the answer to Reverend Mr. Herle's book against the independency of churches* (London, 1646), 465ff.
48. Lechford, *Plain-Dealing*, 42.
49. For a brief discussion see Francis J. Bremer, *Puritanism: A Very Short Introduction* (New York: Oxford University Press, 2009), 82–3.
50. For Dudley see Francis J. Bremer, *First Founders: American Puritans and Puritanism in an Atlantic World* (Hanover, NH: University Press of New England, 2012), 63–78.
51. *Massachusetts Records*, I, 142–3.
52. *Winthrop's Journal*, 173, 184.
53. Don Gleason Hill, ed., *The Record...Transcribed from the Church Records of the Town of Dedham* (Dedham, 1888), 9–10.
54. Hall, *Faithful Shepard*, 127.
55. Hall, *Faithful Shepard*, 168–9.
56. Hall, *Faithful Shepard*, 128–9, where the objections of the Boston church are quoted.
57. Nathaniel B. Shurtleff, ed., *Records of the Governor and Company of the Massachusetts Bay...Vol. IV—Part I* (Boston, 1854), 122. Hereafter cited as MR.
58. *MR*, IV.1, 156–7.
59. Chandler Robbins, *A History of the Second Church, or Old North, in Boston* (Boston, 1852), 4ff.
60. *MR*, III, 293–4.

7 The Role of the Laity in England's Puritan Revolution

1. The uprising against the religious innovations is treated in detail by Laura Stewart in *Urban Politics and British Civil Wars: Edinburgh, 1617–53* (Leiden: Brill, 2006), 172ff.
2. Quoted in Kevin Sharpe, *The Personal Rule of Charles I* (New Haven: Yale University Press, 1992), 788.
3. Michael Braddick, *God's Fury, England's Fire: A New History of the English Civil Wars* (London: Allen Lane, 2008), 128–30.

4. Anthony Fletcher, *The Outbreak of the English Civil War* (New York University Press, 1981), 111–12, 123, 119.
5. Fletcher, *Outbreak*, 112.
6. John Taylor, *The Discovery of a Swarm of Separatists, or, a Leatherseller's Sermon* (1641), a2, a4.
7. John Taylor, *A Swarme of Sectaries and Schismamtics, Wherein is Discovered the Strange Preaching (or Prating) of such as are by their Trades Cobblers, Tinkers, Pedlers, Weavers, Sowgelders, and Chimney Sweepers* (1641), not paginated.
8. This topic is discussed more fully in Francis J. Bremer and Ellen Rydell, "Performance Art? Puritans in the Pulpit," *History Today* (September 1995), 50–4. The quote regarding Rogers, by Sidrach Simpson, and that about Perkins by Samuel Clarke are both to be found in this article.
9. Richard L. Greaves, "The Ordination Controversy and the Spirit of Reform in Puritan England," *Journal of Ecclesiastical History*, 21 (1970), 225–7, from which the quotes are taken.
10. Joel Halcomb, "A Social History of Congregational Religious Practice During the Puritan Revolution" (University of Cambridge PhD, 2009), 57–8.
11. Murray Tolmie, *The Triumph of the Saints: The Separate Churches of London 1616–1649* (Cambridge University Press, 1977), 48–9.
12. Ann Hughes, *Gangraena and the Struggle for the English Revolution* (Oxford University Press, 2004), 37.
13. D'Ewes, quoted in Chad Van Dixhoorn, ed., *The Minutes and Papers of the Westminster Assembly, 1643–1652*, five vols (Oxford University Press, 2012), *Volume I: Introduction*, 9.
14. Information in this paragraph is drawn from Van Dixhoorn, *Westminster Assembly, Volume I*.
15. Van Dixhoorn, *Westminster Assembly, Volume II: Minutes, Sessions 45–119, 155–198 (1643–1644)*, 498.
16. See Francis J. Bremer, *Congregational Communion: Clerical Friendship in the Anglo-American Puritan Community, 1610–1692* (Boston: Northeastern University Press, 1994), 135–43.
17. Van Dixhoorn notes the objections to the term in *Westminster Assembly, Volume I*, 30.
18. Braddick, *God's Fury*, 350–1.
19. Ian Gentles, *The New Model Army in England, Ireland, and Scotland, 1645–1653* (Oxford University Press, 1992), 94.
20. Richard Baxter, quoted in John Donoghue, *Fire Under the Ashes: An Atlantic History of the English Revolution* (University of Chicago Press, 2013), 168, 169, 171, 175.
21. On Rainsborough's regiment see Adrian Tinniswood, *The Rainsborowes: One Family's Quest to Build a New England* (New York: Basic Books, 2013), 138–50.
22. Francis J. Bremer, *First Founders: American Puritans and Puritanism in the Atlantic World* (Hanover, NH: University Press of New England, 2012), 214.
23. Bremer, *First Founders*, 117. For a detailed discussion of colonists who returned to England at this time the most up-to-date examination is to be found in Susan Hardman Moore, *Pilgrims: New World Settlers & the Call of Home* (New Haven: Yale University Press, 2007), and idem, *Abandoning America: Life-Stories from Early New England* (Woodbridge: Boydell, 2013).
24. Quoted in Nuttall, *Holy Spirit*, 78.
25. Gentle, *New Model Army*, 94, where the quotes are to be found.

26. Quoted in Gentle, *New Model Army*, 96, 99.
27. Claire Cross, *Church and People, 1450–1660: The Triumph of the Laity in the English Church* (Hassocks: Harvester, 1976), 211.
28. Gentle, *New Model Army*, 100–3.
29. John Morrill, "Renaming England's Wars of Religion," in Charles A. Prior and Glenn Burgess, eds, *England's Wars of Religion, Revisited* (Farnham: Ashgate, 2013), 312.
30. This paragraph and the next are drawn from the work of John Morrill, particularly "How Oliver Cromwell Thought," in John Morrow and Jonathan Scott, eds, *Liberty, Authority, Formality: Political Ideas and Culture, 1600–1900. Essays in Honour of Colin Davis* (Exeter: Imprint Academic, 2008), 89–112.
31. Morrill, "How Cromwell Thought," 98.
32. John Coffey, "England's Exodus: The Civil War as a War of Deliverance," in Prior and Burgess, *England's Wars of Religion, Revisited*, 268.
33. Quoted in Morrill, "How Cromwell Thought," 90.
34. Lesley Le Claire, "The Survival of the Manuscript," in Michael Mendle, ed., *The Putney Debates of 1647: The Army, the Levelers and the English State* (Cambridge University Press, 2001), 31.
35. Morrill, "How Cromwell Thought," 93.
36. A. S. P. Woodhouse, ed., *Puritanism and Liberty: Being the Army Debates (1647–9) from the Clarke Manuscripts*, with a preface by Ivan Roots (University of Chicago Press, 1974), 19, 38, 95, 99, 101, 103–6, 107–8.
37. Woodhouse, *Puritanism and Liberty*, 127 and 127 n. 1.
38. Walwyn, quoted in Andrew Bradstock, *Radical Religion in Cromwell's England: A Concise History from the English Civil War to the End of the Commonwealth* (London: Tauris, 2011), 37.
39. See Bremer, *First Founders*, 117–22.
40. Donoghue, *Fire Under the Ashes*, 171.
41. Hughes, *Gangraena*, 43.
42. Joel Halcomb, "A Social History of Congregational Religious Practice during the Puritan Revolution" (University of Cambridge PhD, 2009), 56, 64.
43. Halcomb, "Social History," 128.
44. David R. Como, "Radical Puritanism, c. 1558–1660," in John Coffey and Paul C. H. Lim, eds, *The Cambridge Companion to Puritanism* (Cambridge University Press, 2008), 242.
45. Bernard Capp, *England's Culture Wars: Puritan Reformation and its Enemies in the Interregnum, 1649–1660* (Oxford University Press, 2012), 218.
46. Hughes, *Gangraena*, 136, 214.
47. Coffey, "Ticklish Business," 110–11.
48. An outstanding modern assessment of the work is Hughes, *Gangraena*.
49. Elizabeth Clarke, "The Legacy of Mothers and Others: Women's Theological Writing, 1640–1660," in Christopher Durston and Judith Maltby, eds, *Religion in Revolutionary England* (Manchester University Press, 2006), 71.
50. Barbara Taft, "From Reading to Whitehall: Henry Ireton's Journey," in Mendle, *Putney Debates*, 193.
51. Manfred Brod, "Poole, Elizabeth (*bap.* 1622?, *d.* in or after 1668)," *Oxford Dictionary of National Biography*.
52. Quoted in Nuttall, *Holy Spirit*, 87–8.
53. Jung, *Godly Conversation*, 147.

54. Bunyan, *Grace Abounding to the Chief of Sinners* (1966), 10. For a discussion of this experience see Vera J. Camden, "John Bunyan and the Goodwives of Bedford: A Psychoanalytical Approach," in Anne Dunan-Page, *The Cambridge Companion to Bunyan* (Cambridge University Press, 2010), 51–64.
55. Keith Thomas, "Women and the Civil War Sects," *Past & Present*, 13 (1958), 45.
56. Thomas, "Women," 47.
57. Edward Reynolds, *Imitation and Caution for a Christian Woman: or, the Life and Death of that excellent gentlewoman, Mrs. Mary Bewley* (1659), 7–8.
58. Winthrop, quoted in Bremer, *First Founders*, 107; Sarah Keayne is discussed in *First Founders*, 106–10.
59. Halcomb, "Social History," 127.
60. Thomas, "Women," 47.
61. Both tracts quoted in Thomas, "Women," 51.
62. Phyllis Mack, *Visionary Women: Ecstatic Prophecy in Seventeenth-Century England* (Berkeley: University of California Press, 1992), 106–7.
63. Donoghue, *Under the Ashes*, 172–3.
64. Jacqueline Eales, "'So many sects and schisms': Religious Diversity in Revolutionary Kent, 1640–16," in Durston and Maltby, *Religion*, 236, where Coppin is quoted.
65. Hughes, *Gangraena*, 52–3.
66. Clarke, "Women's Writings," 72–3.
67. Katherine Sutton, *A Christian Womans Experiences of the glorious working of Gods free grace* (London, 1663), 40.
68. Anna Trapnell, *A Legacy for Saints* (1654), 23.
69. Baillie, quoted in Nuttall, *Holy Spirit*, 75.
70. Halcomb, "Social History," 67, 73.
71. Halcomb, "Social History," 85–6.
72. Bristol records quoted in Halcomb, "Social History," 125.
73. Halcomb, "Social History," 126.
74. Eales, "Sects and schisms," 227.
75. Thomas Goodwin and Philip Nye, "To the Reader," in John Cotton, *The Keys of the Kingdom of Heaven* (1644), n.p.
76. Samuel Petto, John Martin, and Frederick Woodal, *The Preacher Sent* (London, 1658), quoted in Nuttall, *Holy Spirit*, 79.
77. Petto, Martin, and Woodall, *Preacher*, 21, 34.
78. [Sydrach Simpson], *A Vindication of the Liberty of Public Preaching* (1647), 3, 4, 5, 14.
79. John Owen, *The Duty of Pastors and People Distinguished* (1644), 11.
80. *A Declaration of the Faith and Order Owned and Practiced in the Congregational Churches in England; Agreed upon and consented unto by their Elders and Messengers in Their Meeting at the Savoy, Octob. 12, 1658* (London, 1659), 24.
81. James Fulton Maclear in "'The Heart of New England Rent': The Mystical Element in Early Puritan History," *The Mississippi Valley Historical Review*, 42 (1956), 627.
82. Halcomb, "Social History," 74.
83. Stephen Ford, *An Epistle to the Church in Chipping-Norton* (Oxford, 1657), 41.
84. John Murcot, *Several works of Mr. John Murcot, that eminent and godly preacher of the Word, lately of a Church of Christ at Dublin in Ireland* (1657), 305.

85. Nuttall, *Visible Saints*, 50.
86. Rogers, *Ohel*, 356.
87. Richard Lawrence, *Gospel-separation separated from its abuses; or, The Saints guide in Gospel-fellowship* (1657), 136.
88. John Murcot, *Several Works*, 305.
89. Edward Reynolds, *Israel's Prayer in Time of Trouble, with God's Gracious Answer Thereunto* (1649), 49.
90. For a discussion of Rogers and those who attacked his practices see Crawford Gribben, *God's Irishmen: Theological Debates in Cromwellian Ireland* (Oxford University Press, 2007), 56–76; and Crawford Gribben, "Lay Conversion and Calvinist Doctrine during the English Commonwealth," in Deryck W. Lovegrove, ed., *The Rise of the Laity in Evangelical Protestantism* (London: Routledge, 2002), 40–1.
91. Samuel Petto, *Roses from Sharon, or Sweet Experiences Gathered Up by some precious hearts* (London, 1654), to the reader.
92. See the discussion in Kathleen Lynch, *Protestant Autobiography in the Seventeenth-Century Anglophone World* (Oxford University Press, 2012), especially 122–48.
93. Vavasor Powell, *Spiritual Experiences of Sundry Beleevers held forth by them at severall solemn meetings and conferences* (London, 1651/2), 173. It should be noted that while English puritans published a number of such collections, the only published New England accounts of spiritual experience were those of native American converts. However, it should also be noted that manuscript accounts of spiritual experience also circulated on both sides of the Atlantic.
94. Richard Lawrence, *Gospel-separation separated from its abuses; or The saints guide in Gospel-fellowship. Whereby they may be directed not only to preserve the purity, but withal the unity of Gospel-worship: by a well-wisher to Sion's purity and unity* (1657), 136.

8 Varieties of Lay Enthusiasm in New England and England

1. This was an important insight of James Fulton Maclear in " 'The Heart of New England Rent': The Mystical Element in Early Puritan History," *The Mississippi Valley Historical Review*, 42 (1956), 621–52.
2. John Coffey, "A ticklish business: Defining Heresy and Orthodoxy in the Puritan Revolution," in David Lowenstein and John Marshall, eds, *Heresy, Literature, and Politics in Early Modern English Culture* (Cambridge University Press, 2006), 109.
3. Hall, *The Faithful Shepherd*, 99.
4. Stephen Wright, "Jessey, Henry (1601–1663)," *Oxford Dictionary of National Biography*.
5. Halcomb, "A Social History of Congregational Religious Practice," 47. Petto quoted on 150.
6. Mather, quoted in Carla Pestana, *Quakers and Baptists in Colonial Massachusetts* (New York: Cambridge University Press, 1991), 51.
7. Thomas Lechford, *Plain Dealing, or News from New England* (1642), edited with an introduction by J. Hammond Trumbull (Boston, 1867), 94.

8. Sydney V. James, *John Clarke and His Legacies: Religion and Law in Colonial Rhode Island 1638–1750*, ed. Theodore Dwight Bozeman (University Park, PA: Pennsylvania State University Press, 1999), 21–42, where Clarke is quoted.
9. For Lady Moody see Bremer, *First Founders*, 91–3.
10. Anne Eaton and her views are discussed in Bremer, *Building a New Jerusalem*, 220–5.
11. William G. McLoughlin, *New England Dissent, 1630–1833: The Baptists and the Separation of Church and State*, I (Cambridge, MA: Harvard University Press, 1971), 16, 18.
12. Nathaniel B. Shurtleff, ed., *Records of the Governor and Company of the Massachusetts Bay in New England, Vol. II, 1642–1649* (Boston, 1853), 85. Hereafter cited as *MR*.
13. Philip J. Anderson, "Letters of Henry Jessey and John Tombes to the Churches of New England, 1645," *Baptist Quarterly*, 28 (1979), 30–40, which includes copies of the letters.
14. Bremer, *Building a New Jerusalem*, 269.
15. *MR*, III, 173–4.
16. McLoughlin, *New England Dissent*, 18–20.
17. Pestana, *Quakers and Baptists*, 5.
18. Francis J. Bremer, "Dunster, Henry (bap. 1609, d. 1659)," *Oxford Dictionary of National Biography*. See also Jonathan Den Hartog, " 'National and Provinciall Churches are Nullityes': Henry Dunster's Puritan Argument against the Puritan Established Church," forthcoming in the *Journal of Church and State*. I would like to thank Den Hartog for sharing a copy of his article.
19. Chauncy's stay in Scituate and the split in that congregation are carefully analyzed in Jeremy Dupertius Bangs's introduction to his edition of *The Seventeenth-Century Town Records of Scituate, Massachusetts, Volume One* (Boston: New England Historic and Genealogical Society, 1997), 31–44.
20. McLoughlin, *New England Dissent*, I, 29–30.
21. Winthrop and Downing, quoted in Francis J. Bremer, *John Winthrop: America's Forgotten Founding Father* (New York: Oxford University Press, 2003), 339.
22. Richard S. Dunn, James Savage, and Laetitia Yeandle, eds, *The Journal of John Winthrop, 1630–1649* (Cambridge, MA: Harvard University Press, 1996), 611–12, 629; *MR*, II, 141; *MR*, III, 51, 64.
23. Bremer, *Building a New Jerusalem*, 269.
24. Baxter, quoted in Maclear, "Heart of New England," 630.
25. David R. Como, "Radical Puritanism, c. 1558–1660," in John Coffey and Paul C. H. Lim, eds, *The Cambridge Companion to Puritanism* (Cambridge University Press, 2008), 253.
26. Sibbes, *Bowels Opened*, quoted in Jung, *Godly Conversation*, 97.
27. H. Larry Ingle, "Fox, George (1624–1691)," *Oxford Dictionary of National Biography*.
28. Leo Damrosch, *The Sorrows of the Quaker Jesus: James Nayler and the Puritan Crackdown on the Free Spirit* (Cambridge, MA: Harvard University Press; 1996), 17–18.
29. Fox's *Journal*, quoted in Ingle, "George Fox."
30. Michael R. Watts, *The Dissenters: From the Reformation to the French Revolution* (Oxford University Press, 1978), 198.

31. For an insightful study of Nayler see Damrosch, *Sorrows of the Quaker Jesus*.
32. Clap, quoted in Maclear, "Heart of New England," 651.
33. Quoted in McLoughlin, *New England Dissent*, 6.
34. For the Quakers in New England see Arthur J. Worrall, *Quakers in the Colonial Northeast* (Hanover, NH: University Press of New England, 1980), 1–58.
35. Daniel J. Boorstin, *The Americans: The Colonial Experience* (New York: Random House, 1958), 38.
36. Catie Gill, "Gibbons, Sarah (1634/5–1659)," *Oxford Dictionary of National Biography*.
37. Bremer, *Building a New Jerusalem*, 271–4.
38. Bremer, *Building a New Jerusalem*, 272–6.
39. Quoted in Maclear, "Heart of New England," 649.
40. Maclear, "Heart of New England," 622.
41. See Bremer, *First Founders*, 169–94.
42. William Coddington, *A Demonstration of True Love Unto You the Rulers of the Colony of the Massachusetts in New England* (London, 1674), 6, 10.
43. Coddington, *Demonstration*, 13, 12, 19–20.
44. Information in this and following paragraphs is drawn from Carla Gardina Pestana, "Gorton, Samuel (bap. 1593, d. 1677)," *Oxford Dictionary of National Biography* and Philip Gura, *A Glimpse of Sion's Glory: Puritan Radicalism in New England, 1620–1660* (Middletown, CT: Wesleyan University Press, 1984).
45. Gura, *Sion's Glory*, 62.
46. Gura, *Sion's Glory*, 299.

9 Responding to the Challenges of Diversity, 1640–60

1. John Morrill, "The Puritan Revolution," in Coffey and Lim, eds, *The Cambridge Companion to Puritanism*, 81.
2. Halcomb, "Social History," 256.
3. Richard Lawrence, *Gospel-separation separated from its abuses; or The saints guide in Gospel-fellowship. Whereby they may be directed not only to preserve the purity, but withal the unity of Gospel-worship: by a well-wisher to Sion's purity and unity* (1657), 135–6.
4. Bernard Capp, *England's Culture Wars: Puritan Reformation and Its Enemies in the Interregnum, 1649–1660* (Oxford University Press, 2012), 115.
5. Quoted in Morrill, "How Oliver Cromwell Thought," 108.
6. Quoted in Halcomb, "Social History," 74.
7. Quoted in Geoffrey Nuttall, *Visible Saints: The Congregational Way, 1640–1660*, 2nd edn (Weston Rhyn, UK: Quinta Press, 2001), 115.
8. William Bartlett, *A Model of the Primitive Congregational Way* (London, 1647), 75.
9. Quoted in Nuttall, *Visible Saints*, 116.
10. Baillie, quoted in Geoffrey F. Nuttall, *The Holy Spirit in Puritan Faith and Experience*, with a new introduction by Peter Lake (University of Chicago Press, 1992), 107, where Nuttall discusses this aspect of Congregational thinking.

11. Quoted and discussed in Halcomb, "Social History," 256.
12. Coffey, "A ticklish business," 123.
13. Bremer, *Building a New Jerusalem*, 169–71.
14. David D. Hall, *A Reforming People: Puritanism and the Transformation of Public Life in New England* (New York: Random House, 2011), 108.
15. John Coffey, "The Toleration Controversy during the English Revolution," in Christopher Durston and Judith Maltby, eds, *Religion in Revolutionary England* (Manchester University Press, 2006), 49.
16. Hughes, *Gangraena*, 46.
17. Hall, *Faithful Shepherd*, 209.
18. I have found the concept of a perimeter fence, as discussed by Alexandra Walsham in *Charitable Hatred: Tolerance and Intolerance in England, 1500–1700* (Manchester University Press, 2006), to be a useful tool in dealing with the question of how much latitude of opinion practiced puritans allowed in the public spheres that they created. A similar idea can be found in Kai Ericson's *Wayward Puritans: A Study in the Sociology of Deviance* (New York: Wiley, 1966), in which he discusses conflict as a means of settling boundaries.
19. *MR*, III, 354–5.
20. Hall, *Faithful Shepherd*, 169.
21. *MR*, IV, Pt I, 122.
22. Woburn Petition in *Collections of the Massachusetts Historical Society*, 3rd series, I (1825), 38–45.
23. *MR*, IV, Pt I, 151.
24. J. H. Trumbull, ed., *The Public Records of the Colony of Connecticut* (Hartford, 1850), I, 545, 311, 111–12.
25. Hall, *Faithful Shepherd*, 181–90.
26. This and the following discussion of the Hartford church dispute is treated in Bremer, *Building a New Jerusalem*, 258–62. Hall suggests that Stone and Wigglesworth disagreed on the issue of church membership and allowing all who were baptized to have the rights of membership without submitting themselves to the congregation as adults (*Faithful Shepherd*, 211).
27. Burroughs, quoted in Coffey, "Toleration Controversy," 49.
28. Goodwin, quoted in Coffey, "Toleration Controversy," 49.
29. Francis J. Bremer, *Congregational Communion: Clerical Friendship in the Anglo-American Puritan Community, 1610–1690* (Boston: Northeastern University Press, 1994), 167–8, where Burroughs and Caryl are quoted.
30. Bremer, *Congregational Communion*, 170.
31. This paragraph and the following rely on Halcomb, "Social History," 173–5.
32. Coffey, "A ticklish business," 109.
33. Bremer, *Congregational Communion*, 119–20.
34. Discussion of the associations in this and the following paragraphs is drawn from Halcomb, "Social History," 216ff.
35. Bremer, *Congregational Communion*, 200–1; Halcomb, "Social History," 234–7. See also Hunter Powell, "The Last Confession: A Background Study of the Savoy Declaration of Faith and Order" (University of Cambridge MPhil, 2008).
36. Leverett's letter quoted in Bremer, *Congregational Communion*, 178.

10 Clergy and Laity in the Later Seventeenth Century

1. Report of John Crowe, quoted in Lawrence Shaw Mayo, *John Endecott* (Boston, 1936), 259. The story of the reception of the regicides in New England is told in Bremer, *Building a New Jerusalem*, 282–9. See also Christopher Pagliuco, *The Great Escape of Edward Whalley and William Goffe* (Charleston, SC: History Press, 2012).
2. Some Presbyterians did hope for comprehension within the re-established Church of England, but such an accommodation failed to come about.
3. Michael R. Watts, *The Dissenters: From the Reformation to the French Revolution* (Oxford University Press, 1978), 224–7.
4. The standard listing (with biographical notes) of those ejected is A. G. Matthews, *Calamy Revised: Being a Revision of Edmund Calamy's Account of the Ministers and Others Ejected and Silenced, 1660–1662* (Oxford University Press, 1934, reissued 1988).
5. David J. Appleby, "From Ejectment to Toleration in England, 1662–89," in Alan P. F. Sell, *The Great Ejectment of 1662: Its Antecedents, Aftermath, and Ecumenical Significance* (Eugene, OR: Pickwick, 2012), 79.
6. John Spurr, *English Puritanism, 1603–1689* (Basingstoke: Macmillan, 1998), 134–5.
7. Daniel L. Wykes, "Early Religious Dissent in Surrey after the Restoration," *Southern History*, 33 (2011), 54.
8. In addition to their continuing efforts to shape their lives according to godly imperatives, many lay puritans engaged in efforts to overturn the newly established Restoration settlement. The story of such efforts is discussed in Richard L. Greaves, *Deliver Us from Evil: The Radical Underground in Britain, 1660–1663* (Oxford University Press, 1986), and idem, *Enemies Under His Feet: Radicals and Nonconformists in Britain, 1664–1677* (Stanford University Press, 1990).
9. Anne Dunan-Page, "Letters and Records of Dissenting Congregations: David Crosley, Cripplegate, and Baptist Church Life," in Anne Dunan-Page and Clotilde Prunier, eds, *Debating the Faith: Religion and Letter Writing in Great Britain, 1550–1800* (Dordrecht: Springer, 2013), 70.
10. Samuel S. Thomas, *Creating Communities in Restoration England: Parish and Congregation in Oliver Heywood's Halifax* (Leiden: Brill, 2013), 137–8.
11. Watts, *Dissenters*, 230–1.
12. Wykes, "Early Religious Dissent," 73.
13. Quoted in David L. Wykes, "They 'assemble in greater numbers and [with] more dareing then formerly': The Bishop of Gloucester and Nonconformity in the Late 1660s," *Southern History*, 17 (1995), 30.
14. Brown, *Spirituality*, 102ff.
15. Martin Sutherland's *Peace, Toleration, and Decay: The Ecclesiology of Late Stuart Dissent* (Carlisle: Paternoster Press, 2003) examines the struggles of dissent largely from the perspective of John Howe and other clergy.
16. Wykes, "The Bishop of Gloucester and Nonconformity," 27.
17. As noted in the text, there is no modern study of the institutional life of English Congregationalism in the period from 1660–89. My thoughts in this section have been helped by e-mail communications with Joel Halcomb and Anne Dunan-Page, which I wish to thank them for.

18. Raymond Brown, *Spirituality in Adversity: English Nonconformity in a Period of Repression, 1660–1689* (Milton Keynes: Paternoster, 2012), 88, 318.
19. In Nathaniel Morton, *New England's Memorial…with an appendix*, 6th edn (Boston, 1855), 427.
20. John Owen, *Eshcol:…or Rules of Direction for the Walking of the Saints in Fellowship* (1648), 58.
21. Ann Dunan-Page, "Writing 'things ecclesiastical': The Literary Acts of the Gathered Churches," *Etudies Episteme*, 21, 2012. Acts of Writing, IV—Monumentalization and the Act of Writing, http:??www.etudes-episteme.org/2e/?writing-things-ecclesiastical.
22. Thomas, *Creating Communities*, 131, 133, 127, 141, 135, 152–3.
23. Thomas Watson, *Religion our true interest* (London, 1682), 92–4.
24. John Owen, *A Practical Exposition of the 130th Psalm* (1669), 163.
25. William Hooke, *The priveledge of the saints on earth* (London, 1673), 77–8.
26. Owen, *Eshcol*, 55.
27. Thomas Vincent, *The True Christian's Love of the Unseen Christ* (1677), 157.
28. Thomas Watson, *A body of practical divinity* (1692), 56.
29. Quoted in Brown, *Spirituality*, 101.
30. John Flavel, *The method of grace* (London, 1681), 190–1.
31. Quoted in Nuttall, *The Holy Spirit in Puritan Faith and Experience*, 83.
32. Crawford Gribben, "Lay Conversion and Calvinist Doctrine during the English Commonwealth," in Deryck W. Lovegrove, ed., *The Rise of the Laity in Evangelical Protestantism* (London: Routledge, 2003), 37.
33. Samuel Lee, *The Joy of Faith* (1687), 199.
34. Jung, *Godly Conversation*, viii.
35. Brown, *Spirituality*, 279–80.
36. *Stated Christian Conference Asserted to be a Christian Duty* (1697?), 5, 13, 22–3, 40, 41.
37. Jung, *Conversation*, ix.
38. Clarke, quoted in Jung, *Conversation*, 141.
39. Ted. A. Campbell, *The Religion of the Heart: A Study of European Religious Life in the Seventeenth and Eighteenth Centuries* (Columbia, SC: University of South Carolina Press, 1991), 50.
40. Higginson, quoted in James F. Cooper, Jr., *Tenacious of Their Liberties: The Congregationalists in Colonial Massachusetts* (New York: Oxford University Press, 1999), 92.
41. For the full story of the synod and the resulting controversy see Robert G. Pope, *The Half-Way Covenant: Church Membership in Puritan New England* (Princeton University Press, 1970).
42. Cooper, *Tenacious of their Liberties*, 99.
43. Cooper, *Tenacious of Their Liberties*, 98–101.
44. Hall, *Faithful Shepherd*, 200.
45. John Davenport, " A Third Essay, Containing Replies to the Answer," John Davenport Papers, American Antiquarian Society, Worcester, MA, 156–8.
46. Quoted in Hall, *Faithful Shepherd*, 203.
47. Bremer, *Congregational Communion*, 229.
48. Nathaniel Mather to Increase Mather, March 26, 1684, *Massachusetts Historical Society Collections*, 4th series, VIII, 55. Susan Hardman Moore in *Pilgrims: New World Settlers & the Call of Home* (New Haven: Yale University Press,

2007), 140, claims that Nathaniel Mather was the unidentified author of the preface to Richard Mather's *Disputation concerning Church Members and their Children* (1657), reporting results of that synod, and that Nathaniel Mather supported the Half-Way Covenant. My own reading of the content of the preface makes that unlikely, particularly because the author favors movement toward parish restoration.

49. Wilson, quoted in Nathaniel Morton, *New England's Memorial* (Boston, 1669), 183–4.
50. See Bremer, *Building a New Jerusalem*, 314–38.
51. John Davenport, *A Sermon Preached at the Election of the Governor at Boston in New England, May 19th 1669* (Boston, 1670), 11–26.
52. Bremer, *Building a New Jerusalem*, 348.
53. Bremer, *Building a New Jerusalem*, 348–9.
54. Willard and Woodridge, quoted in Hall, *Faithful Shepherd*, 208.
55. Hall, *Faithful Shepherd*, 217.
56. Wilson, quoted in Bremer, *Building a New Jerusalem*, 316.
57. Though he had originally been allied with John Davenport in opposing the recommendations of the Synod of 1662, Increase Mather had come to support the synod's findings by 1675, when he published *The First Principles of New-England concerning the Subject of Baptism & Communion of Churches*. In that work the Boston clergyman sought to demonstrate that what Davenport and others had considered innovations in the New England Way—broader baptism and consociation of churches—were actually consistent with the ideas of the founders. He successfully mined the writings of the first generation to find passages to buttress his arguments, and also drew on manuscripts to which he had access. According to Mather, John Cotton had urged for a greater use of consociations prior to his death in 1652.
58. Bremer, *First Founders*, 227–32.
59. Bremer, *First Founders*, 230–2.
60. Hall, *Faithful Shepherd*, 209.
61. Thomas M. Davis and Virginia L. Davis, eds, *Edward Taylor's "Church Records" and Related Sermons* (Boston: Twayne, 1981), xxxii.
62. Hall, *Faithful Shepherd*, 212.
63. William G. McLoughlin, *New England Dissent, 1630–1833: The Baptists and the Separation of Church and State*, I (Cambridge, MA: Harvard University Press, 1971), 49–61.
64. McLoughlin, *New England Dissent*, 61–70.
65. McLoughlin, *New England Dissent*, 71–2.
66. The letter, incorrectly dated June 1645, was published in the *Winthrop Papers* (Boston, 1947), Vol. VI, 23–5. The correct date is demonstrated and the mistakes made by historians who accepted that dating explored in Francis J. Bremer, "When? Who? Why? Re-Evaluating a 17th Century Source," in Massachusetts Historical Society, *Proceedings*, 99 (1987), 63–75.
67. Bremer, *Building a New Jerusalem*, 344–5.
68. I would like to thank Joel Halcomb for this information.
69. Bremer, *Building a New Jerusalem*, 345–6; John Oxenbridge, *New England Freemen Warned and Warmed* (Boston, 1673), 19.
70. McLoughlin, *New England Dissent*, I, 74. For Leverett see Bremer, *First Founders*, 213–32.

71. The linkage of lay positions on congregational government and views on dissenting groups is explored in E. Brooks Holifield, "On Toleration in Massachusetts," *Church History*, 38 (June 1969), 188–200.
72. Hall, *Faithful Shepherd*, 220.
73. Quoted in Hall, *Faithful Shepherd*, 221.
74. Cotton Mather, quoted in Hall, *Faithful Shepherd*, 221.
75. Hall, *Faithful Shepherd*, 222.
76. Hall, *Faithful Shepherd*, 222–3.
77. Pope, *Half-Way Covenant*, 76.
78. Paul R. Lucas, "Presbyterianism Comes to Connecticut: The Toleration Act of 1669," *Journal of Presbyterian History*, 50 (1972), 130–1.
79. Paul R. Lucas, *Valley of Discord: Church and Society along the Connecticut River, 1636–1725* (Hanover, NH: University Press of New England, 1976). I have serious questions about his characterization of the laity, particularly the idea that the expansion of membership in the Half-Way Covenant was a lay agenda.
80. Davis and Davis, *Taylor's "Church Records"*, xiv–xv.
81. Francis J. Bremer, *The Puritan Experiment: New England Society from Bradford to Edwards*, rev. edn (Hanover, NH: University Press of New England, 1995), 221–2.
82. Scottow, quoted in Michael P. Winship, *Godly Republicanism: Puritans, Pilgrims, and a City on a Hill* (Cambridge, MA: Harvard University Press, 2012), 3–4.
83. John Davenport, *God's Call to His People* (Cambridge, MA, 1669), 14.
84. Samuel Wakeman, *Sound Repentance, the Right Way to escape deserved Ruin* (Boston, 1685), 25.
85. Jonathan Mitchell, *A Discourse of the glory to which God hath called believers by Jesus Christ* (Cambridge, MA, 1677), 51–2, 15–16.
86. Cotton Mather, *Christianus per Ignem, or, A Disciple Warming of Himself and Owning of his Lord* (Boston, 1702), 84, 126.
87. For a brief discussion see Bremer, *First Founders*, 266–7.

Epilogue: Looking Backwards, and Ahead

1. Nuttall, *The Holy Spirit in Puritan Faith and Experience*, 120.
2. These connections are well demonstrated in David D. Hall, *A Reforming People: Puritanism and the Transformation of Public Life in New England* (New York: Random House, 2011).

Bibliography

Primary (all places of publication London unless otherwise indicated)

A Declaration of the Faith and Order Owned and Practiced in the Congregational Churches in England; Agreed upon and consented unto by their Elders and Messengers in Their Meeting at the Savoy, Octob. 12, 1658 (1659).

A Direction for a Publick Profession in the Church Assembly (Cambridge, MA: 1665).

Ainsworth, Henry *The Confession: A Reply of faith of certain English people living in exile* (1607).

Ainsworth, Henry, *The Confession of faith of certain English people living in exile* (1607).

Anderson, Philip J., ed., "Letters of Henry Jessey and John Tombes to the Churches of New England, 1645," *Baptist Quarterly*, 28 (1979), 30–40.

Baker, Richard, *An Apology for Lay-mens Writing in Divinity* (1641).

Bangs, Jeremy Dupertius, ed., *The Seventeenth-Century Town Records of Scituate, Massachusetts, Volume One* (Boston: New England Historic and Genealogical Societry, 1997).

Bartlett, William, *A Model of the Primitive Congregational Way* (1647).

Bernard, Richard, *Joshua's Resolution for the Well-Ordering of His Household* (1629).

Best, William, *A Just Complaint against an Unjust Doer, wherein is declared the miserable slavery and bondage that the English Church of Amsterdam is now in by reason of the tyrannical government and corrupt doctrine of Mr. John Paget* (1634).

Bicentennial History of the First Congregational Church, Marblehead, Massachusetts (Marblehead, 1884).

Black, Joseph L., ed., *The Martin Marprelate Tracts: A Modernised and Annotated Edition* (Cambridge, UK, 2008).

Bolton, Robert, *Mr. Boltons last and learned worke of the foure last things, death, judgment, hell, and heaven* (1632).

Bradford, John, *The Good Old Way, or, An excellent and profitable treatise on repentance made by John Bradford in the year 1553* (1652).

Bradshaw, William, *English Puritanism, Containing the Main Opinions of the Rigidist Sort of Those that are Called Puritans* (1605).

Bradford, William, *History of Plymouth Plantation, 1620–1647*, 2 vols (Boston: Massachusetts Historical Society 1912).

Bradford, William, *Governor William Bradford's Letter Book* (Bedford, MA; 2001 reprint).

Bray, Gerald, ed., *The Anglican Canons 1529–1947* (Woodbridge: Ashgate, 1998).

Browne, Robert, *A Booke which Sheweth the Life and Manners of All True Christians* (Middelburgh, 1582).

Bunyan, John, *The Pilgrim's Progress from This World to That Which Is to Come; Delivered under the Similitude of a Dream* (1678).

Bunyan, John, *Grace Abounding to the Chief of Sinners* (Oxford University Press, 1966 edition).

Burrage, Champlin, ed., *The Early English Dissenters in the Light of Recent Research (1550–1641)*, 2 vols (Cambridge University Press, 1912).
Bush, Sargent Jr., ed., *The Correspondence of John Cotton* (Chapel Hill: University of North Carolina Press, 2001).
Calder, Isabel M., ed., *The Activities of the Puritan Faction of the Church of England, 1625–1633* (Church Historical Society, 1957).
Calendar of State Papers, Domestic Series, Reign of James I (1857–58).
Calendar of State Papers, Domestic Series, Reign of Charles I (1858–90).
Clap, Roger, *Memoirs of Capt. Roger Clap* (Boston, 1731).
Cob, Christopher, *The Sect Everywhere Spoken Against: or, the Reproached Doctrine of Ely* (1651).
Coddington, William, *A Demonstration of True Love Unto You the Rulers of the Colony of the Massachusetts in New England* (1674).
Collections of the Massachusetts Historical Society, 3rd series, I (1825).
Como, David, ed., *The Early Modern Englishwoman: A Facsimile Library of Essential Works. Series I: Printed Writings, 1500–1640: Part 4, Volume 5: Anne Phoenix* (Ashgate, 2006).
Cooper, James F. Jr., and Kenneth P. Minkema, eds, *The Colonial Church Records of the First Church of Reading (Wakefield) and the First Church of Rumney Marsh (Revere)* (Boston: Colonial Society of Massachusetts, 2006).
Cotton, John, *The True Constitution of a Particular Visible Church* (1642).
Cotton, John, *The Keys of the Kingdom of Heaven* (1644).
[Cotton, John], *A Treatise I. of Faith.... IV. Questions and Answers Upon Church Government Taken from Written Copies long since delivered by the late Reverend Mr. John Cotton* (Boston, 1713).
Culverwell, Ezekiell, *Time Well Spent in Sacred Meditations* (1635).
Davenport, John, *An Apologetical Reply to a Book Called "An Answer to the Unjust Complaint"* (Rotterdam, 1636).
Davenport, John, *The Profession of Faith of That Reverend and Worthy Mr. J. D., Sometimes Preacher of Stevens Coleman-Street, London Made Publiquely Before the Congregation at His Admission into One of the Churches of God in New England* (1642).
Davenport, John, *The Saints Anchor-Hold, in All Storms and Tempests, Preached in Sundry Sermons, and Published for the Support and Comfort of Gods People in All Times of Tryall* (1661).
Davenport, John, *God's Call to His People* (Cambridge, MA, 1669).
Davenport, John, *A Sermon Preached at the Election of the Governor at Boston, in New England, May 19th, 1669* (1670).
Davenport, John, *The power of Congregational churches asserted and vindicated in answer to a treatise of Mr. J. Paget intituled The defence of church-government exercised in classes and synods / by John Davenport* (1672).
Davis, Thomas M., and Virginia L. Davis, eds, *Edward Taylor's "Church Records" and Related Sermons* (Boston: Twayne, 1981).
Dunn, Richard S., James Savage, and Laetitia Yeandle, eds, *The Journal of John Winthrop, 1630–1649* (Cambridge, MA: Harvard University Press, 1996).
Eaton, Samuel, *Defence of Sundry Positions* (1645).
Featley, Daniel, *Threnoikos the House of Mourning ... delivered in sermons preached at the funerals of divers faithful servants of Christ* (1660).

Fincham, Kenneth, ed., *Visitation Articles and Injunctions of the Early Stuart Church, Volume I* (Woodbridge: Boydell, 1994).
Fincham, Kenneth, ed., *Visitation Articles and Injunctions of the Early Stuart Church, Volume II* (Woodbridge: Boydell, 1998).
Firmin, Giles, *The real Christian, or, A treatise of effectual calling wherein the work of God is drawing the soul to Christ...: to which is added, in the epistle to the reader, a few words concerning Socinianisme* (1670).
Flavel, John, *The method of grace* (1681).
Ford, Stephen, *An Epistle to the Church in Chipping-Norton* (Oxford, 1657).
Ford, Worthington Chauncey, et al., eds, *Winthrop Papers*, 6 vols to date (Boston: Massachusetts Historical Society, 1929–).
Geree, Stephene, *The Ornament of Women, Or, A Description of the True Excellency of Women* (1639).
Gilpin, Richard, *Demonologia sacra, or, A treatise of Satan's temptations* (1677).
Goodwin, Thomas, *The Trial of a Christian's Growth* (1650).
Gouge, Thomas, *Christian Directions, Showing how to walk with God all the day long* (1661).
Hall, David D., ed., *The Antinomian Controversy, 1636–1638: A Documentary History* (Middletown, CT: Wesleyan University Press, 1968).
Hill, Don Gleason, ed., *The Record of Baptisms, Marriages, and Deaths... Transcribed from the Church Records in the Town of Dedham, Massachusetts, 1638–1845* (Dedham, 1888).
Hoadley, Charles, ed., *Records of the Colony and Plantation of New Haven, from 1638 to 1649* (Hartford, 1857).
Hooke, William, *The Priviledge of the Saints on Earth Beyond Those in Heaven in Respect of Gifts and Graces Exercised* (1673).
Hooker, Thomas, *A Survey of the Summe of Church Discipline* (1648).
Hooker, Thomas, *The Application of Redemption by the Effectual Work of the Word and Spirit of Christ* (1656).
Hooker, Thomas, *A Comment upon Christ's Last Prayer* (1656).
How, Samuel, *The Sufficiency of the Spirits Teaching without Humane Learning* (1640).
Hubbard, William, *A General History of New England*, 2nd edn (Boston, 1848).
Janeway, James, *Heaven upon Earth, or, The Best Friend in the Worst of Times* (1671).
Janeway, James, *Invisibles, Realities Demonstrated in the holy life and triumphant death of Mr. John Janeway* (1674).
Johnson, Edward, *A History of New-England* (1654).
Lawrence, Richard, *Gospel-separation separated from its abuses; or, The Saints guide in Gospel-fellowship* (1657).
Lechford, Thomas, *Plain Dealing, or, News from New England* (1642).
Lee, Samuel, *The Joy of Faith* (1687).
Longstaffe, W. H. D., ed., *Memoirs of the Life of Mr. Ambrose Barnes*, Surtees Society, Publications, 50 (Durham, 1866).
Mather, Cotton, *Christianus per Ignem, or, A Disciple Warming of Himself and Owning of his Lord* (Boston, 1702).
Mather, Cotton, *Magnalia Christi Americana: The Ecclesiastical History of New England*, 2 vols (Hartford, CT, 1853).
"Mather Papers," *Massachusetts Historical Society Collections*, 4th series, 8.

[Mather, Richard], *Church-Government and Church-Covenant Discussed, in an Answer of the Elders of the Several Churches in New England* (1643).
Mather, Richard, *A Reply to Mr. Rutherford, or, A defence of the answer to Reverend Mr. Herle's book against the independency of churches* (1646).
McGiffert, Michael, ed., *God's Plot: Puritan Spirituality in Thomas Shepard's Cambridge* (Amherst: University of Massachusetts Press, 1994).
Mitchell, Jonathan, *A Discourse of the glory to which God hath called believers by Jesus Christ* (Cambridge, MA, 1677).
Morton, Nathaniel, *New England's Memorial... with Special Reference to the first colony thereof, called New-Plimouth* (Cambridge, MA, 1669).
Murcot, John, *Several works of Mr. John Murcot, that eminent and godly preacher of the Word, lately of a Church of Christ at Dublin in Ireland* (1657).
Orme, William, ed., *Remarkable Passages in the Life of William Kiffin* (1823).
Owen, John, *The Duty of Pastors and People Distinguished* (1644).
Owen, John, *Eschol: a cluster of the fruit of Canaan... or, Rules for Direction for the Walking of Saints in Fellowship* (1648).
Owen, John, *A Practical Exposition of the 130th Psalm* (1669).
Oxenbridge, John, *New England Freemen Warned and Warmed* (Boston, 1673).
Paynall, Thomas, *A fruitfull booke of the common places of all S. Pauls Epistles right necessary for all sortes of people* (1562).
Perkins, William, *The Art of Prophesying* (Edinburgh, 1986 reprint).
Petto, Samuel, *Roses from Sharon, or Sweet Experiences Gathered Up by some precious hearts, whilst they followed on to know the Lord. Published for public soul-advantage* (1654).
Petto, Samuel, John Martin, and Frederick Woodal, *The Preacher Sent* (1658).
Pope, Robert G., ed., *The Notebook of the Reverend John Fiske, 1644–1675*, Publications of the Colonial Society of Massachusetts, 47 (Boston, 1974).
Powel, Vavasor, *Spiritual Experiences of Sundry Believers Held Forth by them at severall solemne meetings and Conferences to that End* (1651/2).
[Rathband, William], *A briefe narration of some church courses held in opinion and practise in the churches lately erected in New England. Collected out of sundry of their own printed papers and manuscripts with other good intelligences. Together with some short hints (given by the way) of their correspondence with the like tenents and practises of the separatists churches. And some short animadversions upon some principall passages for the benefit of the vulgar reader. Presented to publike view for the good of the church of God by W. R.* (1644).
Reynolds, Edward, *Israel's Prayer in Time of Trouble, with God's Gracious Answer Thereunto* (1649).
Reynolds, Edward, *Imitation and Caution for a Christian Woman: or, the Life and Death of that excellent gentlewoman, Mrs. Mary Bewley* (1659).
Robinson, John, *The Peoples Plea for the Exercise of Prophesie* (1618).
Rogers, Richard, *Seven Treatises containing such direction as is gathered out of the holie Scriptures, leading and guiding to true happiness, both in this life and in the life to come* (1603).
Rogers, John, *Ohel, or Beth-shemesh: A Tabernacle for the Sun, or Irenicum Evangelicum. An Idea of Church Discipline* (1653).
Rollock, Robert, *Lectures upon the History of the Passion, Resurrection, and Ascension of our Lord Jesus Christ* (Edinburgh, 1616).

Rutherford, Samuel, *A peaceable and temperate plea for Pauls presbyterie in Scotland* (1642).
Rutherford, Samuel, *Influences of the Life of Grace* (1659).
Saltmarsh, John, *Sparkles of Glory, or Some of beams of the morning-star* (1647).
Selement, George, and Bruce C. Wooley, eds, *Thomas Shepard's Confessions*, Publications of the Colonial Society of Massachusetts, 58 (Boston, 1981).
Scudder, Henry, *The Christian's Daily Walk* (1635 edition).
Sharpless, Stephen, ed., *Records of the Church of Christ at Cambridge in New England, 1632–1830* (Boston, 1906).
Shurtleff, Nathaniel B., ed., *Records of the Governor and Company of the Massachusetts Bay, Vols I–IV* (Boston, 1853/4).
Sibbes, Richard, *Bowels Opened, or, A Discovery of the Near and Dear Love, Union, and Communion Betwixt Christ and the Church* (1639).
Sibbes, Richards, *The Glorious Feast of the Gospel* (1650).
Sibbes, Richards, *The Soules Conflict with itself, and victory over itself* (1635).
[Simpson, Sydrach], *A Vindication of the Liberty of Public Preaching* (1647).
Stated Christian Conference Asserted to be a Christian Duty (1697?).
Sutton, Katherine, *A Christian Womans Experiences of the glorious working of Gods free grace* (1663).
Taylor, John, *The Discovery of a Swarm of Sepratatists, or, a Leatherseller's Sermon* (1641).
Taylor, John, *A Swarme of Sectaries and Schismamtics, Wherein is Discovered the Strange Preaching (or Prating) of such as are by their Trades Cobblers, Tinkers, Pedlers, Weavers, Sowgelders, and Chimney Sweepers* (1641).
Taylor, Thomas, *A Commentary Upon the Epistle of Paul Written to Titus* (1612).
Taylor, Thomas, *Davids learning, or, The way to true happiness* (1617).
The Agreement of the Associated Ministers & Churches of the Counties of Cumberland and Westmorland (1656).
Tipson, Baird, ed., "Samuel Stone's 'Discourse' against Requiring Church Relations," *William and Mary Quarterly*, 3rd series, 46 (1989), 786–99.
Top, Alexander, *St. Peters rocke under which title is deciphered the faith of Peter* (1597).
Trapnell, Anna, *A legacy for saints; being several experiences of the dealings of God with Anna Trapnell* (1654).
Trumbull, J. H., ed., *The Public Records of the Colony of Connecticut* (Hartford, 1850).
Trumbull, J. H., ed., *Plain Dealing by Thomas Lechford* (Boston, 1867).
Tyndale, William, *The Whole Works of W. Tyndall, John Frith, and Doct. Barnes* (1573).
Underhill, Edward, "Anecdotes of Underhill," in John Gough Nichols, *Narratives of the Days of the Reformation*, Camden Society Publications, O.S. 77 (1859).
Van Dixhoorn, Chad, ed., *The Minutes and Papers of the Westminster Assembly, 1643–1652*, 5 vols (Oxford University Press, 2012).
Vincent, Thomas, *The True Christian's Love of the Unseen Christ* (1677).
Vines, Richard, *Gods drawing, and mans coming to Christ discovered* (1662).
Wakeman, Samuel, *Sound Repentance, the Right Way to escape deserved Ruin* (Boston, 1685).
Walker, Williston, ed., *The Creeds and Platforms of Congregationalism* (Boston: Pilgrim Press, 1960).
Watson, Thomas, *Religion our true interest* (1682).
Welde, Thomas, *An Answer to W. E., His Narration* (1644).

White, John, *Direction for the Profitable Reading of the Scriptures* (1647).
White, John, *A Way to the Tree of Life... Wherein is Described Occasionally the Nature of Spiritual Man* (1647).
Woodhouse, A. S. P., ed., *Puritanism and Liberty: Being the Army Debates (1647–9) from the Clarke Manuscripts*, with a preface by Ivan Roots (University of Chicago Press, 1974).

Primary Manuscripts

Boswell Papers, British Library Add Ms 6394.
Davenport, John, "A Third Essay, Containing Replies to the Answer," John Davenport Papers, American Antiquarian Society, Worcester, MA.
Hartlib Papers, Sheffield University.
"John Davenport, Sermons and Writings, 1615–1658," Beinecke Rare Book and Manuscript Library, Yale University, GEN MSS 202.
"Transcript of the Journal of Daniel Bradford of Norwich, 1636–48," Norwich Record Office, MC64/4, 508x8.
William Hubbard to Increase Mather, 29 June 1683, Boston Public Library, MS Am 1502 v.5 no. 16.

Secondary Sources

Books

Andiso, Gabriel, *The Waldensian Dissent* (Cambridge, UK, 1999).
Bangs, Jeremy Dupertuis, *Strangers and Pilgrims, Travellers and Sojourners: Leiden and the Foundations of Plymouth Plantation* (Plymouth, MA: General Society of Mayflower Descendants, 2009).
Boersma, Owe, and A. Jelsma, eds, "Unity in Multiformity, The Minutes of the Coetus of London, 1575 and the Consistory Minutes of the Italian Church of London, 1570–1591," *Publications of the Huguenot Society of Great Britain and Ireland*, 59 (1997).
Boorstin, Daniel J., *The Americans: The Colonial Experience* (New York: Random House, 1958).
Bozeman, Theodore Dwight, *The Precisianist Strain: Disciplinary Religion and Antinomian Backlash in Puritanism to 1683* (Chapel Hill: University of North Carolina Press, 2003).
Brachlow, Stephen, *The Communion of the Saints: Radical Puritan and Separatist Ecclesiology, 1570–1625* (Oxford University Press, 1988).
Braddick, Michael, *God's Fury, England's Fire: A New History of the English Civil Wars* (London: Allen Lane, 2008).
Bradstock, Andrew, *Radical Religion in Cromwell's England: A Concise History from the English Civil War to the End of the Commonwealth* (London: Tauris, 2011).
Bremer, Francis J., *Congregational Communion: Clerical Friendship in the Anglo-American Puritan Community, 1610–1692* (Boston: Northeastern University Press, 1994).
Bremer, Francis J.. *Shaping New Englands: Puritan Clergymen in Seventeenth Century England and New England* (Boston: Twayne 1994).

Bremer, Francis J., *The Puritan Experiment: New England Society from Bradford to Edwards*, revised edn (Hanover, NH: University Press of New England, 1995).
Bremer, Francis J., *John Winthrop: America's Forgotten Founding Father* (New York: Oxford University Press, 2003).
Bremer, Francis J., *Puritanism: A Very Short Introduction* (New York: Oxford University Press, 2009).
Bremer, Francis J., *Building a New Jerusalem: John Davenport, a Puritan in Three Worlds* (New Haven: Yale University Press, 2012).
Bremer, Francis J., *First Founders: American Puritans and Puritanism in an Atlantic World* (Hanover, NH: University Press of New England, 2012).
Bremer, Francis J., and Tom Webster, eds, *Puritans and Puritanism in Europe and America: A Comprehensive Encyclopedia*, 2 vols (Santa Barbara, CA: ABC-Clio, 2006).
Brown, Mathew P., *The Pilgrim and the Bee: Reading Rituals and Book Culture in Early New England* (Philadelphia: University of Pennsylvania Press, 2007).
Brown, Raymond, *Spirituality in Adversity: English Nonconformity in a Period of Repression, 1660–1689* (Milton Keynes: Paternoster, 2012).
Caldwell, Patricia, *The Puritan Conversion Narrative* (Cambridge University Press, 1983).
Cambers, Andrew, *Godly Reading: Print, Manuscript and Puritanism in England, 1580–1720* (Cambridge University Press, 2011).
Campbell, Ted. A., *The Religion of the Heart: A Study of European Religious Life in the Seventeenth and Eighteenth Centuries* (Columbia, SC: University of South Carolina Press, 1991).
Capp, Bernard, *England's Culture Wars: Puritan Reformation and Its Enemies in the Interregnum, 1649–1660* (Oxford University Press, 2012).
Carter, Alice C., *The English Reformed Church in Amsterdam in the Seventeenth Century* (Amsterdam, 1964).
Coffey, John, *Politics, Theology and the British Revolutions: Samuel Rutherford and the Scottish Covenanters* (Cambridge University Press, 1997).
Coffey, John, *John Goodwin and the Puritan Revolution: Religion and Intellectual Change in Seventeenth-Century England* (Woodbridge: Boydell, 2006).
Coffey, John, and Paul Lim, eds, *The Cambridge Companion to Puritanism* (Cambridge University Press, 2008).
Cohen, Charles L., *God's Caress: The Psychology of Puritan Religious Experience* (New York: Oxford University Press, 1988).
Cohen, Daniel A., *Pillars of Salt, Monuments of Grace: New England Crime Literature and the Origins of American Popular Culture* (Amherst, MA: University of Massachusetts Press, 2006).
Collinson, Patrick, *The Elizabethan Puritan Movement* (Oxford University Press, 1967).
Collinson, Parick, *Archbishop Grindal, 1519–1583: The Struggle for a Reformed Church* (Berkeley: University of California Press, 1979).
Collinson, Patrick, *The Religion of Protestants: The Church in English Society 1559–1625* (Oxford University Press, 1982).
Collinson, Patrick, *Godly People: Essays on English Protestantism and Puritanism* (London: Hambledon, 1983).
Collinson, Patrick, *From Cranmer to Sandcroft* (London: Hambledon, 2006).

Collinson, Patrick, *Richard Bancroft and Elizabethan Anti-Puritanism* (Cambridge University Press, 2013).
Como, David, *"Blown by the Spirit": Puritanism and the Emergence of an Antinomian Underground in Pre-Civil-War England* (Stanford University Press, 2004).
Cooper, James F. Jr., *Tenacious of Their Liberties: The Congregationalists in Colonial Massachusetts* (New York: Oxford University Press, 1999).
Cressy, David, *England on Edge: Crisis and Revolution, 1640–1642* (Oxford University Press, 2006).
Cross, Claire, *Church and People, 1450–1660: The Triumph of the Laity in the English Church* (Hassocks: Harvester, 1976).
Damrosch, Leo, *The Sorrows of the Quaker Jesus: James Nayler and the Puritan Crackdown on the Free Spirit* (Cambridge, MA: Harvard University Press, 1996).
Dickens, A. G., *The English Reformation* (London: Collins, 1967).
Donoghue, John, *Fire Under the Ashes: An Atlantic History of the English Revolution* (University of Chicago Press, 2013).
Duffy, Eamon, *The Stripping of the Altars: Traditional Religion in England, 1400–1580* (New Haven: Yale University Press, 1992).
Duffy, Eamon, *The Voices of Morebath: Reformation and Rebellion in an English Village* (New Haven: Yale University Press, 2001).
Dunan-Page, Anne, *The Cambridge Companion to Bunyan* (Cambridge University Press, 2010).
Dunan-Page, Anne, and Clotilde Prunier, eds, *Debating the Faith: Religion and Letter Writing in Great Britain, 1550–1800* (Dordrecht: Springer, 2013).
Durston, Christopher, and Judith Maltby, eds, *Religion in Revolutionary England* (Manchester University Press, 2006).
Ericson, Kai, *Wayward Puritans: A Study in the Sociology of Deviance* (New York: Wiley, 1966).
Fletcher, Anthony, *The Outbreak of the English Civil War* (New York University Press, 1981).
Foster, Stephen, *The Long Argument: English Puritanism and the Shaping of New England Culture, 1500–1700* (Chapel Hill: University of North Carolina Press, 1991).
Gentles, Ian, *The New Model Army in England, Ireland, and Scotland, 1645–1653* (Oxford University Press, 1992).
Gildrie, Richard, *Salem, Massachusetts 1626–1683: A Covenanted Community* (Charlottesville, VA: University of Virginia Press, 1975).
Greaves, Richard L., *Deliver Us from Evil: The Radical Underground in Britain, 1660–1663* (Oxford University Press, 1986).
Greaves, Richard L., *Enemies Under His Feet: Radicals and Nonconformists in Britain, 1664–1677* (Stanford University Press, 1990).
Green, Ian, *Print and Protestantism in Early Modern England* (Oxford University Press, 2000).
Gribben, Crawford, *God's Irishmen: Theological Debates in Cromwellian Ireland* (Oxford University Press, 2007).
Gura, Philip F., *A Glimpse of Sion's Glory: Puritan Radicalism in New England, 1620–1660* (Middletown, CT: Wesleyan University Press, 1984).
Ha, Polly, *English Presbyterianism, 1580–1640* (Stanford University Press, 2011).
Haigh, Christopher, *The Plaine Man's Pathways to Heaven: Kinds of Christianity in Post-Reformation England* (Oxford University Press, 2007).

Halcomb, Joel, "A Social History of Congregational Religious Practice During the Puritan Revolution" (University of Cambridge PhD, 2009).
Hall, David D., *The Faithful Shepherd: A History of the New England Ministry in the Seventeenth Century* (Chapel Hill: University of North Carolina Press, 1972).
Hall, David D., *Worlds of Wonder, Days of Judgment: Popular Religious Belief in Early New England* (Cambridge, MA: Harvard University Press, 1990).
Hall, David D., ed., *Lived Religion in America: Toward a History of Practice* (Princeton University Press, 1997).
Hall, David D., *Ways of Writing: The Practice and Politics of Text-Making in Seventeenth-Century New England* (Philadelphia: University of Pennsylvania Press, 2008).
Hall, David D., *A Reforming People: Puritanism and the Transformation of Public Life in New England* (New York: Random House, 2011).
Hambrick-Stowe, Charles E., *Practice of Piety: Puritan Devotional Disciplines in Seventeenth-Century New England* (Chapel Hill: University of North Carolina Press, 1985).
Hill, Christopher, *Society & Puritanism in Pre-Revolutionary England* (New York: Schocken, 1964).
Hill, Christopher, *The World Turned Upside Down* (New York: Penguin, 1972).
Hallett, A. C. Hollis, *Chronicle of a Colonial Church; 1612–1826, Bermuda* (Bermuda: Juniper Hill Press, 1993).
Hughes, Ann, *Gangraena and the Struggle for the English Revolution* (Oxford University Press, 2004).
Hunt, Arnold, *The Art of Hearing: English Preachers and Their Audiences, 1590–1640* (Cambridge University Press, 2010).
James, Sydney V., *John Clarke and His Legacies: Religion and Law in Colonial Rhode Island 1638–1750*, ed. Theodore Dwight Bozeman (University Park, PA: Penn State University Press, 1999).
Jung, Joanne J., *Godly Conversation: Rediscovering the Puritan Practice of Conference* (Grand Rapids: Reformation Heritage Books, 2011).
Kapic, Kelly M., and Randall C. Gleason, eds, *The Devoted Life: An Invitation to the Puritan Classics* (Downers Grove, IL: IVP Academic, 2004).
Kaufman, Peter Iver, *Thinking of the Laity in Late Tudor England* (Notre Dame, IN: University of Notre Dame Press, 2004).
Kaufman, Peter Iver, ed., *Leadership and Elizabethan Culture* (New York: Palgrave Macmillan, 2013).
Lake, Peter, *Moderate Puritans and the Elizabethan Church* (Cambridge University Press, 1982).
Lake, Peter, *The Boxmaker's Revenge: "Orthodoxy," "Heterodoxy," and the Politics of the Parish in Early Modern London* (Manchester University Press, 2001).
Lake, Peter, and Michael Questier, eds, *Conformity and Orthodoxy in the English Church, c. 1560–1660* (Woodbridge: Boydell, 2000).
Lake, Peter, with Michael Questier, *The Antichrist's Lewd Hat: Protestants, Papists & Players in Post-Reformation England* (New Haven: Yale University Press, 2002).
Littleton, Charles, "Geneva on Threadneedle Street: The French Church of London and Its Congregation, 1560–1625" (University of Michigan PhD, 1996).
Loades, David, ed., *John Foxe and the English Reformation* (Aldershot: Ashgate, 1997).

Loades, David, ed., *John Foxe: an Historical Perspective* (Aldershot: Ashgate, 1999).
Lovegrove, Deryck W., ed., *The Rise of the Laity in Evangelical Protestantism* (London: Routledge, 2002).
Lowenstein, David, and John Marshall, eds, *Heresy, Literature, and Politics in Early Modern English Culture* (Cambridge University Press, 2006).
Lucas, Paul R., *Valley of Discord: Church and Society along the Connecticut River, 1636–1725* (Hanover, NH: University Press of New England, 1976).
Lynch, Kathleen, *Protestant Autobiography in the Seventeenth Century Anglophone World* (Oxford University Press, 2012).
MacCulloch, Diarmaid, *Thomas Cranmer* (New Haven: Yale University Press, 1996).
MacCulloch, Diarmaid, *Tudor Church Militant: Edward VI and the Protestant Reformation* (London: Allen Lane, 1999).
MacCulloch, Diarmaid, *A History of Christianity: The First Three Thousand Years* (London: Penguin, 2009).
MacCulloch, Diarmaid, *Silence: A Christian History* (London: Allen Lane, 2013).
Mack, Phyllis, *Visionary Women: Ecstatic Prophecy in Seventeenth-Century England* (Berkeley: University of California Press, 1992).
Marsh, Christopher, *Popular Religion in Sixteenth-Century England* (Basingstoke: Macmillan, 1998).
Martin, Jessica, and Alec Ryrie, eds, *Private and Domestic Devotion in Early Modern Britain* (Farnham: Ashgate, 2012).
Matthews, A. G., *Calamy Revised: Being a Revision of Edmund Calamy's Account of the Ministers and Others Ejected and Silenced, 1660–1662* (Oxford University Press, 1934, reissued 1988).
Mayo, Lawrence Shaw, *John Endecott* (Boston, 1936).
McLoughlin, William G., *New England Dissent, 1630–1833: The Baptists and the Separation of Church and State*, vol. I (Cambridge, MA: Harvard University Press, 1971).
Mears, Natalie, and Alec Ryrie, eds, *Worship and the Parish Church in Early Modern Britain* (Farnham: Ashgate, 2013).
Mendle, Michael, ed., *The Putney Debates of 1647: The Army, the Levelers and the English State* (Cambridge University Press, 2001).
Miller, Perry, *Orthodoxy in Massachusetts, 1630–1650* (Boston: Beacon, 1933).
Moore, Susan Hardman, *Pilgrims: New World Settlers & the Call of Home* (New Haven: Yale University Press, 2007).
Moore, Susan Hardman, *Abandoning America: Life-Stories from Early New England* (Woodbridge: Boydell, 2013).
Morgan, Edmund S., *Visible Saints: the History of a Puritan Idea* (Ithaca: Cornell University Press, 1963).
Morison, Samuel Eliot, *The Founding of Harvard College* (Cambridge, MA: Harvard University Press, 1935).
Morison, Samuel Eliot, *Harvard College in the Seventeenth Century* (Cambridge, MA: Harvard University Press, 1936).
Morrill, John, *The Nature of the English Revolution* (Harlow: Longman, 1993).
Morrill, John, *Oliver Cromwell* (Oxford University Press, 2007).
Morrow, John, and Jonathan Scott, eds, *Liberty, Authority, Formality: Political Ideas and Culture, 1600–1900. Essays in Honour of Colin Davis* (Exeter: Imprint Academic, 2008).

Mullan, David George, *Episcopacy in Scotland: The History of an Idea, 1560–1638* (Edinburgh: John Donald, 1986).
Mullan, David George, *Narratives of the Religious Self in Early-Modern Scotland* (Farnham: Ashgate, 2010).
Narveson, Kate, *Bible Readers and Lay Writers in Early Modern England: Gender and Self-Definition in an Emergent Writing Culture* (Farnham: Ashgate, 2012).
Neuman, Meredith Marien, *Jeremiah's Scribes: Creating Sermon Literature in Puritan New England* (Philadelphia: University of Pennsylvania Press, 2013).
Nuttall, Geoffrey F., *The Holy Spirit in Puritan Faith and Experience*, with a new introduction by Peter Lake (University of Chicago Press, 1992).
Nuttall, Geoffrey F., *Visible Saints: The Congregational Way, 1640–1660*, 2nd edn (Weston Rhyn, UK: Quinta Press, 2001).
Opitz, P., and E. Campi, eds, *Heinrich Bullinger: Life–Thought–Influence*, 2 vols (Leiden: Theologischer Verlag, 2006).
Ortman, Susan B., "Gadding about London in search of a Proper Sermon: How Robert Keayne's Sermon Notes from 1627–28 Inform Us about the Religious and Political Issues Facing the London Puritan Community" (Millersville University of Pennsylvania MA thesis, 2004).
Pagels, Elaine, *The Gnostic Gospels* (New York: Random House, 1979).
Pagliuco, Christopher, *The Great Escape of Edward Whalley and William Goffe* (Charleston, SC: History Press, 2012).
Pestana, Carla, *Quakers and Baptists in Colonial Massachusetts* (New York: Cambridge University Press, 1991).
Peterson, Mark, *The Price of Redemption: The Spiritual Economy of Puritan New England* (Stanford University Press, 1997).
Pettegree, Andrew, *Foreign Protestant Communities in Sixteenth-Century London* (Oxford University Press, 1986).
Powell, Hunter, "The Last Confession: A Background Study of the Savoy Declaration of Faith and Order" (University of Cambridge MPhil thesis, 2008).
Powell, Hunter, *The Crisis of British Protestantism, 1638–1644* (Manchester University Press, forthcoming).
Prior, Charles A., and Glenn Burgess, eds, *England's Wars of Religion, Revisited* (Farnham: Ashgate, 2013).
Rambo, Lewis R., *Understanding Religious Conversion* (New Haven: Yale University Press, 1993).
Rex, Richard, *Henry VIII and the English Reformation*, 2nd edn (Basingstoke: Macmillan, 2006).
Robbins, Chandler, *A History of the Second Church, or Old North, in Boston* (Boston, 1852).
Rosenmeir, Jesper, *"Spiritual Concupiscence": John Cotton's English Years, 1584–1633* (Boston, UK: Richard Kay, 2012).
Rutman, Darrett B., *American Puritanism* (Philadelphia: Lippincott, 1977).
Ryrie, Alec, *Being Protestant in Reformation Britain* (Oxford University Press, 2013).
St. George, Robert Blair, *Conversing by Signs: Poetics of Implication in Colonial New England Culture* (Chapel Hill: University of North Carolina Press, 1998).
Seaver, Paul, *The Puritan Lectureships: The Politics of Religious Dissent, 1560–1662* (Stanford University Press, 1970).
Sell, Alan P. F., *The Great Ejectment of 1662: Its Antecedents, Aftermath, and Ecumenical Significance* (Eugene, OR: Pickwick, 2012).

Sharpe, Kevin, *The Personal Rule of Charles I* (New Haven: Yale University Press, 1992).
Sprunger, Keith L., *The Learned Doctor William Ames: Dutch Backgrounds of English and American Puritanism* (Urbana: University of Illinois Press, 1972).
Sprunger, Keith L., *Dutch Puritanism: A History of English and Scottish Churches of the Netherlands in the Sixteenth and Seventeenth Centuries* (Leiden: Brill, 1982).
Spurr, John, *English Puritanism, 1603–1689* (Basingstoke: Macmillan, 1998).
Stewart, Laura A. M., *Urban Politics and British Civil Wars: Edinburgh, 1617–53* (Leiden: Brill, 2006).
Stuart, Robert Ork, "The Breaking of the Elizabethan Settlement of Religion: Puritan Spiritual Experience and the Theological Division of the English Church" (Yale University PhD, 1976).
Sutherland, Martin, *Peace, Toleration, and Decay: The Ecclesiology of Late Stuart Dissent* (Carlisle: Paternoster Press, 2003).
Thomas, Samuel S., *Creating Communities in Restoration England: Parish and Congregation in Oliver Heywood's Halifax* (Leiden: Brill, 2013).
Tinniswood, Adrian, *The Rainsborowes: One Family's Quest to Build a New England* (New York: Basic Books, 2013).
Tipson, Lynn Baird, "The Development of a Puritan Understanding of Conversion" (Yale University PhD, 1972).
Tipson, Baird, *Hartford Puritanism: Thomas Hooker, Samuel Stone, Their Terrible God, and the Roots of Evangelicalism in America* (Manchester University Press, forthcoming).
Todd, Margo, *The Culture of Protestantism in Early Modern Scotland* (New Haven: Yale University Press, 2002).
Tolmie, Murray, *The Triumph of the Saints: The Separate Churches of London 1616–1649* (Cambridge University Press, 1977).
Tyacke, Nicholas, *Anti-Calvinists: The Rise of Arminianism c.1590–1640* (Oxford University Press, 1990).
Van Dijk, Ger, *History of the Beguinage in Amsterdam from 1307 to the Present* (Amsterdam, 2005).
Van Engen, Abram C., *Sympathetic Puritans: Calvinist Fellow Feeling in Early New England* (New York: Oxford University Press, 2014).
Walsham, Alexandra, *Charitable Hatred: Tolerance and Intolerance in England, 1500–1700* (Manchester University Press, 2006).
Webster, Tom, *Godly Clergy in Early Stuart England: The Caroline Puritan Movement, c. 1620–1643* (Cambridge University Press, 1997).
Winship, Michael P., *Making Heretics: Militant Protestantism and Free Grace in Massachusetts, 1636–1641* (Princeton University Press, 2002).
Winship, Michael P., *Godly Republicanism: Puritans, Pilgrims, and a City on a Hill* (Cambridge, MA: Harvard Univ ersity Press, 2012).
Worrall, Arthur J., *Quakers in the Colonial Northeast* (Hanover, NH: University of New England Press 1980).
Worthley, Harold, *An Inventory of the Records of the Particular (Congregational) Churches of Massachusetts Gathered 1620–1805*, Proceedings of the Unitarian Historical Society (Cambridge, MA, 1970).
Wright, Stephen, *The Early English Baptists, 1603–1649* (Woodbridge: Boydell, 2006).
Wunderli, Richard, *Peasant Fires: The Drummer of Niklashausen* (Bloomington: Indiana University Press, 1992).

Essays and Articles

Abbott, William M., "Ruling Eldership in Civil War England, the Scottish Kirk, and Early New England: A Comparative Study of Secular and Spiritual Aspects," *Church History*, 75 (2006).
Appleby, David J., "From Ejectment to Toleration in England, 1662–89," in Sell, *Great Ejectment*.
Bremer, Francis J., "When? Who? Why? Re-Evaluating a 17th Century Source," in Massachusetts Historical Society, *Proceedings*, 99 (1987).
Bremer, Francis J., "William Winthrop and Religious Reform in London, 1529–1582," *The London Journal*, 24 (1999).
Bremer, Francis J., "'To tell what God hath done for thy soul': Puritan Spiritual Testimonies as Admission Tests and Means of Edification," *New England Quarterly* (2014).
Bremer, Francis J., and Ellen Rydell, "Performance Art? Puritans in the Pulpit," *History Today*, 45 (September 1995).
Camden, Vera J., "John Bunyan and the Goodwives of Bedford: A Psychoanalytical Approach," in Dunan-Page, *Cambridge Companion to Bunyan*.
Clarke, Elizabeth, "The Legacy of Mothers and Others: Women's Theological Writing, 1640–1660," in Durston and Maltby, *Religion in Revolutionary England*.
Coffey, John, "A Ticklish Business: Defining Heresy and Orthodoxy in the Puritan Revolution," in Lowenstein and Marshall, *Heresy, Literature, and Politics*.
Coffey, John, "The Toleration Controversy during the English Revolution," in Durston and Maltby, *Religion in Revolutionary England*.
Coffey, John, "England's Exodus: The Civil War as a War of Deliverance," in Prior and Burgess, *England's Wars of Religion, Revisited*.
Collinson, Patrick, "Cranbrook and the Fletchers: Popular and Unpopular Religion in the Kentish Weald," in Collinson, *Godly People*.
Collinson, Patrick, "The English Conventicle," in Collinson, *Cranmer to Sandcroft*.
Collinson, Patrick, "The Godly: Aspects of Popular Puritanism," in Collinson, *Godly People*.
Collinson, Patrick, "Lectures by Combination: Structures and Characteristics of Church Life in 17th Century England," in Collinson, *Godly People*.
Como, David R., "Women, Prophecy, and Authority in Early Stuart Puritanism," *Huntington Library Quarterly*, 61 (1998).
Como, David R., "Radical Puritanism, c. 1558–1660," in Coffey and Lim, *Companion to Puritanism*.
Craig, John, "The Growth of English Puritanism," in Coffey and Lim, *Companion to Puritanism*.
Craig, John, "Bodies at Prayer in Early Modern England," in Mears and Ryrie, *Worship and the Parish Church*.
Den Hartog, Jonathan, "'National and Provinciall Churches are Nullityes': Henry Dunster's Puritan Argument against the Puritan Established Church," *Journal of Church and State*, forthcoming.
Ditmore, Michael, "A Prophetess in Her Own Country: An Exegesis of Anne Hutchinson's 'Immediate Revelation'," *The William and Mary Quarterly*, 3rd series, 57 (2000), 349–92.

Dorsey, Andy, "A Rhetoric of American Experience: Thomas Shepard's Cambridge Confgessions and the Discourse of Spiritual Hypocrisy," *Early American Literature*, 49 (2014).

Dunan-Page, Anne, "Writing 'things ecclesiastical': The Literary Acts of the Gathered Churches," *Etudies Episteme*, 21, 2012. Acts of Writing, IV—Monumentalization and the Act of Writing, http:??www.etudes-episteme.org/2e/? writing-things-ecclesiastical.

Dunan-Page, Anne, "Letters and Records of Dissenting Congregations: David Crosley, Cripplegate, and Baptist Church Life," in Dunan-Page and Prunier, *Debating the Faith*.

Eales, Jacqueline, "'So many sects and schisms': Religious Diversity in Revolutionary Kent, 1640–16," in Durston and Maltby, *Religion in Revolutionary England*.

Foster, Stephen, "New England and the Challenge of Heresy: 1630–1660: The Puritan Crisis in Transatlantic Perspective," *The William and Mary Quarterly*, 3rd series, 38 (1981).

Greaves, Richard L., "The Ordination Controversy and the Spirit of Reform in Puritan England," *Journal of Ecclesiastical History*, 21 (1970).

Green, Ian, "Varieties of Domestic Devotion in Early Modern English Protestantism," in Martin and Ryrie, *Private and Domestic Devotion in Early Modern Britain*.

Gribben, Crawford, "Lay Conversion and Calvinist Doctrine During the English Commonwealth," in Lovegrove, *Rise of the Laity*.

Hall, David D., "John Cotton's Letter to Samuel Skelton," *William and Mary Quarterly*, 3rd series, 22 (1965), 478–85.

Hall, David D., "Review Essay: What is the Place of 'Experience' in Religious History?," *Religion and American Culture: A Journal of Interpretation*, 13 (2003).

Hambrick-Stowe, Charles, "Christ the Fountain of Life by John Cotton," in Kapic and Gleason, *The Devoted Life*.

Holifield, E. Brooks, "On Toleration in Massachusetts," *Church History* 38 (June 1969), 188–200.

Hughes, Ann, "Puritanism and Gender," in Coffey and Lim, *Companion to Puritganism*.

Jones, John Gwynfor, "The Growth of Puritanism c. 1559–1662," in Sell, *Great Ejectment*.

Kobrin, David, "The Expansion of the Visible Church in New England: 1629–1650," *Church History*, 36 (1967).

Lake, Peter, "Feminine Piety and Personal Potency: The 'Emancipation' of Mrs. Jane Radcliffe," *The Seventeenth Century*, 2 (1987), 143–65.

Lake, Peter, "Defining Puritanism—Again?," in Francis J. Bremer, ed., *Puritanism: Transatlantic Perspectives on a Seventeenth-Century Anglo-American Faith* (Boston, Massachusetts Historical Society, 1993).

Lake, Peter, "Puritanism, Familism, and Heresy in Early Stuart England: The Case of John Etherington Revisited," in Lowenstein and Marshall, *Heresy, Literature, and Politics*.

Lake, Peter, and David Como, "'Orthodoxy' and Its Discontents: Dispute Settlement and the Production of 'Consensus' in the London (Puritan) Underground," *Journal of British Studies*, 39 (2000).

Le Claire, Lesley, "The Survival of the Manuscript," in Mendle, *The Putney Debates*.

Lucas, Paul R., "Presbyterianism Comes to Connecticut: The Toleration Act of 1669," *Journal of Presbyterian History*, 50 (1972).
MacCulloch, Diarmaid, "Catholic and Puritans in Elizabethan Suffolk: A County Community Polarizes," *Archiv fur Reformationsgeschichte*, 72 (1981).
MacCulloch, Diarmaid, "The Impact of the Reformation on Suffolk Parish Life," *Suffolk Review*, n.s., 15 (1990).
MacCulloch, Diarmaid, "Heinrich Bullinger and the English Speaking World," in Opitz and Campi, *Bullinger*.
Maclear, James Fulton, " 'The Heart of New England Rent': The Mystical Element in Early Puritan History," *The Mississippi Valley Historical Review*, 42 (1956), 621–52.
Marsh, Christopher, " 'Common Prayer' in England 1560–1640: The View from the Pew," *Past & Present*, 171 (2001).
Marsh, Christopher, "Sacred Space in England, 1560–1640: The View from the Pew," *Journal of Ecclesiastical History*, 53 (2002).
Marsh, Christopher, "Order and Place in England, 1580–1640: The View from the Pew," *Journal of British Studies*, 39 (2005).
Martin, J. W., "The Protestant Underground Congregations of Mary's Reign," *Journal of Ecclesiastical History* 35 (1984), 319–38.
McGinnis, Timothy Scott, "Swingebreeches and Schollers: Images of Pastoral Leadership in Elizabethan Puritan Dialogues," in Kaufman, *Leadership and Elizabethan Culture*.
Morrill, John, "How Oliver Cromwell Thought," in Morrow and Scott, *Liberty, Authority, Formality*.
Morrill, John, "The Puritan Revolution," in Coffey and Lim, *Cambridge Companion to Puritanism*.
Morrill, John, "Renaming England's Wars of Religion," in Prior and Burgess, *England's Wars of Religion, Revisited*.
Murray, Ian H., "Thomas Hooker and the Doctrine of Conversion," *Banner of Truth Magazine*, 195 (1979).
Narveson, Kate, " 'Their Practice bringeth little profit': Clerical Anxieties about Lay Scripture Reading in Early Modern England," in Martin and Ryrie, *Private and Domestic Devotion*.
Neuman, Meredith M., "Beyond Narrative: The Conversion Plot of John Dane's 'A Declaration of Remarkable Providences'," *Early American Literature*, 40 (2005).
Peterson, Mark A., "The Plymouth Church and the Evolution of Puritan Religious Culture," *The New England Quarterly*, 66 (December 1993).
Ryrie, Alec, "Congregations, Conventicles, and the Nature of Early Scottish Protestantism," *Past & Present*, 191 (2006).
Simmons, Richard C. "Richard Sadler's Account of the Massachusetts Churches," *The New England Quarterly*, 42 (1969).
Stearns, Raymond Phineas, and David Holmes Brawner, "New England Church 'Relations' and Continuity in Early Congregational History," *Proceedings of the American Antiquarian Society*, 75 (1965).
Taft, Barbara, "From Reading to Whitehall: Henry Ireton's Journey," in Mendle, *Putney Debates*.
Thomas, Keith, "Women and the Civil War Sects," *Past & Present*, 13 (1958).

Tipson, Baird, "The 'Judgment of Charity' in the Early New England Churches," *Church History*, 44 (1975).
Tipson, Baird, "The Elusiveness of 'Puritanism'," *Religious Studies Review*, 11 (1985).
Usher, Brett, "Backing Protestantism: The London Godly, the Exchequer and the Foxe Circle," in Loades, *John Foxe: an Historical Perspective*.
Usher, Brett, "In a Time of Persecution: New Light on the Secret Protestant Congregation in Marian London," in Loades, *John Foxe and the English Reformation*.
Walsham, Alexandra, "The Godly and Popular Culture," in Coffey and Lim, *Companion to Puritanism*.
Webster, Tom, "Early Stuart Puritanism," in Coffey and Lim, *Companion to Puritanism*.
Westerkamp, Marilyn J., "Anne Hutchinson, Sectarian Mysticism, and the Puritan Order," *Church History*, 59 (1990).
Westerkamp, Marilyn J., "Puritan Patriarchy and the Problem of Revelation," *Journal of Interdisciplinary History*, 23 (1993), 571–95.
Willen, Diane, "Godly Women in Early Modern England, Puritanism and Gender," *Journal of Ecclesiastical History*, 43 (1992).
Willen, Diane, "'Communion of the Saints': Spiritual Reciprocity and the Godly Community in Early Modern England," *Albion*, 27 (1995).
Williams, Daniel E., "'Behold a Tragic Scene Strangely Changed into a Theater of Mercy': the Structure and Significance of Criminal Conversion Narratives in Early New England," *American Quarterly*, 38 (1986), 827–47.
Winship, Michael P., "Brigit Cooke and the Art of Female Self-Advancement," *The Sixteenth Century Journal*, 33 (2002), 1045–59.
Winship, Michael P., "'The Most Glorious Church in the World': The Unity of the Godly in Boston, Massachusetts, in the 1630s," *Journal of British Studies*, 39 (2005), 71–98.
Wykes, David L., "They 'assemble in greater numbers and [with] more dareing then formerly': The Bishop of Gloucester and Nonconformity in the Late 1660s," *Southern History*, 17 (1995).
Wykes, Daniel L., "Early Religious Dissent in Surrey after the Restoration," *Southern History*, 33 (2011).

Entries in *The Oxford Dictionary of National Biography* (Oxford University Press, 2004 (and available online))

Bremer, Francis J., "Dunster, Henry (bap. 1609, d. 1659)."
Brod, Manfred, "Poole, Elizabeth (bap. 1622?, d. in or after 1668)."
Collinson, Patrick, "Barrow, Henry (c.1550–1593)."
Gill, Cartie, "Gibbons, Sarah (1634/5–1659)."
Gregory, Victoria, "Bradshaw, William (bap. 1570, d. 1618)."
House, Seymour Baker, "Becon, Thomas (1512/3–1567)."
Ingle, H. Larry, "Fox, George (1624–1691)."
Moody, Michael E., "Browne, Robert (1550?–1633)'.
Moody, Michael E., "Johnson, Francis (bap.1562, d. 1617)."

Morgan, Basil, "Crowley, Robert (1517–1588)."
Morrill, John, "Cromwell, Oliver (1599–1658)."
Pestana, Carla, "Gorton, Samuel (bap. 1593, d. 1677)."
Sprunger, Keith L., "Paget, John (d. 1638)."
Sprunger, Keith L., "Parker, Robert (c.1564–1614)."
Wright, Stephen, "Helwys, Thomas (c.1575–c.1614)."
Wright, Stephen, "Jacob, Henry (1562/3–1624)."
Wright, Stephen, "Jessey, Henry (1601–1663)."
Wright, Stephen, "Smyth, John (d. 1612)."

Index

Actes and Monuments (also *Book of Martyrs*), 13, 14, 32
Admonition to Parliament, 24
Ainsworth, Henry, 59, 61, 63, 67
Alcock, John, 13
Allen, Edmund, 13, 15
Allen, James, 171–2
Allerton, Isaac, 78
Allerton, Ralph, 13
Ames, William, 54–5, 56, 57, 74
Ames, William, Jr., 85
Ancient Church, 52, 53, 58, 61, 62, 63
Apologetical Narration, 110, 116, 146
Army Debates (Putney and Whitehall), 113–16
Ashe, Simeon, 108
Ashwood, Bartholomew, 160
Aspinwall, William, 93–4
Attaway, Mrs., 119

Baillie, Robert, 8, 58, 108, 118, 120, 146
Baker, Sir Richard, 38
Bancroft, Richard, 31
Bancroft, Timothy, 160
Banford, Joan, 120
Bangs, Jeremy, 60
Baptists (Anabaptists), 117, 127–35, 153, 158, 170–2, 177
Barrington, Lady Joan, 30
Barrow, Henry, 38, 51–2, 78
Bartlett, William, 146
Baxter, Richard, 135, 161
Baynes, Paul, 74
Beaumont, Richard, 112
Becon, Thomas, 20, 38
Beford Church, 118
Bellingham, Richard, 140
Bennet, Sir John, 38
Bernard, Richard, 30, 50
Best, John, 64
Betts, William, 15
Bewley, Mary, 118–19

Bible, availability of, 12, 19
Bird, Samuel, 16
Bishops Wars, 106
Bohm (also Behem), Hans, 11
Bolton, Robert, 35
Book of Martyrs, see *Actes and Monuments*
Boorstin, Daniel, 137
Bowes, Lady Elizabeth, 50
Boston, First Church (originally Charlestown), 78, 165–6, 171
Boston, Second Church, 103–4, 150
Boston, Third Church, 167
Boston Ministerial Association (see also clerical conferences), 172–3
Bourne, Nathaniel, 134
Bourne, Nehemiah, 171
Bowers, Benanual, 170
Bownd, Nicholas, 29
Bradford, Daniel, 66
Bradford, John, 14
Bradford, William, 70, 71, 72, 133
Bradshaw, William, 50, 57, 70–2
Bradstreet, Simon, 140
Brawner, David, 71
Brewster, William, 2, 39, 60, 63, 69–70, 75, 81
Bridge, William, 66, 108, 110, 120, 145, 147
Bright, Francis, 73
Brightman, Thomas, 147
Browne, Richard, 77
Browne, Robert, 49–50, 51
Browne brothers, Samuel and John, 75
Bruen, John, 17, 38
Bucer, Martin, 12
Bunyan, John, 118, 162, 176
Burgess, John, 28
Burroughes, Jeremiah, 66–7, 110, 153
Byfield, Nathaniel, 37

Calamy House Accord, 108–9
Calamy, Edmund, 108

233

Cambridge Assembly and Platform, 97–8, 102, 154, 163, 169, 173
Capp, Bernard, 117
Carnsew, William, 17
Cartwright, Thomas, 18, 21, 22, 57, 65
Caryl, Joseph, 153
Cawdrey, Daniel, 108
Cawdrey, Robert, 50
ceremonies, opposition to, 23
Chaderton, Lawrence, 22
Charles I, 105–6
Charles II, 138, 142
Chauncy, Charles, 98, 133, 149, 163
Chesire, Thomas, 107
Chidley, Katherine, 62, 120
church covenants, 51, 52, 56, 61, 65–6, 73, 77, 78, 79
Clap, Roger, 83–4, 137
Clarendon Codes, 158–9
Clarke, John, 114, 129–30, 132, 142, 153
Clarke, Samuel, 1, 162
clergy, role enhanced, 95–8, 101, 148–52, 163, 168, 169, 172–4, 180
clergy confronted in pulpit (see also lay questioning of clergy), 23, 93, 116, 166, 168
clerical conferencing (also assemblies, councils, synods), 89, 102, 152, 154, 164, 167
clerical resistance to lay power, 24, 42, 94–5, 115, 120–1, 151–2, 164, 166, 178
Clifton, Richard, 53, 70
Cob, Christopher, 39
Coddington, William, 76, 78, 139–41
Coffey, John, 127, 146
Coggeshall, John, 93–4
Coleman Street ward, 11, 27, 29, 42, 46, 47–8, 111, 116, 119
Collett, William, 38
Collings, John, 41
Collins, Edward, 84
Collinson, Patrick, 2, 18, 23, 25, 38, 41
Colman, Benjamin, 173
Como, David, 41, 47, 116, 135
Conant, Roger, 75

conferencing, 9, 23, 29–33, 34–7, 44–7, 79–81, 85, 91, 124, 135, 145, 150, 160–3, 174–6, 178, 180
confession (or profession) of faith, 53, 66, 73, 79
Congregationalism, 54–9, 65, 74, 77, 80, 89, 108, 110, 121, 146–8, 158, 168, 177
conventicles, 11, 25, 30–1, 159
Cook, John, 146
Cooke, Brigit, 40
Cooper, James F., 3, 164
Cooper, Thomas, 50
Coppin, Richard, 120
Cornwell, Francis, 120
Cotton, John, 28, 29, 31, 49, 57, 76, 77, 78, 80, 83, 85, 89, 90, 91, 95–7, 98, 99, 109, 122, 123, 132, 140, 142, 146, 165–6, 178
covenants of believers (see also church covenants), 13, 33, 65–6, 77, 79, 81, 90
Craddock, Walter, 37, 71, 108
Crandall, John, 132, 170–1
Cranmer, Thomas, 10, 12, 19
Cromwell, Henry, 133
Cromwell, Oliver, 39, 72, 110–11, 112–14, 136, 145–6, 148, 155
Cromwell, Thomas, 10
Cross, Claire, 3
Crowley, Robert, 20
Culverwell, Ezekiel, 33
Cushman, Robert, 60, 70
Cutter, Barbary, 84
Cutter, Richard, 84–5

Davenport, James, 181
Davenport, John, 7, 27, 29, 42, 44, 45, 46, 49, 64–6, 72, 85, 93–5, 97, 103, 109, 131, 132, 138, 139, 146–7, 152, 163, 164–7, 169, 171, 174
Davis, Nicholas, 138
Dedham Church, 79–80
Dedham Conference, 25
Dell, William, 111
Dennison, Stephen, 47
Dent, Arthur, 21
D'Ewes, Simonds, 37

Dickens, A. G., 3
Directory of Church Government, 24
Dissenting Brethren, 110, 153
Dod, John, 50
Dominion of New England, 172
Dorchester Church, 83–4
Downane, John, 38
Downing, Emmanuel, 134
Downing, George, 134
Dudley, Thomas, 76, 78, 82, 100
Duffy, Eamon, 3
Dunan-Page, Anne, 160
Dunster, Henry, 84, 133
Duppa, John, 62
Durant, John, 109
Dyer, Mary, 1, 89, 138
Dyer, William, 89

Eaton, Anne, 130–1, 147
Eaton, Samuel, 65
Eaton, Theophilus, 131
education, value of, 9, 98, 100, 115, 151, 180
Edwards, Jonathan, 181
Edwards, Thomas, 117, 128, 147
Eliot, John, 31
Elton, Edward, 88
Endecott, John, 71–2, 74, 75, 78, 82–3, 132, 140
English Church in Amsterdam, 63–5
Erasmus, Desiderius, 6
Etherington, John, 47
Ewins, Thomas, 146
Exercises of prophesying, 18–19

Fairclough, Samuel, 28
fasts, 26, 34, 169
Fenn, Humphrey, 50
Fenner, Dudley, 65
Fenton, Edward, 23
Fenwick, Anne, 41
Feoffees for Impropriations, 28
Firmin, Giles, 91, 93
Flavel, John, 161
Fletcher, Richard, 22
Forbes, John, 65, 67
Ford, Stephen, 124
Foster, Stephen, 2, 74, 79
Fowle, Thomas, 134

Fox, George, 117, 135, 139
Foxe, John, 13
Foxley, Thomas, 44
Fulke, William, 17, 22
Fuller, Samuel, 71, 72, 73, 77, 78

gadding to sermons, 13, 23, 44, 88, 160, 178
Gataker, Thomas, 46
Gifford, George, 20, 38
Gilby, Anthony, 20, 38
Gilpin, Richard, 35
Gnostics, 5
Goffe, Stephen, 65
Goffe, William, 114, 157
Goodwin, Christopher, 134
Goodwin, John, 37, 46, 47–8, 115, 118, 146
Goodwin, Thomas, 7, 67, 108, 110, 115, 122, 128, 153, 155, 171, 178
Goold, Thomas, 170–1
Gorton, Samuel, 120, 140, 141–2
Gott, Charles, 72
Gouge, Thomas, 36
Green, John, 109, 116
Greenhill, William, 116
Greenwood, John, 51
Griffith, George, 155
Grindal, Edmund, 15, 19

Half-Way Covenant, 163, 164, 168
Haigh, Christopher, 3
Halcomb, Joel, 116, 145, 159
Hall, David D., 96, 127, 151, 168
Hampton Court Conference, 27
Harley, Sir Robert, 46
Harriman, Anne, 119
Harrison, Robert, 23, 50, 51
Harrison, William, 18–19
Hartlib, Samuel, 29, 147
Harvard College, 98, 100, 151, 165, 180
Hastings, Henry, Earl of Huntingdon, 16–17
Hathorne, William, 140
Helwys, Thomas, 50, 62
Henry VIII, 10
Herring, Julines, 28, 32
Heywood, Oliver, 159, 160

Hicks, Samuel, 70
Higginson, Francis, 72–3, 75
Higginson, Francis, Jr., 163
Higham, Sir John, 16
Hildersham, Arthur, 50
Hill, Christopher, 1, 3
Hilton, William, 69–70
Hinde, William, 38
Hobson, Paul, 111, 112
Hoby, Margaret, 40
Holcroft, Francis, 160
Holmes, Nathaniel, 116
Holmes, Obadiah, 132
Hooke, William, 85, 131, 155, 161
Hooker, Thomas, 30, 31, 64, 71, 109
Hooper, Hester, 159
Hooper, John, 14
household exercises, 16–17, 160, 162, 175–6
How, Samuel, 46, 47–8, 62, 107
Howgill, Francis, 135
Hubbard, William, 1, 70, 96
Hull, John, 138
Hurst, Geoffrey, 15
Hutchinson, Anne, 1, 8, 40–1, 89, 91–5, 131, 135, 140, 147
Hutchinson, Edward, 167
Hutchinson, William, 89

iconoclasm, 13, 106–7
Independents, 110, 116
Inner Light, 136
inspiration of the Spirit, 5, 7–8, 38, 39, 51, 62, 88, 90–1, 113–16, 122–6, 127, 134, 135–6, 147, 162, 165, 181
Ipswich Church, 82
Ives, Jeremiah, 111

Jacob, Henry, 45, 55–6, 58, 62, 63, 128
James I, 27
Janeway, James, 36
Jenison, Robert, 41
Jermyn, Sir Robert, 16
Jessey, Henry, 128, 129, 132
Jewell, John, 17
Johnson, Edward, 87, 98
Johnson, Francis, 52, 59, 61
Johnson, George, 61

Johnson, Isaac, 78
Jollie, Thomas, 159
Jubbes, John, 114

Keayne, Robert, 43, 119
Keayne, Sarah Dudley, 119, 131
Kiffin, William, 44, 45, 128
King, John, 312
Knewstub, John, 16, 33, 34
Knollys, Hanserd, 128
Knox, John, 49

Lake, Peter, 46, 47
Lambe, Thomas, 111, 116, 119
Langford, Jonas, 139
Langland, William, 20
Lathrop, John, 45, 62
Latimer, Hugh, 20
Laud, William, 105
Lawrence, Richard, 124–5, 145
lay evangelizing (see also testimonies), 20, 36, 58, 59, 123–6, 160–1
lay governance of congregations (see also Congregationalism), 22, 50, 57, 59, 73–4, 78–80, 95, 110, 166, 168
lay patronage, 12, 13, 16, 28, 159
lay power, limitation on (see also clerical resistance to lay power), 101, 103–4, 163, 167, 169, 173–4
lay preaching (see also prophesying), 9, 39, 46, 47–8, 70, 76, 82–3, 102–3, 107–9, 111–12, 116–26, 149–50, 155, 157, 159, 178
lay pressure on clergy, 23, 107, 178
lay questioning of clergy, 18, 82–3, 98–9, 117, 121
lay religious gatherings (see also conferencing, conventicles, household exercises), 14–15, 25, 26
Leach, John, 38
Lechford, Thomas, 82, 100, 130
L'Ecluse, Jean de, 62
lectureships, 28, 42
Ledra, William, 138
Lee, Richard, 46
Lee, Samuel, 161
Leighton, Alexander, 45

Levellers, 1, 113
Lever, Thomas, 17
Leverett, John, 111, 155, 167, 169, 172
Lollards, 11
London, as center of puritan activity, 42–8
Lucas, Paul, 173–4
Luther, Martin, 6, 11
Lyle, Francis, 99

MacCulloch, Diarmaid, 1
Maclear, James Fulton, 2
Mansell, Robert, 58
Marbury, Francis, 90
Marshall, Stephen, 132
Martin, Henry, 51
Martyr, Peter, 12
Mary Tudor, 13
Mather, Cotton, 1, 129, 137, 173, 175, 180
Mather, Eleazar, 163
Mather, Increase, 163, 169, 80
Mather, Nathaniel, 165
Mather, Richard, 98–9, 101, 151, 163
Mather, Samuel, 103
Matthew, Tobie, 32
May, Susan, 120
Melville, Elizabeth, 40
membership requirements in Congregational churches, 55, 56, 65, 71, 73, 79, 165, 181
Middle Advent, 146–7
Mildmay, Lady Joan, 38
Miller, Perry, 2, 74
Mitchell, Jonathan, 151, 175
Montagu, Edward, Viscount Mandeville, 43
Montagu, Richard, 32
Moody, Lady Deborah, 130–1
Morrill, John, 42, 114, 145
Morton, Nathaniel, 160
Morton, Thomas, 71
Murcot, John, 124

Narveson, Kate, 39
Nayler, James, 135, 136–7
Neile, Richard, 41

Netherlands as refuge for puritans, 54–68
New Model Army, 108, 110–11
Nicene Creed, 5
Norton, Humphrey, 138, 141
Norton, John, 97, 103, 138, 165–6
Norwood, Robert, 153
Nowell, Increase, 82
Noyse, James, 97, 147–8
Nuttall, Geoffrey, 181
Nye, Philip, 67, 110, 115, 122, 128, 165, 171

Oates, Samuel, 111
Oliver, John, 82
Overall, John, 32
Owen, John, 36, 123, 153, 155, 160
Oxenbridge, John, 171–2

Paget, John, 54, 63–5
Pagitt, Ephraim, 117–18
Painter, Thomas, 131, 147–8
Parker, Matthew, 15
Parker, Robert, 54–5, 56, 57
Penn, James, 167, 173–4
Perkins, William, 21, 65, 98, 108
Peter, Hugh, 64, 65–6, 111, 113, 115, 155
Petto, Samuel, 35, 125, 128
Phillips, George, 77, 96
Pickereing, John, 112
Pike, Robert, 102, 149
Plymouth church, 69–70, 77, 78
Poole, Elizabeth, 118
Pope, Robert, 173
Potts, Thomas, 63–4
Powel, Vavasor, 34, 125
Powell, Michael, 103–4, 150
prayer, extemporaneous, 32, 36, 160
Presbyterianism, 25, 35–6, 58, 108, 110, 147–8, 153, 168
prophesying (see also exercises of prophesying), 9, 18, 58, 59–62, 73, 81–3, 99–100, 103–4, 114–26, 127, 129–30, 146, 149, 157, 160, 175–6, 178
publications, lay, 38, 120
puritanism, 15–16, 21–2, 23, 27, 179

Quakers, 1, 8, 107, 130, 135–41, 155, 157, 170, 178
Quartermayne, Roger, 34

Radcliffe, Jane, 40
radical sectaries, 117, 127
Rathband, William, 84
Reforming Synod (1679), 169–70
Reynolds, Edward, 118–19, 124
Richardson, Walter, 15
Ritor, Andrew, 131
Robinson, John, 8, 28, 53, 54, 56, 59, 63, 67, 69
Robinson, William, 138
Rogers, Ezekiel, 30
Rogers, John (of Dedham), 28, 30, 40, 108
Rogers, John (of Dublin), 35, 118, 124–5
Rogers, Richard (of London), 62
Rogers, Richard (of Wethersfield), 33, 34, 37, 39–40
Rollock, Robert, 36
Rosier, Edmund, 62
Rotterdam Church, 65–7, 108
Rutherford, Samuel, 36, 100
Rutman, Darrett, 1
Ryrie, Alec, 35–6

sacraments, 63, 75, 120, 155, 165
Salem Church, 71–5, 80, 100
Saltmarsh, John, 37, 71, 108, 120, 12
Saltonstall, Gurdon, 1741
Sandes, Henry, 33, 34
Savoy Conference and Declaration, 123, 129, 155, 159
Saybrook Platform, 174
Saye and Sele, Lord, 58
Scobell, Henry, 155
Scottish National Covenant, 1056
Scottow, Joshua, 85, 174
Scripture, interpretation of, 17, 19, 38, 51
Scudder, Henry, 44
Sedgwick, Robert, 134
separatism, 49ff.
sermon notes, 32
Settle, Thomas, 25
Sewall, Samuel, 175–6, 180

Shaw, Peter, 47
Shepard, Thomas, 84, 91–2, 96, 133
Sibbes, Richard, 7, 30, 35, 36, 44, 45, 135
Simpson, John, 146
Simpson, Mary, 41
Simpson, Sidrach, 66–7, 108, 110, 122, 128, 147, 153
Skelton, Samuel, 72–3, 76, 89, 96
Smith, Ralph, 81
Smyth, John, 50, 53, 59, 61, 62, 67
Society of Negroes, 175
Spilsbury, John, 128
Stearns, Raymond Phineas, 71
Stedman, Alice, 84
Stevenson, Marmaduke, 138, 141
Stoddard, Solomon, 174
Stone, Samuel, 85, 151, 170, 173
Stranger Churches, 12, 18, 42
Sutton, Katherine, 41, 120
Symonds, Joseph, 66–7
Synod of 1637, 93–4
Synod of 1662, 163, 164–6

Taylor, Edward, 174
Taylor, John, 107
Taylor, Thomas, 34, 44, 45, 47
Temple, Thomas, 139
testimonies of religious experience, 14, 34–7, 66, 83–5, 122–6, 161–2
Thomas, Samuel, 160
Tombes, John, 129, 132
Topp, Alexander, 17
Trapnell, Anna, 41, 120
Travers, Walter, 22, 24, 41
Tyndale, William, 12
Tyng, Edward, 167

Udall, John, 32
Udall, Ralph, 22
Underhill, Edward, 15
Upcher, Thomas, 15

Valdes (also Waldo), Peter, 11
Van Engen, Abram C., 2
Vane, Henry, 89, 91, 93, 153
Vaughan, Richard, 31
Vere, Lady Mary, 43

Vincent, Thomas, 161
Vines, Richard, 35

Wakeman, Samuel, 174–5
Walker, George, 46–7
Wallington, Nehemiah, 38, 39, 42
Walton, William, 82
Walwyn, William, 115, 153
Ward, John, 66
Ward, Samuel, 16, 36, 36
Warham, John, 77
Watson, Thomas, 30, 161
Watts, Thomas, 15
Weld, Lady Mary, 28
Welde, Thomas, 64, 84, 93–4
Westminster Assembly, 105, 109
Whalley, Edward, 112, 157
Wheelwright, John, 82, 90, 94, 135, 140
White, John, 7
Whitefield, George, 181
Wigglesworth, Michael, 151
Wildman, John, 114
Willard, Samuel, 168, 170
Williams, Roger, 80–1, 89, 100–1, 130, 140, 141–3, 154

Wilson, John (of Sudbury and Boston), 27, 49, 78, 81, 82, 89, 91–3, 96, 138, 165–6, 168
Wilson, John (of Yorkshire), 25
Winship, Michael, 51, 74, 87, 90
Winslow, Edward, 70, 78, 142
Winthrop, John, 1, 8, 33, 76, 77, 78, 80, 82, 89, 91–3, 100, 105, 124, 128, 134, 143
Winthrop, John, Jr., 82, 139, 140
Winthrop, Margaret, 29
Winthrop, Samuel, 139, 141
Winthrop, Stephen, 111, 115–16, 119, 134, 171
Winthrop, William, 12, 14, 18
Witaker, William, 17
Withers, George, 23
Witter, William, 131, 132, 134–5
women, role in religion, 11, 39–42, 53, 65–7, 85, 90, 117–20, 125, 159
Woodbridge, John, 168
Wotton , Anthony, 46–7

Yale College, 180
Yates, John, 59
Youngs, John, 138

The manufacturer's authorised representative in the EU is Springer Nature Customer Service Centre GmbH, Europaplatz 3, 69115 Heidelberg, Germany. If you have any concerns regarding our products, please contact ProductSafety@springernature.com

Printed and bound by CPI Group (UK) Ltd, Croydon, CR0 4YY

23/03/2026

02076662-0014